And Still
It Goes On

ACKNOWLEDGMENT

To my family: Sister Michelle Palmer, children David Bond and Nichola Sobie, husband Jim Vesterinen, and grandchildren David, Sydney, Benjamin, and Chloe. Thank you for your patience, love, and support.

DEDICATION

Dedicated to my father, Sydney L. Palmer. Without his daily writings, this book would not have been possible. Thank you, Dad, for allowing me to tell your story. Also dedicated to his grandchildren, great-grandchildren, and future descendants.

Table of Contents

FORWARD

In this war Sept 3, 1939, Great Britain, France, Poland versus Germany, and later, Italy. To the blind, the obvious, a maniac with a fanatical desire for power. I can't look at it in that light. A war of invested interests, power, money, fear, domination, etc. It will be to no avail, will end nothing, nor do any good. I am no fatalist or pessimist, but I can see history repeating itself. There will be many more, for the sake of money and interest as to its conduct and conclusion and to that of my part in it. I pen the following, being very optimistic as to my coming through it. I state in all truth and sincerity that I have no desire to kill, to fight, or to defend this country. I owe nothing.

I have no reason other than the fact that I was trapped and yet a desire for a change for a while. This is not my home or my happiness. I left that behind in the beauty and ruggedness of Canada, which were some of my happiest and carefree days. Someday, though, I might see that beautiful country again and fulfil my greatest desire.

Opening for a period of military training and my part as a soldier in this war of 1939 between 2 social systems.

Chapter 1:
Basic Training July 18, 1940 - January 30, 1941
1940 JULY

THURSDAY, 18th,

Registered for service.

21/10/39 Called up

18/7/40 Army R.A.

Being above day Thursday, which day being filled with much excitement and experience. An uneventful trip by train to a somewhat wild part of "Surrey, England." Destination being naught but military area. After unravelling much red tape, we were issued with Kit, Squad, living quarters, Sergeant, etc. It was very amusing all of it, and yet this isn't all. I have a sense of time wasted. Of course, we are like a herd of sheep. Ordered. Commanded. Shouted at. Still, the novelty of it all tempers the sting. Parade for all meals. Rough but substantial. Blocks of barracks, two floors - 4 rooms to each block. 14 to a room. Iron spring beds lights out at 10:15.

FRIDAY, 19th

Spent a bad night. Window caused a draft. Woke up several times. Bomb call 5:30, Shave (cold water), but was pleasantly surprised finding I shaved without discomfort. Drill to 7:30. Parade, Breakfast, More drill. Marching, wheeling, forming. Sergeant is a decent chap with a bull-like voice, which, of course, is natural in a sergeant. Blasted navy boots, heavy, but will get used to them. Lecture by C.O. Ditto by Sgt. every 5 minutes, ha! I laugh. The different specimens of men gathered here. Especially when drilling. There's one guy, short, and as stupid as you get them, he can't do a thing. Bit of a sing-song tonight. Jock used my mouth organ, sang like hell.

SATURDAY, 20th

Had a much better night. Should explain, perhaps. Squad of 28 men, Sergeant and Bombardier. Sgt. does drill, and Bdr. Keeps order and watches men. Went through some procedures. Breakfast, Respirator drill (amusing, complicated) Issued with a second suit, (rough) Test in Kit Inspection (hell of a job), rolling up in order and display - 2 pairs of socks, 2 shirts, uniform, 2 gym outfits, shorts, jersey, and underwear. Take all kit - toothbrush, shaving kit, soap, button stick, brushes (hair and boot), silver kit bag - great coat, helmet, scarf, forage hat, 2 pairs of heavy boots, gym boots, etc. Off for the rest of the day.

SUNDAY, 21st

Up at 6:00, nothing of import. Cleaned buttons, etc., with articles supplied. Lay about. Don't know how to fill in time. Some life, alright in a way. It's a big experience for me. It's a step towards my achievements. Something I haven't done, new. Walked down to the town. A hell of a dump. Funny in uniform.

MONDAY, 22nd

What a hell of a feeling. It's tired, dry, nasty, and altogether, you know, it's reminiscent of Quebec and Half Moon Bay in Canada. Gas drill, marching, slow, halting, about turn. Sgt. yelling like a bull. Men like dogs, with exceptions, on the hungry side. Meal in the canteen at 6:00.

TUESDAY, 23rd

Boy some day. Slow march up and down for an hour, gas drill, gym. Sod of an instructor and filled with his own importance. Gas chamber, rifle drill. Give me a kick to use ye gun again (303 service). Poor old D. had to run around the football field with a rifle in the air above his head. Played football and sprained ankle.

Boy, am I worn out? So's the rest; some can hardly move. Poor buggers. 1 shilling a day for what, half-baked patriotism? They are treated as scum and yet are looked upon for the protection of the country. I'm settling down to it.

Recruits "Deepcut" 1940

WEDNESDAY, 24th

Nothing much to report. Hell, on twisted foot marching. Not much of interest.

THURSDAY, 25th

All the same again. Air raid at 12:00, down to shelter. Don't like ye shelters. Very lightly constructed. Getting on okay.

FRIDAY, 26th

Saw dentist, looked over teeth. A result later. Big event this afternoon. I don't know whether this thought frightens me or not. I've had a blood test, etc. Well, had inoculation, guys passing out all over. Hardly felt needle, aches a bit. Went to bed early.

SATURDAY, JULY 27th

Hell, of a night, stiff arm aching, cold, had Sgt. in, no work, and rest 48 hours. Felt sick after breakfast, weary, etc. Okay now. Lousy blasted grub. 2 sausages for breakfast. Went for a walk with the boys. "Frimley, " what a dump. Arm aches.

SUNDAY, 28th

Tea in bed. Some laugh, a guy came around with pot and offered cake; it was alright. Some guys still laid up. Kipper for breakfast, bit turned bad, but guys too soft, they ate it and liked it. Played cards, Joan and Vi, came on bikes, a nice surprise. Spent the day with them, showed them around. Damn pity, all that long ride, could see that I was miserable at parting, but after all, life at best was miserable. Glad to hear of allowance, etc. Nice of boys to collect. Lousy meals, cold meat for dinner, tea, and supper, cost me 10/1 a week for sundries and food. Can't see much hope, tied left and right. Pain is gone, ok now, bit dizzy when with Joan in canteen. Long week of drills next. Have the natural human vanity in uniform, say I look alright, but what are we, scum.

MONDAY, 29th

Same stuff, nothing of interest. Getting along pretty well, figured I am equal to any in squad. 3 or 4 dopes to cover my average intelligence. Bdr. a sod, stands a foot away and shouts and roars. Little man, ignorant, self-important. Knows his job and expects us to complete in 2 weeks, that which took him 10 years.

TUESDAY, 30th

Same as above. 4 men made L.Bdrs. 2 earned it, others pretty hopeless. No method in proving their worth Pretty unfair. Still, what is it to me? This is another phase in life; maybe I'll prove myself.

WEDNESDAY, 31st

Again, the same. Got caught at Port Arms with a mask on and felt pretty much like a fool. But there's nuttin' to it, serving something for you and get nothing. Ah, well! As I said above, I'm trying something new.

AUGUST

THURSDAY, 1ˢᵗ

Gonna make a stab for a trip Sunday. What have I to lose? Where do I gain? Who cares? It will come, something new, grasping it ok. By hell, I don't know. I'm fancy; I've got no more than I would normally do.

FRIDAY, 2ⁿᵈ

Yessir, some life. The pains they go to for a miserable stripe. The difference in class, amongst the poor sods. Oh ah! I laugh at the way of all flesh. Me too!

SATURDAY, 3ʳᵈ

Nothing of interest. Looking forward to Sunday. A bit of a sweat for fatigue made it ok. Blast, Bdr. makes me howl. He's like a short-ass bull. Haha.

SUNDAY, 4ᵗʰ

Well, I made it ok. Nice to see her., I enjoyed the day very much. One hell of a foot slog home. Family tickled to death. Same here. Bit of an interest for me, like old times. Surprises.

MONDAY, 5ᵗʰ

Well, still battering away. Marvellous the things one can do if forced. Nothing of interest today. The blasted class and differences in mere stripes. All are very self-important. You can't turn one blasted way or another. You're trapped.

TUESDAY, 6ᵗʰ

Some day. Yessir. Large scale battle between two armies, marched 10 miles to open country, pretty rough, hard. Well weighted down. Had to crawl, rush, and duck to the objective. I lay down in the shade, waited till they had advanced, then made a dash for it and laughed.

WEDNESDAY, 7th

Tetanus inoculation. Not bad. P. T. right after. Damned laughable P. T. instructor. Walked to the village, and had a photo.

THURSDAY, 8th

Great day. Rifle ranges. 100 yards, 200-300 yards. Boy! What a difference! Some kicks gave me a horrible reality and impression of warfare. Noises like heavy detonations, ears jump. Had fair averages. Lousy dinner after going a stretch of 6 ½ hours. Dinner-cold meat, spuds, beets, no tea, dry bread. Oh, it's terrific the way they're kicked about. Still, ye rifle range was worth noting for my store of experience. I guess this takes the unreality of it out now. Yeah, I guess I realize.

FRIDAY, 9th

I've done it before, yeah. It's the same, different characters, but I've come out of my shell. It does that sort of thing for you. Broadens one's mind. Teaches you to take them as they come. Also, to look after yourself. Had preliminary to march past.

SATURDAY, 10th

No march past cancelled. Lads going out on manoeuvres. Missed it. Laid about all day.

SUNDAY, 11th

Pops birthday. Bought a card, also, dear Joan. Yeah, time marches on. Pity, though, youth slips by. God to be without the beauty of youth, the lovely world about us, the beauty of music. I could weep, and I yearned for that, which I could not understand. I shall never cease marvelling. I look around me. Young men, just the sort you'd find in a bunch anywhere: the noisy guy, the smiler, the darky, the ginger, the quiet, reserved guy. Yeah, it's all here again. They hardly realize what the purpose of it all is. But better they don't; ignorance is bliss. I wonder what will happen to each individual. We shall see. Went to "Camberley" with Mish, queer guy, not fast enough. Picked up a blonde. No, it wasn't the same. I used to connect once. I failed. She was a bit drunk though'.

MONDAY, 12th

Preparing for the march past.

TUESDAY, 13th

All ok. Had R.A. band. Crowd to watch. Done it without a hitch. C.O. said good, fastest lot yet. Had the rest of the day off.

WEDNESDAY, 14th

Final get out. Marched uphill, full kit. I had blasted overcoat on. Boy! Some sweat. Then back with biscuits. New place, ok. Usual scramble for beds, camp canvas. 20 to a hut, low adjoining other. 10 squads were split up. Pity. Still, we were still together. Got Mish alongside me. Sgt, ugly sod, but ok. It's surprising. Bdr. ok. Drills are ok, not so hard. Food is better.

With some of the boys. I'm seated in 1st row in the middle.

THURSDAY, 15th

On R.A. guns. Damned interesting, yeah. Some weapon, a B marvel, lectures on A.A sighting, etc. Officers are ok. Had 2 air raids, 3 Nazi bombers passed over, and dropped 2 pills. Boy, some commotion. Some kick to hear them.

FRIDAY, 16th

Not much to relate. Pretty intensive training now and more tomorrow. Expect to have two months here. I must try to get home on Sunday. To hell with the army. Can understand Jack now. Discipline, stupid fads. What do you think? Towel around blankets? I groan. Grub has improved. I'm ok, still have dopes to cover me.

SATURDAY, 17th

Had inoculation, wasn't too bad. Excused duties for 48 hours. Hung about all day. Illness came on about 4:00. Boy, I felt rough then. Played checkers and beat all comers. Still feel damn rough.

SUNDAY, 18th

Feel lousy. Limb's ache. Started out for home, a 4-mile walk to "Brookwood." Don't know how I did it, sweat. Got home without mishap. Joan, glad to see me. Yeah, sure was good to be home. Small interest in folk. Oh, I don't know. The welcome is stale. Damn, and blast it. I've changed, and something or another has left me. Got back ok. Mess where the bomb fell at "Woking."

MONDAY, 19th

Nothing new, more gunnery than anything. I might try for something, but somehow, I don't see the result.

TUESDAY, 20th

Again, a blank. It goes on without fail. Blasted Sergeant reminds me of a bullfrog with a wart on his jaw, squat, and all teeth.

WEDNESDAY, 21st

Nothing of interest.

THURSDAY, 22nd

It's getting damned cold at night, and 2 blankets are not adequate. Slept in pants, much warmer. Joan is very effusive in letters. By hell, she means it, too. What love to bear one, a man should be proud to be the object of such feeling. Woke at about 2:00 in the middle of the night to explosions. 5 incendiary bombs dropped by the Nazis. Heard drones peculiar to their planes. Heard it die off. Marvellous, no opposition. Britain has bitten off a lot this time. It will last some time, for years, I believe. We shall see.

FRIDAY, 23rd

Still at it, mostly gun drill. Mobile and static very interesting. Shall get on, no doubt. I always seem to have confidence in myself, which I know to be a valuable asset. God, sometimes I feel it; my heart breaks. I am lonely and weak. I visualize and dream of the past and see so many things that it hurts, and I feel as though I'm missing something. The world is so great, and there are so many beautiful things. I want it all, but am defeated. But I am grateful to a great god. Security tonight. It will pass.

SATURDAY, 24th

Messed about. Inspection, talk by C.O. Off at 1:00. Made up my mind to beat it. Did so. Different way of route. "Frimley" to "Richmond" better. Saw no one. I got oiled, Pop and me, I laugh, walked home in a raid, got sick in the garden, and went through the lavatory window to bed. Ha. Joan was surprised to see me. Had a good day. Safe home. Boy, some raid.

MONDAY, 26th

Nothing of importance. Time bombs going off from last night. Feel damned tired today. Blasted slave drivers.

TUESDAY, 27th

Nothing out of the usual. Stuck into the guts of autoloader etc. Few bombs dropped. Impressive. Red flash, large detonation, hum of Bosch motors recedes and smells of oil, diesel.

WEDNESDAY, 28th

Vaccination, not much to it, got used to it. I had momentary qualms.

THURSDAY, 29th

Nothing of import.

FRIDAY, 30th

Blasted Sgt. had us on double, ignorant sod. Say it sure is some life, your times gone, freedoms gone. I laugh. I fear for this country. Wonder how she'll fare. I think Hitler had more than any other leader alive. Say what organization. Pay. Kit tomorrow. Getting ready for it. Damn things we gotta do. Of all the childish simple fads. Boy it's some experience. Worth money. Joan is very effusive. Still getting on, marking time with the rest of the gun fodder. Say, are they sucked in.

Gas Equipment. In training. Deepcut

SATURDAY, 31st

Messed about in general. Talk by Major. Usual bull. Gave an indication of pass out. Done 7 weeks now, more or less an old sweat. On security, not bad.

SEPTEMBER

SUNDAY, 1st

War a year old today. Doesn't seem like it. Bombing like hell now. London is subject to it. Bombs on "Hayes" gramophone company. Hundreds per day. Marvellous how its civilization marches on to its own destruction. Bombers are fine pieces of work, but they must hand it to Gerry, the smart guy. Walked around finally with "Mish." Lousy dump.

MONDAY, 2nd

Nothing much. Went to "Aldershot" on fatigue. Not a bad town. Saw a tank hit a car and boxed it up—peeled spuds in the cookhouse. "Anderson" had me on double today. Sod. Because of the contradiction between Sgt. and him, I suffer. He saw it, though, got messed up on deflections.

SATURDAY, 7th

Was rejoicing in fact of no fatigues or duties. Went to "Blackdown, " fixed up with A.T.S. Came home. Trapped for general mobilization of men, ammo, and rifle. Road blocking. Bloody cold. Slept in kit, cape, harness, both masks, helmet, no blankets. Dozed off for ½ hour. Got up cold. Up and down, on the march. Great raid on London. Could see the anti-aircraft barrage. Me and "Darky" slept side by side for warmth.

SUNDAY, 8th

Didn't think I'd make it. Got back at 8:00 and messed about. "Oz" came after dinner. How about it, ok? Thumbed 3 rides. Got in at 4:00, not bad. Home from "Hammersmith" by rail. Hell, of a raid over London, could see East India docks ablaze. "Poplar" smashed up, P.O. Victoria, Waterloo. Still, they retaliated in London.

MONDAY, 9th

Hard at the gun, getting on fairly well. I'm just messing along with the rest now. I don't give two hoots for any of it as long as I just keep the pace ok.

TUESDAY, 10th

Of no import, except guard duty 24 hours. Sgt. a louse tried to be funny, wouldn't work. Stripes too big for him. Nothing to report. The off-and-on are a bit difficult. Felt foolish first. I was first relieved. 50 Dornier planes passed over all silver, marvellous sight, going like hell. Spitfires on their tails, we brought 1 down.

THURSDAY, 12th

The usual drills, more lectures than anything. Went into the store and changed boots. 3rd time. Can't bloody well get a decent fit. Bdr. is a decent chap. New men coming in, poor sods, and from the point of view of an old sweat now. Forgot to note, moved to married quarters. 15 to a house, a row of houses. Brick, all conveniences, 4 in rooms 1-5. Mish, Blondie, Perty, and myself. Ok, beds on the floor, fine. Wash the house with cold water. I hoof it to another wash house. Much too cold to shave. My mug(face) won't take it. Had marched again and was on sentry duty. To hell with that and the army!

FRIDAY, 13th

Ah payday 7 shillings and 6 pence. They've taken another shilling from us. Sods. Somebody wants a week off. 6- a day extra, they said, but keen to take it back with the other hand

SATURDAY, 14th

Started off alright. Not much to relate to. Started early for home, me and Ozzy. Got a van right home, lucky. Saw time bombs on our way, craters, etc. Boy, some damage! Saw Joan, blasted kids, some racket when I came in, made me feel like going back.

SUNDAY, 15th

Jock, Oz, and I set out again. Made it ok. Arrived safe, early, decent day. Brother Jack is out of work, a hell of a lad. Don't blame him. He wants to join the Air Force. Harry is growing up now, and Vi. Gee, I think of when I was like Harry, tall, good-looking, bloody shame. It's there passing me now, but what glory I had once. Got home after a 5-mile walk. Bloody shoes hurt, and I can't seem to get a pair to fit.

MONDAY, 16th

Up at 4:00 on guard. Just like a week on Saturday. Turned out full Kit for road blocking party (invasion scare) etc. Raining like hell ah! Was it miserable, and yet I like to see how much I can stick it. It took 3 hours for them to get out there, and the patrol lasted ¾ of an hour. They're overconfident. I fail to see it.

TUESDAY, 17th

Nothing of interest. Getting along fairly well. London being blasted. Brought down 185 planes yesterday. My pal Cled in R.A. Signals.

WEDNESDAY, 18th

On security, nothing happened, day as usual. Had a go on Predictor, broke down a bit, went alright with me. Swell job.

THURSDAY, 19th

Rain setting in. Stopping the Germans a bit. Attempt at invasion 150, 000 used. Repulsed. He'll try again. Used gas. "London" getting hit bad. Docks, main stores. 45 bombs on "Southall." Naval and A.A at "Southall" used. Joan said the noise was terrible. Getting on well with training. Got wet on field training today, and Anderson made us work after. Boy, it was uncomfortable. By the way, I got home alright by road too, nuttin to it.

FRIDAY, 20th

Nothing of importance.

SATURDAY, 21st.

Thought of going home but changed my mind. Went to the" Woking" dance. Not bad, had a decent dance. What a difference, freedom. Got away ok. Didn't think I'd make it.

SUNDAY, 22nd.

Had pain again. Gee, I don't know, and I can't understand it. It is agonizing. To think I used to be ok. I'll make it. Folks, ok, "West Ealing" hit and "Heston." Boy "London" is going. I am convinced she'll be ruined. Poor old "London, " she can't stand much more. Those big bombers come over with their deadly loads, oil bombs, aerial torpedoes, land mines, 8 feet by 4 feet, laid out 4 streets at "Kew." Getting nearer to "Southall." Almost finished training. Shall be glad. Kids ship hit; kids lost. 4, 000 Gerry's on transport sunk. That's retaliation. French coast being battered. A new Predictor is being used. They can't stop us.

MONDAY, 23rd

Bad pains still. Enough to drive one nuts. Poor Joan guessed she felt it. Drilled hard today, yeah, held up. Nothing to report except the pain again. God, it drives me nuts, but I shall laugh soon.

TUESDAY, 24th

Gun manning. Not bad at all, easy 24 hours. Went on guard 1:00-2:00. Bombs dropped nearby. Heard the whining, whistle. Boy! Unnerving! Yeah, I guess I was scared. Hell, of a thing to realize.

WEDNESDAY, 25th

Not much. Went to dance at "Woking, " crowded, borrowed a bike, me, Mish, Oz and Jock. Had a good time, jaunt going home. Poor old "London" still getting it mighty heavy. "Oxford" street, all big stores hit. Looks as though "Japan" and "Spain" will be in it. "Dakar French West Africa" lost. Hell, of a mix-up.

THURSDAY, 26th

Went sick. Treat you like cattle. What can you expect from the British army or the British? Had an easy day today. Missed digging. Had afternoon. I went down and changed boots. Forth pair. I laugh. Ah, nuts to the army! Got a pass for Sunday.

FRIDAY, 27th

Always like Fridays, short days. Finished at 4:00. Pay. Not much to say for today except that I received 10 shillings. I mentioned the rise some weeks ago. Yeah. 3/6- and they've already taken 1/- a week away.

SATURDAY, 28th

Went sick again. Didn't want to but can't see M.O. otherwise. He's alright, giving me Bismol for the pain. Bloody pain. It drives me nuts. I'll beat it though. On guard patrol tonight, stood on road Oz and me from 8:00-11:00. Stop cars etc. Lousy job, cold, pain. Say, I won't forget.

SUNDAY, 29th

Started out early and caught the car. Brig. Gen. decent head, army car right to the Ace of Spades. Nice day. Got a car from Colonel Hammond, right home. Boy "Oz" and I are lucky. Woolworths hit a time bomb at Greenford Hotel. Say, it hasn't started yet. He'll smack it flat. He's got it all.

MONDAY, 30th

Usual drill. Got a damn fine pair of boots. Yessir! Ok now.

OCTOBER

TUESDAY, 1st

Nothing of import. The usual drills, etc.

WEDNESDAY, 2nd

Pain persists. I sometimes wonder if ever I shall be free of it. I hope for the best. It can't go on. Field training is easy. I like to be out amongst nature; my memory is sweet yet sad. Got a letter from Joan. A bomb dropped at Seagull (pub) hurt her slightly. God! To have the constant reminder that they may be wiped out at any moment. Still, I'll look at it with philosophy. Yes, I think I could make it. Still, I know it's nothing compared to what they will get. We're up against a mighty brain and its organization. I doubt if "London" will come through it. Reports of being sent to "Egypt." OK. It's working around for me. I said it would come. The kid will look into the sun again.

THURSDAY, 3rd

Bad weather is settling in. I think the enemy has not located Deep Cut, etc. Some heavy stuff dropped, and I felt a terrific concussion. I guess they'll lay it out. I think the people are now accepting Hitler as a great genius. The government is now revealing a few things. The sight in "London" is pretty bad. People of all descriptions line up early, 2:00-5:00, for the best positions in shelters, plus their blankets, food, etc. Pitiful sight! Still, they are plucky, with plenty of wit and philosophy. Lots of people are getting out. The bus line charges 2 shillings and 6 pence for a safety trip into the country for the night and return in the morning. They're charging for reservation of places or concrete in underground shelters. I jot these down as a future reminiscence.

FRIDAY, 4th

Big day. Pay. 10/-. Received the same without much enthusiasm. It's certainly well-earned.

SATURDAY, 5th

Sweated on being free this weekend. (gun mg) 1st Sat and 1st Sun. By hell of all the lousy luck. Raining like hell. Messed about lining up, etc. On guard 10:00 -11:00. Heavy barrage over London. Still knocking the hell out of her. Dropping stuff here, too. Yeah! Anderson got excited over the flight of "Huns."

SUNDAY, 6th

Still raining. Damned uncomfortable. Big, great coats on. Saw Junker 88 by himself, daring sod. Sent Joan wire can't come, too bad.

MONDAY, 7th

Preparation for passout. Will be glad to move to new hunting grounds. Boys are getting excited over it. Sheriff wants us perfect. Blanco, shine, hair, etc. Hell's delight, all this for an hour's drill.

TUESDAY, 8th

Drilling pretty hard now. It'll be easy. Nothing of import.

WEDNESDAY, 9th

Half day off for clean up, etc. Worked up to 11:30 preparing for it. Taking stuff for gut for 2 weeks, hardly any improvement.

THURSDAY, 10th

Passed ok, drilled well. Squad done its stuff, fell on the gun a bit though. I was ok on Predictor. Colonel said Ok, half day off. Beat it home by road. Went for Joan in the factory. Terrific at night, gunfire, bombs, by hell. I didn't realize it. Poor bloody people, no rest or sleep. Scream of shrapnel, planes flying low. Joan is sticking it well, though. Waited hours for trains and got in at 10:00. Sgt. Major played hell! Nothing was done about it, though. Packing tonight.

SATURDAY, 12th

Started at 6:30. Up at 4:00. Marched to "Farnborough." Started from "Farnborough" at 9:30. Me, Mish and Blonde in 1st class coach together. Not bad, usual cheering, etc. Rations of 2 sandwiches, meat, and pasta. Passed through "Salisbury, " "Exeter, " "Truro, " "Plymouth, " "Devonport." Decent trip, a nice country, a nice town, and a waterfront in "Plymouth." Good to see the sea and tubs. Wild country "Cornwall, " old houses, thatched, the pretty seaside town here. Arrived at "Perranporth" at 6:30. 10 hours travelling then a march, by hell, it was terrible, up and down. 50 lbs or more of a pack and harness on the back. I sweat, the straps were cutting my shoulders, cold and sweaty. 6 miles on rough, stony road. But by hell, we made it. Had good supper. Mish and I worked 2 meals, and so went to bed.

SUNDAY, 13th

Slept well, except for cold at times, on bare springs. Breakfast. Few orders. Had a look at the surroundings, pretty bleak and wild. The sea looks good, with huge rugged cliffs and a nice sandy beach. Small camp, 600 men and plenty of guns, though. Had a walk with Mish. Nice walks here, lovely scenery. Well, I'm glad it's only for 2 weeks. It's a bit too wild, etc., although I love the sea and its rugged beauty, reminds me of "Half Moon Bay" in Canada, Yessir. Still working on my grub racket. Good grub. All in together now, the squad. It looks to be easy here. Monday will bring new things. Lousy weather, wind, and rain.

MONDAY, 14th

Caught duty first thing. Gun manning. Say, is it windy up in this burg? Blows like hell. Easy time today. Laying about doing nothing. Small dug out with Lewis gun, telephone. Overlooking the sea, lovely view. Done 2 hours of night guard. I received calls of warnings, saw lights over the airdrome, and reported the same. Rained and blew a gale.

TUESDAY, 15th

Still on guard. Fairly calm today. Boys on Predictors now. I think we're on a shoot tomorrow. They are fairly slack here, not half the discipline as at "Deepcut." Sea smells good.

WEDNESDAY, 16th

Didn't do march. Played in a match for C.3. Our half lost 3-1. I played a decent game, according to the boys. Very easy here. This town "Penhale" is situated on a high cliff overlooking the sea. "Newquay" 6 miles off. Beaches on either side.

THURSDAY, 17th

Boy! Do I feel that game? Stiff all over. Firing today. Rumours detailed for "Egypt." I knew it. All along, I have felt it. Persecutes me, the lust. I said the chance would come. Leaving tonight at 7:00 this day of Thursday the 17th of October 1940. I also passed out as a Layer Gunner after 20 rounds, numbers 2&3. Elevation, and Traversing on Predictor. God knows how long for. Now it has come, I am sore at heart. Loneliness overcomes me. That sense of desolation I've always felt whilst starting again. But I reckon it's my lot, though, wanderlust.

FRIDAY, 18th

Started out by Lorry last night, 80 of us. Mish wasn't keen. Blondie lost the toss, later voluntarily. Charlie, George. 4 of us out of Company 3. Boys felt it, well, we all did. Didn't like being split up. I shan't forget. We may meet again. Yeah, I'd like to see them all again. We got the train at 9:00 from "Perranporth." Went as far as "Truro" in a luggage van, then changed into a mixed passenger. Me and George in compartment with two Sailors, both drunk. Slept. Passed through "Bristol, " "Redding, " "Swindon, " G.W.R. 16 hours travelling. Arrived at "Farnborough" 9:00. Got lorries to "Blackdown." By the way, they gave us two lousy sandwiches for the whole trip. No drink of any kind. Anyway, after going through 5 hours of red tape we eventually got our leave passes and money, 30 shillings and travelling warrant. They took us by army lorry to "Brookwood." Boy that was a ride. What a driver. 1/2 hour to get

8 miles (he done it). Got train ok, and so home, about 7:00. That made it 30 hours moving. Full Kit all the time. Harness, big pack and Kit, boy!

SATURDAY, 19th

Didn't do much just took it easy. Went to dance, got boozed. Changed into civvies. Sure, was a change.

SUNDAY, 20th

I'm damned restless. Miss the boys a hell of a lot. The Gerry is pretty busy over here. Yeah. Just after dark. Everything from bombs to shrapnel guns, planes low. Bomb fell near Mrs. Whites' house, smashed the whole street. Untenable now. Also, bottom of the street by Townhall. Smashed house flat.

MONDAY, 21st

Feeling damned queer. Sore throat, pains in all my joints. Forgot to mention for Sunday, the guy at the dance getting familiar with Joan. I didn't like it. No! So, I fix. Oh yeah. Guy was scared. Only bravado, absolutely. Spent a hell of a night, illness taking grip.

TUESDAY, 22nd

Spent a lousy night again. Throat pretty bad. Bloody rough, on leave, too. Guess I'll get over it soon. Still, I'm restless. Being used to the boys and having plenty to do, I guess, is what it is.

WEDNESDAY, 23rd

Feel much better now. Of all the luck, being ill on leave! I reckon I shouldn't have changed into civvies and a different air from "Cornwall" too.

THURSDAY, 24th

Well, this is the last day of my leave. Feel damned restless. Don't like the idea of going back at all. Joan very effusive. She's late with monthly, a bit worrying. I made myself look silly on Sunday. I guess the guy won't bother her again. She looked good, though. I couldn't help it. Went around to see the boys. They're bashing the hell out of London still.

FRIDAY, 25th

Left at 8:00, got a train to "Paddington." Had to change at "Piccadilly" for "Waterloo." Raid, saw them above. Bomb fell at the station. Got to "Blackdown, " blasted dump. Cold and miserable, rotten grub and beds. Froze during the night. Fried roll for breakfast and all bloody stuff to give us. Went and saw Sgt. and Rodgers for the last time. Haven't heard from the rest of the squad.

SATURDAY, 26th

Got together again. All kit. Started at 1:00, by army bus. Got to "North Farnborough." In train me, Blondie, Charlie, and George, still together, started away. Well, of all the blinding rides. "Waterloo, " 40 miles away. We went dead slow, though, through "Southampton" then "Chatham, " "Gravesend, " "Dartford." Took 8 hours. Clear the lines, they said, we haven't had anything to eat yet. Good god, the British army is horrible. What a waste of time and expense. Got off at "Dartford." By lorry to barracks, through shot and shell, so to speak. Arrived at H.Q at 11:00. Familiar red tape, lined up for bedding, full Kit on, too. Palliasse of straw, good god, we were faint with hunger. Had supper, pretty good. 12:00, so to bed. What a bed. I laugh.

SUNDAY, 27th

Breakfast, good. Sort out. The 4 of us split up. Me with 40 others. Put in the stable of old horse artillery. Stone floors, crammed together. The worst yet. Candle for light, cold shave. Big place, though. 5, 000 men barracked. Went out. 2 bombs dropped while I was in the street. Bit of a scare. It's quite a change from the strict training regiments.

MONDAY, 28th

Getting cold now. Milled about a bit in the usual herd manner. Signed Declaration of Loyalty to conform with the draft. Don't know how long we're here for, docks close by. Short arm inspection

TUESDAY, 29th

Up at 6:00, breakfast at 6:30, dinner at 11:30, and tea at 5:30. That's just to demonstrate the system here. They have loudspeakers for all calls or orders. We seem to line up for everything. I don't know. For a long-established Depot and H.Q of the R.A it's lousy. I'm afraid the lousy organization is general of the British army. Broke off early, and went out with some boys for a walk. Not a bad town "Woolwich." Using starlight here. Arsenal close by. Some pretty heavy guns here 6 inch-7 inch. What a laugh, conditions, blasted stables, straw. Some get up, some don't. I didn't shave till 11:00. Nobody seems to care. Why does old Charlie know more than some Sergeants? Issued with Tropical Kit, all canvas. Say! It's light - shorts, topee etc.

WEDNESDAY, 30th

Could easily make a dash home, via "East Ham." Think I'll try Sunday. Would be nice for Joan. The old basking feeling is present. Just to sit in the sun, near water, and dream. I crave that. Oh, "Half Moon Bay"! Long pants, ok. Grub darned good here. Met Frankie. Expect to pull out soon. Pay 10/-. I'm just following the rest of the herd. I'm interested in nothing but the new hunting grounds. To hell with the army. I shall await my opportunity. They actually inspect the stables for all the dopes. Blankets checked and other silly things of that calibre.

THURSDAY, 31st

Nought of import. Drill yesterday. Expect we shall move off next week. The weather is fair now for November. I guess we shan't see Xmas here. I shall have to figure out the different Xmas I've spent abroad, in all conditions. It's funny, though, I should move again. I figured I would never be settled for long. Talk of wanderlust! The comparison is small; I am more or less forced into it.

NOVEMBER

FRIDAY, 1ˢᵗ

Done nothing again today, but hang about. It's alright here, no work, but a crummy marching drill. Finished at 2:00. No to the Express Dairy-to hell with Frankie. Shall make a break for it tomorrow. They're blasting away now, here. But hell, they came over today and dropped bombs without a siren. It's a lot of bull. Did I mention "Greece" had been invaded by "Italy"? Well, that is the start of the finish, I guess. We shall see.

SATURDAY, 2ⁿᵈ

Pretty wet. Guess I'll beat it in the afternoon. Bomb fell 10 yards away from the door of our stable. It was a small one, though. Bloody good thing it was, also, on the Canteen. It's alright here. Yea, good grub. An hour's marching drill and were finished. Frankie didn't come, nuts! Express Dairy is alright. Took 2.5 hours to get home, a 15-mile journey. Boy is the East End bashed about; whole streets smashed down. Gee, is it tough on the poor sods? There they lie on the stone floors in the tube stations, on blankets, trains running about 2 feet away. Cold and draft, young girls, kids, and babies. They had to get up at 4:30 as that's when trains start, you see. It's a hell of a sight, civilization. That's all this country offers the people here: misery and an existence. Mind you, they take it, yeah, they got to. Poor old "London, " old and dirty, wounded and hurt, but she'll make it, yeah. She gets nasty at times; she shrieks her hate and defiance by siren and gun and then laughs at the tragedy of it all.

SUNDAY, 3ʳᵈ

I spent the night with Joan. Up at 4:00, got back to find nobody had bothered, so back to Joan again. Had a decent stay, nothing unusual. Harry doing well with the accordion, Jack also on it. Mention of Vi getting engaged to Gordon. I don't like it, Gordon's alright, but there's something uncertain about it.

MONDAY, 4th

Started early and got back ok. Nothing doing much. Went out with the boys, saw a good show. Not much change here, an hour's march, drill, finish. I just putter along. I don't give a damn.

TUESDAY, 5th

Usual procedure. 9 bombs on "Woolwich." Here now in barracks. Thought of something today, you know I think I know what's wrong. No ambition. When I was young, I had ambition, you know, I mean about 14-20. I wanted to travel, make new trips, get home, and see the folks. My eyes were continually being opened. I don't seem to have the same love for it. Ah well, it's got to end sometime. I wonder if I'll have it back.

WEDNESDAY, 6th

Charlie getting on well with the squad. Surprised the boys. Word came in today, yeah detailed for the East. Pity, though, different draft. I guess we won't be together now. Good to see Mish. Ah, well, it's a small world, so we might meet over there. Still easy here. Nothing to do all day.

THURSDAY, 7th

Got paid, usual. Let down for Express Dairy, something wrong somewhere. This blasted outfit. What can one expect, no headway?

FRIDAY, 8th

Route march. Good. Got a funeral escort. I guess I'll get home tomorrow if all's well, I think. Mish, Draft will be away soon. Toby, North, and Spott at "Deepcut." Nicklin and Pittam are on staff at "Blackdown." Morrison, Philips, and Bateman at "Newcastle." Perty and Parrect at "Glasgow." Some more in some other countries Just to illustrate where some have gone. Went to a funeral, very impressive. Bombardier killed in cinema by bomb. First, the firing party, then the full band, then the gun wagon with a coffin covered with a flag, then mourners. Slow march. Band good. Damn it, I felt sad. To think of a young chap on such a lovely day. There are 2 more besides. Still, 1000s have died like this, purposeless. What a lousy way to die.

SATURDAY, 9th

Got away at 11:30. went via "Charring X. East Court." 2 hours travel. Nice to see Joan. Went to L. Hall. Had good singsong, got slightly oiled, also danced. Wore P. Cap felt a fool in it. Jack pretty tight, I laugh. A good evening. Well worth the risk.

SUNDAY, 10th

Up at 4:00. Went via "Ealing." Got through ok. Had breakfast. About 4, 000 men lined up for it. Made it, though. 26 missing from the squad. Result: Parade 2:15. got away at 3:00. Home again, played cards at brother Bert's. 5/- win, helpful. Vi thinking of engagement to Gordon. Shock to me. I shall try and dissuade her. Only 18, hell not yet. Harry in a new squadron, getting on well. Jack also. Haven't heard from May or Norman. I ought to mention May has 3 kids. Norman about to get married. Now a pastor. Cled in signals, still R.A. Chamberlain dead. Roosevelt in again. Greeks driving Italians back. Good day.

MONDAY, 11th

Good weather. Italian planes used, 16 brought down. Almost 3000 lost up to date. Lots of our shipping lost. Bit of shrapnel hit me, bounced off the window. Say, they won't get me. The boys have changed yeah! Don't see em much now. I guess the squad tie is broken. Blondie, Charlie, and me are all that's left. Good guys. How long is this bloody waste of time for? I'm doing nothing. Time is valuable. Where will it end? We may move tomorrow.

TUESDAY, 12th

Nothing. Funeral again. Damned sake. Well, I guess I'll see a lot of this. I haven't changed or had a bath for 3 weeks. No facilities.

WEDNESDAY, 13th

Well, I guess we're away. Ordered to be ready in full Kit by 3:00. Blankets etc. by 11:30. Damned shame, I intended to get home last night but left it till tonight. Too late now. I would have liked to have seen Joan though. God knows how long before I see her again. Well, I liked" Woolwich, " near home, good grub. Still, it'll work. Good to get away from stables and candlelight. Supposed to be going to "Glasgow." Tea at 2:30. Wrote to Joan. Couldn't get letters or sugar. Saw the last of Mish, Jock, and Tick. 10 coaches took us to "Earls Court." Waited about like sheep, full Kit, in the rain. Holy bloody smoke, they took us to public shelters, crammed up. I'll go nuts. Mad dash for the train. Away at 9:00.

THURSDAY, 14th

Slept brokenly. Fast train this. "Midlands," "Crewe" and "Carlisle, " are all I saw. Came into "Glasgow" docks at 9:00, hung about. 3 ships alongside. Otranto is our boat. Went into the bowels of the boat, on Hold deck, filled with hooks for hammocks, bunged in anyhow. Swore and blinded for dinner, finally got it at 12:00. First meal for 24 hours. Lousy meal spuds with jackets, peas (dry), and beef. Had to walk up 4 decks to get it. I dished it out, and the bloody swine grabbed all the rice. Never again, canteen under customs. Waited, the boat filled all sorts, about 3, 000 men. Hell, slung hammocks touching each other. I laugh. Guys falling out. But so help me, it's a death trap. Not a guy would get out if anything happened. If we've got 7 weeks in this Tubb, then it's gonna be hell. Boy, what an experience. To hell with this Army.

FRIDAY, 15th

What a lousy night! Cold, hammock broke my back almost. Guys gambling. It seems as though nobody knows anything aboard. They're milling about like lost sheep. I've been right through here, fore and aft. Nice fittings, etc. Aussies gone on strike. Kick about quarters. Say it's a death trap. Don't blame them! Me and Blonde in the cabin. New orders, all J.A draft to get out. Too many aboard.

Bloody good job. It's all to hell. All officers and no one responsible. All line up on keys. 16 buses took us. Arrive at 6:00 at Billets, an old school suburb of "Glasgow." Boy were we hungry. 50 in a large room. Blondie and me together went into town. Say, are these Scotts alright, and how? Give you anything. Women gave us chips on the street. Plenty of dames, civil dames. We shall see. I reckon it will be ok here. Waiting for the next convoy and new boat.

SATURDAY, 16th

Had a good night. Blondie and I together. Revelry at 7:00, breakfast at 7:30. Not bad. One sergeant in charge of 350 men. Me and Charlie got out into "Glasgow." Not bad, big streets, taverns. "Argyle St." Lot of tenements here, 4 stories high, solid. Something like "New York." Hard to understand the Scotts. Forces can go anywhere for 1 penny (bus). I felt like a foreigner, all staring at us. Dames' sassy, and they are all so damned cheerful and sociable. To pass over the "Clyde" is something like the "Thames." Fine big store "Lewiss." Think I'll make the grade here.

SUNDAY, 17th

Fire picket duty today. As a point of interest, I shall set down my various addresses from training on. – R.10 Squad. A Battery. - 2nd L.T Training Reg. R.A. – "Deepcut Camp, Aldershot" (Sgt. Cook). – "Hants, " 2 months drill, all sorts (toughest of all). - C3 Squad - C Battery (on a plateau). Finishing of drill and intensive gunnery (Sgt. Hulme, 2 months) Firing course (40 mm) Steels Battery- "Perranporth, Penhale" (Capt. Steele) near "Torquay Cornwall" (1 week). Detailed for East. 8th reserve Reg. R.A. Blackdown "Hants, " "Aldershot" (2 days). D Subsection, C Battery. R.A Depot "Woolwich London" (3 weeks). – For Convoy, King George 5th Docks, "Glasgow, " S.S Otranto (convoy not ready) – R.C.L. J.A L 12 Langside Transit camp "Glasgow" (Sgt. Potts 10 weeks). Bound for the East. H.M.S. Glenhearn (ex Merchantman) Feb 1st, 5 1/2 weeks. – "Amirya" Transit camp (near "Alexandria") 5 weeks. (B.S.M. Potts) 12 march-18 April. –

H.M.S. Glenhearn bound for "Malta" via the Mediterranean on April 18 (Potts) for 2 days. –St. Georges barracks "Valletta Malta" 21/4/41(2 days) - B.H.Q. 59th Battery, 74th Regiment, Fort Kapsali "Malta" 23/4/41 – T.H.Q.(B.S.M. East) Ta Kali Drome (fighter) near "Musta, Malta" 28/4/41 - Gun Sight "Marsa Sorrosso Malta" 7/5/41 (Sarge Guest) – Gun sight Stoneheap, "Luqa" (Bomber Drome) 5/41-8/41 (3 months) _ "Luqa" rest camp "Birkirkara" 2 weeks (august). – Gun Sight Kennleworth

MONDAY, 18th

Weather keeping well. No raids as yet here. Damned peaceful compared to London. Grub lousy. Spend a lot on food, but the freedom and dames make up for it. Route march, games. There is a certain amount of amenity here in Scotland. They want independence. Well, why not? Each country for itself. Why should one be under domination? It's happening all over Europe. Same here in a different sense. Rumours of leaving soon, maybe "Woolwich" again. Alright, that good grub, get home easy, nice for Joan. 4 weeks till Xmas. Italians driven out of "Greece." War there going well for the Greeks. Our convoy left. Kit bags aboard.

TUESDAY, 19th

Me and Blondie skipped after the roll call. Had a walk to the city. Alright, though, no Khaki about. Dames ok. It's nice to be noticed, though, in this manner. Just follow the rest still. Don't care much what happens. It's got what you can for yourself primarily. Played football. It's just a matter of doing what you like here. Use your head. Rumours of a move. Bert lost a brother, tough! Only 4 weeks till Xmas, might be here yet, perhaps 7 days leave. Swell! The weather is keeping well. Greeks take "Durazzo." Into "Albania" now. Doing well there. Blitzkrieg still on "London." 200 killed in "Coventry." Well, I like "Glasgow" and the people, a vast difference from "Southall." Different classes of people altogether. Pretty rough at night, lots of drunks, brawls, etc.

WEDNESDAY, 20th

Payday, good. I'm flat broke, owing to football, slid out of it easy. So, to bed. Central heating ok.

THURSDAY, 21st

Got out of route march. Walk with Blondie. Damned nice here still. Grub lousy. Had the first air raid for a week.

FRIDAY, 22nd

Of no importance. Letter from Joan, very nice too, sure would like to be back home. Life's funny. The novelty wears off. I would hate the routine of home life later, I know, but one appreciates a lot of things missing. The Armies lousy at all times. Where a man is anchored down, one will always find it. I shall always be restless in this manner. Had free tea at Methodist church, like old times again. Something for nothing.

SATURDAY, 23rd

Saw Rangers & Falkirk, damned fine match. Swell football, "Ibrox Park."

SUNDAY, 24th

Greeks doing well in "Albania." The Europa sunk. We're having Kit renewed. Wonder if we'll see our old Kit. My best suit is in it, guess it's in "Cairo" by now. No news yet of how we'll end up. Got our old officers back. Squad drill in the morning, one laugh. Still bombing London. "Southall" hit. What a lousy war! don't seem to be any gain so far. Gerry establishing himself. I guess it will end up out East. Either that or peace, by Britain. They'll never get "Germany" back to her same status.

MONDAY, 25th

Officers tightening up. Drill morning, off in the afternoon. Me and Blondie went to church. Alright there. Free supper and games, played darts, etc. Women contribute towards food. Damned nice of them. Am broke, hell like this.

TUESDAY, 26th

Usual thing. Very wet now. Went to church again. Saw boys football match, bit lousy. Busted glass of my watch. No news as yet. Received a letter from Joan. Bombs on Palace, few killed. Poor kid must be nerve-wracking for them. Officers came around with a fire bell to wake us. Made a hell of a noise. Pounced on me. I said I was on guard. I laugh. Wrote to Joan. Weather lousy but the grub better now.

WEDNESDAY, 27th

4 weeks till Xmas, might get leave yet. Boy, I hope so. Payday. Usual 10 bob. Do I need it? Yessir sure gets an appetite in the Army. Guard tomorrow had a shuffle.

THURSDAY, 28th

Bloody Captain is nuts, a long streak of shit, like a schoolboy. Took us on route march. Kept up a fast pace. Almost done. Played match, won 3-1. Went to Glasgow, not bad, saw ME. 109, was surprised. Boy, it's appearance is far inferior to British planes. Greeks driving into Albania. Still battering London.

FRIDAY, 29th

Just the same, no change. Weather not bad.

SATURDAY, 30th

"Coventry" and "Birmingham hit badly." Saw a match on Ranger's ground. Army in England versus Army in Scotland. Fine Football, England won. Joan wants to come here but can't be done. I would love it, so help me. It would be lovely for her.

DECEMBER

SUNDAY, 1st

Xmas close, looks as though no leave. Still free grub at Church. New Captain is pretty strict. Went to Baptist Church. Decided to have Joan up for a week. Fixed up rooms for her by Mrs. Wright. Langside Hall free for a week.

MONDAY, 2nd

Fixed details of Joan's coming. Shuffle not bad. Still carrying on as usual here. Weather very good.

TUESDAY, 3rd

Sent latter shall now await wire from Joan. Sure, she'll be happy about it. Rumours of India now. Greeks nearly have Albania now.

WEDNESDAY, 4th

Pay early by half a day. Went into the city, crowded. Weather wet. We're here for a while yet. Okay by me. Shall be alright for Xmas, drinks etc., also sweets, I laugh, easily influenced. Norman got married. Huh? In October. New Kit came in. Damned good job, old Kit, all to hell. Grub ok now. Managing ok on 10 shillings. Game not expensive.

THURSDAY, 5th

Still awaiting wire from Joan. Nothing unusual today. Route march, tour of Art Galleries and Cathedral, very nice too.

FRIDAY, 6th

No wire as yet. Can't understand it should have come. Must see Mrs. Wright. Went to Church supper. Got Kit. Still Uncertain about us.

SATURDAY, 7th

Route march ok, through town. People like to see us. Got telegram from Joan, ok, arriving Sunday. Went to Match with Blondie. Rangers and Motherwell. Not bad. Spent the evening with Mrs. Wright.

SUNDAY, 8th

Church Parade ok. Slept afternoon. Waited 4 hours for Joan. Nice to see her. First long trip for her. Scottish dame helped her. Had a nice trip, she said. I am glad. Mrs. Wright fixed supper for us.

MONDAY, 9th

Fixed up ok now. Joan was provided a night pass. Good room and meals. Had a good night. Went Pictures.

TUESDAY, 10th

Went on a tour of Cotton Mills. Damned interesting. Amusing girls walking about barefoot. Wax floors are the reason. Marvelous machinery. Directors gave us a lovely tea. Fine bus ride, too. This was at "Paisley, East Glasgow." 8, 000 workers. Our bus held up. Got back at 7:00.

WEDNESDAY, 11th

Payday, great! Showed Joan about today. Joan impressed by the city. We went for pictures, tea at Lewis's. Argyle Street, Empire Theatre, Sauchiehall Street, very good enjoyed it thoroughly. Wrights are ok. Joan might stay for Xmas.

THURSDAY, 12th

Ah well, move again. Draft split up into sections for various ports and ships. Blondie and me parted, and both Mitchells. Leaving weekend, I think. Took Kit bags to the Station. Poor old Joan. What a life. Might be out there for years. Going to Greece, I think. Still, I'll come through it ok. I know it. Maybe the opportunity will arrive as yet. Tours, dances, and dinners organized for us. Damn decent of them here!

FRIDAY, 13th

Joan and I went to Pantomime "Babes in Woods." Not so hot. Went pictures. Booked for a show next day. Not a bad day.

SATURDAY, 14th

Draft day cancelled. 50 only going. Blondie, one of them, not me. I don't know what to think now. I guess I'd rather stay. Went show. Lousy, all Scottish, couldn't catch the jokes. Having a nice time with Joan. Mr. and Mrs. Wright very nice, we have a good room, good grub.

SUNDAY, 15th

Stayed in today, had fireside. Joan feeling lousy about her going. Yeah, this time, I feel it. Back with 3 other women, she'll be alright. Goodbye kid. Hurt pretty bad.

MONDAY, 16th

Weather lousy, rain. Not much of interest today. Went church. Can't find "Gone with the wind, " so we shall see.

TUESDAY, 17th

11 gone today. Blondie, Cutter, Jock, M, Deen, Lang, too bad. All split up again. I expect we shall meet again. Xmas week off. No leave. This Institute is located on a hill. Langside suburb of Glasgow. I ride into town. Parks all around us. Queens Park, Kings Hampden Park. International football ground. Plenty of dames, grub better now. Conditions good. No duty. Draft cancelled.

WEDNESDAY, 18th

Payday. Fatigues. Miss Blonde a bit. More rain. Peeled 3 cwt spuds. Miss Joan a hell of a lot. 3 deserters caught, 12 still at large. Must go see Mr. and Mrs. Wright. Bugger football. Saw Mrs. Wright, had tea. Joan got home alright, early too, 8:30 in morn. Very glad.

THURSDAY, 19th

Not much of import. Weather cold, damp now. Xmas, week to go. I expect we'll spend it here. Not unusual for me. No air raids whatsoever here. British advance into Libya, Somaliland, and

Algeria. Greeks advance rapidly to the Albanian coast. Revolt in Abyssinia and other countries. War costing 15 million a day. Raids on London easier now, going for midland cities. Britain playing hell with Gerry. Towns of all calibre.

FRIDAY, 20th

Nothing of importance today. The usual route march from 9:30-11:00, then break. March and rifle drill to 12:30, then dinner. Parade 2:15. Usually football between squads, very amusing the different guys play. Still it's ok. I usually work up a sweat and then wish I hadn't played. Went to pictures, very good.

SATURDAY, 21st

Should have a letter from Joan soon. Half day today. Pass comes in very useful. Weathers not too bad, not too cold, a bit damp. Miss Blonde a bit, guess he's mid-ocean now. We're getting plenty of invitations from people now, for tea, supper, dances, etc., very generous of them. The 6 toughs got sentenced today: Marriot -30 days, Parks – 21, Davis -24, etc. This is a glasshouse. They'll find it pretty tough. No, it's not worth a few days away like that, especially when their wives suffer too. I hope I can consider Joan a little more than that.

SUNDAY, 22nd

Church parade, nice chap, Mortimer. Good service. Had a nap in the afternoon. Found H ok, we went Jewish society tea and social, very nice, all Jews and how, but certainly very sociable, nice serving.

MONDAY, 23rd

Received card, parcel, and letters from Joan, Mum, and Twins. I greatly appreciate this. What a lovely card Joan's is. I felt remorse over the difference in myself. I must write letters of thanks. I have tons of chocolate now, writing material, etc., thanks to Joan how I've learned to appreciate her. Ah! Well, there are more Xmases to come.

TUESDAY, 24th

This is Xmas Eve. This is not the Scotsman's week. They celebrate New Year. The weather is good, no snow. Half day. Slept. Went to flicks, not bad.

WEDNESDAY, 25th

Day off. Good breakfast, porridge, bacon, chips, etc. Read till 12:00. I am reading a lot now. Dinner very good, baked spuds, peas, pork, apple sauce, etc., plum pudding, mince tarts, tea, very good. Was surprised at lines of dames. Went to pictures, darn good show, and got in for 8 pence. Thoroughly enjoyed it. Bert and I went to social. Hell's delight, it was bloody awful. About 60 old crows sitting about drinking tea and knitting, while we had tea. After, with a piano, they tried to get us to dance, not hope. No single women allowed. I laughed. What do they think we are made of, holy ol doodle! One old hen was a secretary. Kept on ringing a bell like a fire alarm. I had a dance, the only good one. I happened to be the only one on the floor. Ouch! Bussed off about 10:00. Went over to Canteen. Ok there, party going, joined in.

THURSDAY, 26th

Weather holds good. On guard tonight, don't mind. I've escaped fairly well. Route march. Afternoon off to clean up. Got the first guard. Went to meeting with Feury. After 7:00, singing, tea, and a parcel each for us. Beat it back. Say, some gift! Boot polish, socks, toothpaste, 20 Players, Box of Matadors, handkerchief, pad, box of sweets, shaving soap, duster, inner pads. Not bad! Damn good of the people, what! Got through guard ok, nothing to it. Forgot to mention the presents from Mrs. Sommerella. Yes, damn nice of her. I shan't forget.

FRIDAY, 27th

Got invite to New Year's party. Finish off guard. Well, this is Xmas over. I shall remember it for many reasons. Haven't heard from Joan yet. I guess I will soon.

SATURDAY, 28th

Half day. Haven't anything to do. Guess I'll go to the pictures. Things going on as usual, no difference. Pretty dreary here. Wet and damp, cold, grey, miserable. Then I think of the warm south with its sunshine and soft background. What a contrast. Saw a good picture, came out, had to try for supper rather in the YMCA. Thought I'd get away with it, but she caught me, cost a bob. Wandered about. Plenty of drunks, fights, etc. Got in at 11:00. Using a permanent pass.

SUNDAY, 29th

Church, parade, slept afternoon. Went to the Jewish Institute, social, and dance. Very good. Letter from Joan. Very good Xmas. Good!

MONDAY, 30th

As above. New Year soon, 1941. Guess it won't be much for me. Who cares?

TUESDAY, 31st

New Year's Eve. Pretty cold. Got invited to a party. Went to Gorbals, had a couple of pints, ex-serviceman treat. Plenty of booze. Had a good supper, whiskey, etc. Old tradition of coal. Almost spewed my tea up after whiskey. Boy, was it hot. Stayed till 5:00. So, to bed. Percy tried to use his jack-knife in the cafe. Some fight left him in the passageway. He went to sleep, we forgot him.

JANUARY

WEDNESDAY, 1st

Another New Year. Wonder what's ahead. How long must I waste time here? Rumour says we move again soon. Snowing like hell, boy, and is it cold. Went to Y.M.CA. Play on, very good, fine big place it is. In Sauchiehall street. Big Theatre and cafe etc. Had a good meal for 6 pence. Got in fairly early, with lots of drunks, but still not as bad as it's cracked up to be.

THURSDAY, 2nd

A letter from Joan saying they had a good time Xmas. Nothing of importance here.

FRIDAY, 3rd

Had alarm. You know it was quite nice to have them. When I think back to the sirens 5-6 a day, the guns, the fires and flashes, great bombs going off, ruined buildings. It all seems like a dream now. The shells burst, flashes. Well, I can't forget it. Ozzie and I go home Sundays. I got to like it, yeah, and how. I'm homesick for this. Air shelters and tubes with people sleeping in them. Marvellous. The hum of the bomber came closer and lower, waiting for the scream of the bomb. Scared that it may fall your way. No, not yet. It falls nearby. Boom, Good god, what power and it's still going on. On Sunday, they dropped 2-3, 000 lb fire bombs on London. Destroyed Churches and public buildings. Disastrous. The British are pounding away. Entry of "Bardia" and we are still here.

SATURDAY, 4th

Half day. I went small stamp. No signs of leaving yet. It doesn't look like it either. Received a parcel as a present from Violet. Very nice of her.

SUNDAY, 5th

Church Parade, alright. Boy, it sure is cold. Now cold and frost penetrates all these clothes. Well, we have nothing else at the moment. Jewish Institute tonight. Stamp, ok.

MONDAY, 6th

Usual stuff. Mighty cold also yellow fogs. Most of the boys are down with flu and colds. At night, they cough incessantly, waking you up. Draughts and no fresh air. Cold weather, standing about, Route march, they get hot and then cold, no wonder. I've got another cold again and am just getting over one. Went to Methodist Church. Wrote letters. Am on my own now, much better.

TUESDAY, 7th

Order to carry a side pack with eating tools. Out for long march. Walked a good 15 miles, I reckon, hell, it was tiring. Had dinner in a Public Park. Some laugh lifted about a half dozen bottles of mineral and 1 lb sweets. Went to bun fight and a concert. Damned good.

WEDNESDAY, 8th

Half day. Pay. Went to see "Great Dictator." Very good, his speech was amazing. Went to the Empire Garrison Theatre. Not bad. Letter from Joan, enclosed letters from Dorothy and Norm. Very good, too, married 2 months now, trying to graduate. Let's hope he makes it. Funny though, I'll never forget that once members of our family were in need of help. It never came. It might spiritually but never materially from any sod. It's all very well, but you cannot eat that stuff. They didn't know, I guess. I shall remember, though.

THURSDAY, 9th

Weather warmer now. Usual stuff. Air raid, and nothing happened. Dance for the boys at Dixson's Hall, "Cathcart Road." Very good.

Had to wear gym slippers. Good time. Reminds me of the Locarno in "Southall." Yeah, decent joint. It's that good. They are too fond of Reels up here. Very few decent dancers.

FRIDAY, 10th

D section gym.

SATURDAY, 11th

Half day, on guard too, worse luck. Must go to Scouts Club tonight. Shall try and get the first shift. Cleaned up all afternoon. I shall never try to attend, man, again. Guy with unsightly boots got it. I got the first shift. Scouts club, ok. Good fun. Spent a decent guard.

SUNDAY, 12th

Easy guard. Jewish Institute tonight. Very good, too. I'm still in working order. Technique is ok. Lovely weather now, fairly warm, sunlight. London bashed about.

MONDAY, 13th

Lots of rumours still as regards leave. Usual stuff. Mighty awkward route march. Ice on the road, very slippery. Wrote a letter to Joan and Norman. Norman and Dorothy are both studying for pass out. They seem to be quite happy together. They have been married 3 months now. Bit worried about Joan's periods.

TUESDAY, 14th

Long march, bloody tiring. Marched 10 miles. Dinner of sandwiches. Don't know what for. Received a nice parcel from Joan. Chocolates, Cigarettes, and very handy things. Everything's ok regarding her period. Very relieved. "Plymouth" bashed about. 10, 000 incendiary bombs dropped and tons of bombs. Hellish. Land mines at "Ealing." British advance in "Libya." Greeks doing well. Most of Company 3, (old squad) in "Glasgow." Haven't seen them yet. Pretty much by myself now. Miss Old Blonde. Can't seem to pick a companion, damn and blast it. My former solitude is showing itself. I pay for it.

WEDNESDAY, 15th

Pay day. On fatigues, easy. Finished at 10:00. Pay 11.50 Went to city. Pictures, show at WMCA very good. Have good tea there. Lovely moonlight nights now. So endeth this day.

THURSDAY, 16th

Tour of Lochs today at 9:30, in coaches. Held up, waited until 11:00. Cause- Let down by dinner arrangements. Had to bring grub. Freezing in coach. Sat with Shieshard, went through "Glasgow." Surprised at the size of city. Very dirty, drab, crowded. Reminded me of "Southampton." Out in the country was very nice. Joan's chocolate came in handy. Lovely scenery near Lochs. Finally, "Loch Lomond, " lovely. A lake hemmed in by mountains and hills. Snow on tops glistening in the sunlight, very pretty. Water calm, it winds in and out and reappears way off. Lovely road winding around its edges. Stopped once at "Luss, " near "Loch Long." Stop for lunch. Hell, what a lunch. Bread, bully beef, about 2 inches of it, a bit of cheese about the same size, tea in rusty bowls. But I was bloody starving, glad of it. Keen air there, very healthy. Mountains, same proportion covered with bracken, still it's got nothing on the Rockies. Hell no! Beats it to a frazzle. On the way home, the road ran along "Loch Long" (salt water). Saw convoys also, seaplane bases, shipyards, and so home. Wrote letters, etc., early at night. Damned good day, seeing the best beauty spot in Scotland. Funny to think Rob Roy once strode these highlands.

FRIDAY, 17th

Usual stuff, route march, squad drill. Fairhead gone. Damn, good job, he wasn't liked. Played the footer for the D section draw. 4-4 good game. Parcel from Joan, fags and chocs. Good kid! Night in, read a book by service. Good kip. Pretty cold still. Southampton bombed and sunk by 50 Gerry bombers. Too bad, damned fine cruiser. 20 Stukas brought down in revenge. Illustrious bombed, damaged, ok though. British at "Tobruk" in "Libya." Greeks advancing slowly. 80, 000 Italian prisoners in "Libya." "Bristol" and "Plymouth" bashed about. Britain retaliated at the "Wilhelmina" U-boat base, causing much damage. They're knocking the hell out of each other, and I'm damned if I can see them getting anywhere by it. I don't think they'll subdue Germany. Ah, they'll come to an agreement, I guess. Britain's got too big a bite.

SATURDAY, 18th

Same again. Half day. Went to see Rangers-Hearts at Ibrox. Good show. Pitch- snow and very slippery. Amusing to see em sliding about. Rangers all creamed em 2-0. Walker playing for Rangers. Good front line. Tea at church canteen. Went stamp. Scouts Hall. Tiny and gang quite good. Lots of fun. Boys on the new draft back from leave. Say London's damaged, and all large cities getting it now.

SUNDAY, 19th

Church, not bad. Afternoon in. Boys made too much damned noise to sleep. Went to the Jewish Institute with Tiny and gang. Good tea and dance, very warm though in clothes and boots are heavy. Mighty cold, wow! Colder than the south

MONDAY, 20th

E section to have a course at college for a refresher course in Glasgow. Pity we can't have some form of education. Waste of good time here doing nothing useful or good. Had a hot bath at the baths on Calder St. Very nice, too. Bitterly cold, though, now. The other draft might move off soon. Also, up for leave. Hell, and how? Joans brother Wally called up. Pioneer company, poor sod, rough outfit. His eye trouble let him down. Still, he'll get on with his education.

TUESDAY, 21st

Gym ok, the rain washed all the snow away. Very wet and muddy. Glasgow is mud and slime. Bert in Hospital broken rib, poor sod. "Tobruk" taken by the British. Raids less over Britain now. Glasgow not touched yet. Went to pictures and church hall. Ping pong with boys, ok. Have a good book.

WEDNESDAY, 22nd

Too wet for a route march. Pay 11/- saved 4/- for a gift for Joan, got scent, etc. Gave me much pleasure. Pictures Jamaica St. Good. Came back and went to free with Tiny and the gang. Bun fight and Social, evening ok too.

THURSDAY, 23rd

Not a bad day, looking forward to tonight. It turned out to be a momentous day. Got to the do me, and gang just going to start the fun when the Staff called me aside. He had received a telegram from Joan, accident. Say, some shock. It scared me. Couldn't make it out. It could be anything. Staff arranged with O.C. for 4 days of compassionate leave. All fixed. Left Central 9:30 train. Packed. Sat in the lavatory nearly all night, had the usual gutache to keep me company. Lost grub I had given to me. Chap gave me some bread and cheese, though, so I wasn't too bad. I lay down in the corridor. Wow, a draft almost cut me in half. Well, got there at 11:00. Joan's face was badly cut, etc. Poor sod fell off the bike. Couldn't be helped.

FRIDAY, 24th

As I stated above, I arrived at 11:00. Right side of Joan's face scraped. Deep cut on nose and lip. Still, it will heal up ok. Saw folks. All living apart now, the usual thing of course. Can't figure it out, but nothing hopeless. Vi and Harry are fine kids, rapidly approaching maturity. Yeah, reminds me of myself at that age. Mrs. Puddy down with pneumonia in bed. Peggy running the house.

SATURDAY, 25th

Slept lots. Good to have some peace and freedom and grub. Had a few drinks, went to the pictures. Joan out. Brave kid to come out.

SUNDAY, 26th

Slept late. Good dinner. Vi came over, helped. Messed about. Jack came over, and Harry. Took Harry in darts. Went with Harry first to Bert's (not in), and he promised he would be too. Ah, well, it's not worth thinking about. Met Pop and the crowd at the White Hart. Had much beer. Lots of noise. Went to a café, had some fun there. So that was a decent gathering.

MONDAY, 27th

Mrs. Puddy (Daisy) got up. Joan is much better. Yeah, it'll soon heal up. Norrie is homesick. Vi at Hoover's. Stayed in all day. Pretty wet out. Got to leave at 7:00 train from "Euston Station" at 9:15. Too bad, but these things must be done. They cut "Southall" out of the London area. Joan loses 3 and 6pence. Blast their hides, dirty swine. Proficiency Pay will make up for it said Harwell. Another session over. Got seat ok. Bloody hell, draughts, I almost froze. Why was the first trip far better? as bad as it was. Fast train, do it in 11 hours. No raids whatsoever on London for 7 days.

TUESDAY, 28th

Got to Central at 8:00. YMCA, ok. Got in the Barracks to find all the guys on leave for 4 days. We were supposed to be sailing Thursday or this week anyway. What do you think of that? That week off, they didn't telegraph me. Otherwise, I could have stayed until Wednesday. Ah, well, so be it. We shall see. It'll all turn out ok.

WEDNESDAY, 29th

Slept well. Blasted mice woke me up at 3:00. Bit cold, put an overcoat on. Parade at the same time. Nothing to do. Wrote Joan and Vi letters. Didn't send it, though, until I knew what's doing. Pay ok. Made query as to repayment warrant. We shall see. Some of the boys coming in from leave didn't have long. I was lucky in a way to have 6 days. Medical ok. Packed kit, labelled etc. Guard cancelled. New proclamation by King 18-40-year old's. Harry is in it. Went to Empire, good. Revelry 6:00 tomorrow. So, I guess we move. Ok. Must mention Harry and Jack getting on well with recorders. All doing well. Mighty wet and muddy here. No regrets.

Chapter 2:
At Sea January 30, 1941 -
February 19, 1941

JANUARY

THURSDAY, 30th
"Aboard ship"

Reveille 6:00, blankets in at 7:00, breakfast 8:00, a gathering of various things such as laundry, boots, handing in plates, cups, etc. Some boys still coming in. All packed now. Dinner at 11:00. Ok. Master parade, full war kit. By hell, enough of it, too. Beginning to weaken already. Found I've packed Joan's letter, must write another. Glad I'm leaving Glasgow. Ah, well, the great adventure begins. Should be some interesting material. Marched to Pollock Shaw Station. Got troop train to "Greenock." Border tender to be taken out to troop ships. Waited an hour or two. Few Air Force and Sailors aboard. Not many of us, 350, I think. Me and Charlie together. Bert still in hospital. Me and Charlie were last of the crowd. Just to think of it, 30 of us, and this book records how we were all split up and parted. Still, there is a good chance of seeing them. Tender moved up along side ship, big convoy gathered here, Destroyers, etc. Waited an hour, blasted freezing, and the usual gut ache before we boarded the ship. Aboard, we were herded into hold, fed corned beef, and tea was much better than "Otranto." This boat, which is 13, 000 tons in size, is clean and warm, like the "Taranaki." Tiny and boys on the other deck. Good Naafi and restroom. Below boys all gambling. Got a letter off to Joan, at least. I hope that guy posted it. It will be a shock for her poor kid.

Ah, well, we'll have our day yet. Headed for "Alexandria," I think. We shall see. Now, I shall enlarge my experience and knowledge.

FRIDAY, 31st

"Aboard ship." H.M.S. Glenearn

Me and Charlie kipped on deck. Nuts to ye hammocks. It was fine on deck, cool, etc., but a bit hard. Reveille 7:00. Staff Sgt. came around, warning they found water from the sink had flowed under my bed. Lovely! Had breakfast. Holy smoke, eggs, and sausages, wonders will never cease. Wrote a letter to Joan. Had a look around. Films, canteen, fags cheap- 6 pence for 20, Woodbines were 20 for 4 pence, not bad. Beer was cheap, too. Boys are playing cards, reading, etc. It is fairly crowded, but still not bad. Navy boat this, 6" guns aboard. "H.M.S Glenearn" 10, 000 tons.

FEBRUARY

SATURDAY, 1st
"At Sea"

Pretty damned hard sleeping last night. Ship got underway about 2:00, down the Clyde River. We are flanked by Destroyers, Cruisers, and Merchantmen. Pretty rough now, running a gale, some tub this, it rolls and pitches like a barrel, worse I've been on. Good breakfast. Ah, boy, all the boys are sick. I laughed like hell. As usual, it hasn't affected me. It won't either. I'm a Seaman first. Dolphin, he looked horrible. Out he went, and gradually, the rest vanished out on deck. They're lying about in all altitudes like dead sheep. Green, yellow, what ghastly pallor's. They've spewed everywhere, on companionways, tables, decks, lavatories, hammocks. Its everywhere. Some don't bother to move; just spew where they sit. #4 deck next to me is awash, yeah! About a foot of water, everything is afloat. The boys are walking around barefooted. George is mighty bad, and Charlie. Good dinner. Had blasted row over plates. Ah, nuts to em, they can't intimidate me. "One first, always". Must sling my hammock somewhere tonight, too, blasted hard on the deck. The water runs from the sink, too, under us. Boy, its good to be back at sea again. Like old times again. The old roll and thump of engines. She's MV, by the way. Don't know how many ships are in convoy, can't see em all. Were headed straight out now, off the coast of Ireland.

SUNDAY, 2nd
Slept in a hammock last night because of the sink running over on the deck. Hammock almost broke my back. Cold wow, the draught from the hatch. Boys still sick. Boy, are some of them bad. Lots of grub now, yeah! Grub very good, plenty of good bread and butter. Me and Charlie together. Ok. 18 to a table. Cross in charge of it. 4 meals a day, supper- like dinner. Today's weather was good, chilly, though, but out of gale. Much better speed. We have 6-gun boats with us. I don't know where we are. I'm sure nobody knows where we are headed for yet. Boat drill on rafts, rather. 18 to a raft,

it's like a huge tire with paddles and rings on. Abandon ship, we dash to it. It's dumped into the water and we dive into the sea after it. There are huge bulletproof boats aboard, holding 100 men, used for invasions or landings. Nuts to that! Plenty of hot water for shaving. Lavatories were a bit crowded, no privacy at all. Still, it's only for a while. Must see films tonight. Plenty of cards, Housey Housey etc. Fixed up hammock again, blasted things, don't like them.

MONDAY, 3rd

Not a bad night. Pretty rough this weather, mist and rain, not so rocky though. Left "Georgie" at midnight, she's going on to New York. Destroyers also gone. Left with one Cruiser now. We're out in mid-Atlantic, so it's not so dangerous. Getting much warmer. Grub is excellent today. Plenty of it, too. Nothing to do all day. I read a lot, up on deck, too. Smoking heavy, I'm putting a few away. They're so damned cheap. Cleaned up a few bobs at cards. No duties yet, so we've lots of time. Sleep like hell and eat. Guts still worry me, though. Should hit "Freetown" Saturday. Well, I'm certainly adding to my stock of foreign Ports I've seen. Yessir! Boy, I can consider myself well-travelled after this. Went to see films(forward), alright, Donald Duck, etc. Bit warm. They're getting a concert up now. They reckon we were 200 miles off New York last night. Holy smoke, think of it, so near yet so far. Yeah, it's good to be back at sea. I always said I would. It's no fault of mine. It just won't leave me alone.

TUESDAY, 4th

Clocks back an hour. It was light at 7:00 this morn. So, I guess we're not so far off. Sea is about the same. Had a descent sleep last night. Much warmer. Grub good still. Boys are over their sickness now. Don't know where we are headed for yet. Got paid yesterday 10/-. Nothing to spend it on, so we shall save it. Wonder how Joan and folks are? Won't know for some time. Knocking out a good 18 knots now. Very calm. Cruiser uses her plane, and she catapults it. It cruises about observing. Is taken aboard by derricks. Had a smack at Housey Housey. 1 Shilling, no good. Very interesting, lots of Brag, etc. Spend a lot of time on deck. Gradually stripping down now.

WEDNESDAY, 5th

Average of 450 miles in 24 hours. Not bad. The 3 vessels are all motor. One Cruiser keeps ahead of us. Water cut off today, getting short. Our steering gear broke down, using an auxiliary. The weather is drying things up a lot. Tiny's feeling a bit rough. I must see my M.O. on my guts soon. What in hell's wrong with me anyway? I've got to get rid of it. Posted a letter for Censor today. Got posted at "Freetown, Sierra Leonne, South Africa". New for me. Packed most of the heavy dress, damned glad to get it off. Shall don light stuff soon, same though better. This is our 6th day at sea now. I'm enjoying it immensely, yessir! It's great, with the open air, the sea, sun, and breezes. It all comes back to me. I remember I mentioned to Joan that it would not leave me. Oh yes, I said, I shall go to sea again, soon too, mark me. And it has. It's not me, it's circumstances. Think I'll read tonight. Couldn't pass the time better. I like the hammock now. Getting news from London, ok. Italians are retreating fast in all sectors. Hmm, we might help that.

THURSDAY, 6th
"At Sea"

Good night last night. Weather is nice, sunny. Making good time. 18 knots. All boats tried out their guns today. The Destroyer first. Boy, did her guns kick up a noise? And our 18 and 12-pounders, holy smoke, almost busted our eardrums. The Pompoms also. Me and Tiny and gang were reading on the well deck quietly when they suddenly let off a Parachute flare. Wow! I went weak. The noise was just like a bomb. Everybody dived for shelter. It was quite a display, like engaging. Gee! When I think of Glasgow, or England, for that matter, I get a sense of desolation. The cold, grey, damp climate compared to this. I still harbour thoughts of the great slide. Yep. We shall see. Opportunity awaits me, I'm sure. It's opening up before me. I can see it. Food is very good. Canned pears for tea today. No duties yet. Plenty to read, Yessir, it's alright. Saw M.O. on gut. Usual stuff, Bismuth. It will ease it for a while, but it will return. Cleaned up 2 shillings on Ponti and lost it on Housey. Housey Boys are getting like dogs now, fighting and arguing over nothing. Familiarity. It's damned warm between decks, especially in hammocks. I'm alongside a hotplate with Charlie and chaps.

FRIDAY, 7th

Nothing much today. Sea is very good. The sun is hot. Making a good 18 knots now. West African Patrol has joined us. Cruiser. Me and Charlie got a fatigue job in the restroom. That's alright. Keep us out of other jobs and PT. Reading on deck a lot now. Boys are lying about like sheep. Must get the old tan on again yessir. Still taking bismuth and doubt it will work. A week today at sea. One hell of a long week. Poor old Dougal down with gastric ulcer. Holy smoke, by the way, he used to bolt down his grub it's no wonder. Chaplain picked up 3 pounds on Housey Housey. Must have a smack myself. Growing ye mustache. Not a bad kid.

SATURDAY, 8th

Getting mighty hot, wow! Sweating in hammock, no wonder, me and Charlie right on top of hot plate. Boys washing hanging all around us. What a sight, Kit bags, webbing, everything hanging about. Went forward for a while. No smoking after dark. See phosphorous fish. Changing into tropical Kit tomorrow. Got it all out and ready. Boys running about like kids. Grub still good. I've got a lovely boil on my neck, rotten blood. Concert on, too damned hot, left early. Johnny the Greek took part. I laugh.

SUNDAY, 9th
"At Sea".

Still pushing along. Lovely today, hot as hell. All in tropical Kit. Yep, mine fits swell. Shorts, shirt, topee. Wearing my patent shoes. Some look good. Spindly legs, etc. George's topee doesn't fit.

What a sight, I laugh. It sits on his head. Fixed my camera, must take some snaps soon, unless the film is bad. Had a bath, washed clothes every half hour and less, water shut off. Holy o'doodle, what a game. The lavatories are all open, stinking horribly. Saw Porpoises and Flying Fish.

MONDAY, 10th

"At Anchor, Freetown".

Sighted land at about 10:00. Good to see it again. Sailed in slowly, anchored at 11:00. Boy, some sight, must be about 200 ships of all sizes and class. Tramps, liners, yachts, etc., and the Royal Navy are dominant. "Freetown" is set upon a hill or mountainside, very pretty. Not very large, though. All 3 of us boats are close to each other with our escort all around us. We had a water ship pumping water out as the natives came out in their canoes with oranges, mangoes, bananas, coconuts, and a few Knick-knacks. Oranges and bananas were 12 & 6 pence. Some of the boys got whole sacks for old shirts and shoes and old watches. I bought oranges, damned nice too. Boy, do the natives look queer? They dress in anything, some with caps, straw hats, forage caps, scotch tams, and turbans. Wear shirts pullovers with bathing suits over slacks. One wore an overcoat, and it was blistering hot. Their canoes are cut out of logs. Generally, have 4 or 5 in it, paddling while one acts as a salesman does all the wrangling. They use baskets for their transactions. Some dive for coins. They sure are fine swimmers and have fine bodies. Bill got 41 dozen oranges for a shirt. I took some snaps. Let's hope they turn out. It's sweltering, 10 degrees from the line. 60 miles. Taking oil aboard.

Freetown, Sierra Leonne, West Africa. With our escort, the
Dorsetshire in the foreground. Aboard ship.

Below: The 2 sister ships of the Glenearn M.V. The 3 of them comprised the Convoy. Taken as we crossed the line. We were the fastest convoy to get through. Average 18 knots, 4 and a half weeks. Bitter Lake Suez

Taken at Freetown, West Africa, Sierra Leonne.

This Boat sold me 10 dozen oranges for 1 shilling. A fellow in the stern of the boat is naked.

Natives of Freetown selling fruit, curios, etc. to Ships Company

TUESDAY, 11th
"At Sea".

What a hell of a night. Good God! I was up 6 times, screaming shits. The fruit did it. I had to stop 4 times to squeeze it back. Wow, and what a gutache there is with it. It's terrific. I was in a cold sweat each time. Also, it worked on others, too. The lavatory was full each time, all through the night. I got back to my hammock but lay and sweat like a pig. Good God! Awful. Left "Freetown" at 6:00, well out to sea now. Getting warmer each hour. Sweltering below decks. We eat naked. The smell of food and sweaty bodies is nauseating at times. At night, holy smoke is terrific. Won't be able to sleep in a hammock tonight.

WEDNESDAY, 12th

Much better sleep last night, slept on deck with Charlie and Wally. Near the companionway, got air from stairs and a draft chimney. Still bouncing along at 18 knots. I reckon it's over the line now. Getting fruit for sweat ration of lime juice each day. Got paid yesterday, but haven't touched last week yet. Chappy is a lucky sod. 30/- again, Housey Housey. No news of home as yet, or anything for that matter. Seeing plenty of sharks, porpoises, flying fish etc. Done some washing; about ten articles certainly needed it.

THURSDAY, 13th

Good sleep again last night. Still mighty hot. Eating an average of 4 oranges a day. Rations aboard are short and cutting down on grub. Boys quarreling and fighting like hell, over grub mostly. It breaks out everywhere. I seem to lash out at everyone. It's the old story, familiarity. It's the bottom end of our table, Slim, John, Porky, and swine's! Always short of grub. Had rain today. I'm breaking out into a rash and whiteheads. Joan should be with me; she'd get em out. Read an average of 1 penguin (book) a day. Lovely on deck, I often drop off to sleep for hours. My hair growing fine now, nice mustache coming on. Joan would like it, ha-ha. On deck now, weathers not as hot as last time I was up this way. Plane from Cruiser practised dive bombing on us today.

Getting overseas news is okay. 3 days off "Cape Town" now. I think we'll get shore leave. Wrote letter for "Cape Town". Bought fruit at the Canteen, okay too, biscuits, etc. Went to pictures. So hot I thought I'd melt. Holy Jack fish, it was horrible. The boys were naked, with sweaty bodies wow. Reckon I'm putting on weight now.

FRIDAY, 14th

Good night again last night. Get the air from the companionway and air chute. Fine weather. Got long pants out, etc. Must get em fixed up tomorrow. Took a snap of myself and Ozzy. Guys got cameras, so I guess there's not much to worry about.

Ozzy and Myself. At sea. Whilst in the tropics. Taken on well deck just above #4 mess deck, companionway. Pretty damned hot, then.

SATURDAY, 15th

Cruiser laid a smoke screen today. She dashed about at full speed, and then the whole convoy took a sharp turn. Boy, did we heel over? I was standing on the well deck near the aft deck when suddenly, the 12-pounders opened up. Good God, I was almost flung into the sea. My head swelled up, and my ears sang. She sent out 4 rounds and put the smoke screen right out. Had eggs for supper tonight, amazing. Fixed long pants up. Shortened them also buttons. Cleaned toppee for shore leave at "Cape Town." News over the radio says 12, 000 troops landed in "South Italy, " British troops. Trouble between Johnson and Cross over lights out. Blasted kids.

SUNDAY, 16th

Good Sleep. I've got 2 hammocks above me touching my face. Charlie at my head, Dolphin at my feet, and so crowded, with feet and fart. Much cooler, heavier seas. Inspection by C.O. of men's walking out Kit. I was on duty, so I kept out of the way in the restroom. Damned good grub still. No gut ache now, Boy! What a relief. Jimmy collapsed, sunburned. Some are in hellish pain with it. My former experience made me wise to it, and yet I look back and am amazed I used to revel in it. I laid it out to get tanned. Maybe I am tough? Played cards with Ozzie Charlie. Lost 2/-. Nice game. Lent me Decameron(book), I always wanted one. George gave me a beauty, too. Hot and how.

MONDAY, 17th

By myself on the floor last night, I prefer it like that. Hell, it gets colder. Target practise by ships, guns, etc. What a racket. We were all kept below. The 12-pounders shook the ship. The Pom Poms, wow! Had good rest in R.'s room. Wrote a letter to Pop for "Cape Town." Getting bored with all this inactivity, though. I wonder how things are at home. I guess Joan is carrying on as usual. Wonder how long I'll be out here? Years maybe. It looks as though this bloody, useless war will go on for years. Good God, what a fool I am to be mixed up in it. Me, a soldier in Foreign Service for what? By hell, I must keep my eyes open. I'm not sacrificing myself for no lousy administration or country, for that matter. I shan't gain whichever way it turns out. Me for myself. Yowsah! Had a shot at H.H. Shared line with Charlie. 13 + 6 Pence not bad, will help at "Cape Town".

TUESDAY, 18th

Should get in tomorrow. Getting colder and rougher. Can expect that off the "Cape", great currents. Changed money, got 15 shillings pay -10 shillings African, rest in silver. lecture by M.O. on venereal diseases, etc. Well, I don't need the warning. I guess I can handle that. Sailors get issued French letters (condoms). Most of the boys are after some. They figure they'll need em. Read a good yarn today. Some descent books aboard. The LT. caught us slack this morning. Blasted Chappie as mean as hell; didn't want to lend me polish. Gave the 4 quid he won to "Viera for safety. Afraid to spend, the lousy sod. I have a great appetite these days. Tried H.H. again tonight.

Chapter 3:
South Africa February 19, 1941 -
February 21, 1941

WEDNESDAY, 19th
Tied up "Cape Town"

Revelry at 6:00. Land in sight. Moving into "Table Bay." Tied up at 8:00. Lovely morning. A beautiful sight, the big bay. "Table Mountain" and others in the background. The town itself spread out all in its shadow. Town runs around its base for miles. Huge power station near large docks. I remember it quite well from last time. City is bigger than I remember it. Tug pushed us in, we tied up, alongside "Carnarvon Castle." Can see the scars of the battle she was in. Also, "Somerset, " a troop ship, is now a hospital ship. Took two snaps of the city and Mountain. Must get another roll. Boys chucking coins to natives on Key. They are nice fellows. Good to see cities, trains, buses, and life. Marvelous to think of a huge modern city in once darkest Africa. It's a beautiful setting. There are many ships here, and it's nice and warm. They're giving us up to 10:30 tonight, shore leave. Great Joy amongst all the boys, all dressed. Taking 25 shillings with me. Charlie, Oz, and I lined up together on the Key side for inspection, ratings, etc. Warmer in long pants and jackets. Marched to gates, then broke off. Holy smokes, the boys scattered. We walked to Main Street, Adderley Street. Everybody is in a state of undress. It's their summer here. Some fine streets, big buildings, and little shopping centers are running off. We had a drink, 9 pence a quart. Good beer, like cider, is off the ice. No treat in bars, not allowed. Felt damned good after it. Dames okay. Hell, of a lot of Half Castes, Black, Yellow, etc. The woman has big breasts. The cops look like army officers. Lots of Soldiers, Sailors. There were 16, 000 who came off our convoy. We stopped for a drink every 1/4 hour. Good Beer. Big Woolworths. We tramped all over the city. Big as "Cardiff" nearly. 12 Main streets: all modern Flats, Hotels, Veranda Cafes. Feeling the beer. Met Aussy. Went to tea, four of us. Big place, band. Damn, fine feed. Left Aussy. Looking for more beer. Went to the Main Streets singing arm in arm. Lovely and warm here. Met a few girls, Dutch. Took us in a Taxi to their home. Had more beer food. Got back to the city on a bus, free for Service. All 3 of us watered the grass in the street. They wouldn't allow us in after 8:30, Police orders. So, we went to the hotel. Plenty more beer. Went to a café. Good feed. Charlie paid, and Ozz ate his grub. Ozz was blind drunk. Charlie was sick in a hotel three times. I soaked his head in the wash basin. Me, I'm okay. I've never laughed so much in all my life. Good God, it was funny. Ozz sleeping with fag in mouth. I woke him up, and he asked for a light. First step, get us on the Docks. Broke into offices and slept on the floor. Got on the Ship at 6:30

Table Mountain, Bay, and Cape Town with dock and power station. Taken from Ship as we entered Harbour.

Combined, Table Mountain, Table Bay, and the city are at the base of Table Mountain. The huge smokestack of Cape Town power station can be seen beside city buildings, cranes, etc., of the docks. The tug in the foreground is pushing us into the dock. Taken from ship

THURSDAY, 20th
Tied up "Cape Town".

Holy smokes, my head and guts! Did we all stink? Oh my. Ozz is ill. I'm dead. I can't move my system. It's choked. Got screaming shits. What a great day yesterday. Getting leave again. Nothing was said as regards last night. Going out in shorts this time. Much cooler. Took 2 snaps of us. Way to go. Had more beer. Went and saw Betty at Woolworths. Had a good laugh, and bought films. Knocked off lighter. More beer. Some beautiful gardens here. And cars, good gosh, beauties. Buick, Nash, Bentleys, and Plymouths. Had Tea, fine. Saw Tiny and Gang. Good band. More beer. Walked a bit. Lost the boys. Went to dance. Had a damn nice dance with a half-caste. Ok. Went for more refreshments. No blackout, gosh, it's great. It's all lit up with signs, lamps, and neon. Went hotel, 2 quarts. In some boys with the doctor. 1ST Lieutenant, nice guy, fixed the boys up, lots of dough. Wandered about. Beer tap costs 35 bob a barrel. I rode my bike all over the streets, staggered back to Docks, had grub, lovely. Took Bus 29 Bree Street. Got aboard at 3:00 a.m.

 Didn't turn out so good. Glaring sun. Ozz and Charlie before going ashore to Cape Town for the day. Taken on well deck. Sacks of spuds included. 2nd picture is Supposed to be me! Pretty bad what! Taken on well deck in my best Tropical Kit. Just before going to Cape Town for a day's leave.

Chapter 4:
At Sea February 21, 1941 -
March 11, 1941

FRIDAY, 21st

"At Sea"

Left at 9:00. I'm all to hell, shaky, tired, and so on. Well, I guess you can't drink from 2:00-11:30 and get away with it. Messed about, watched us pull out, all together. Big Docks here, a natural bay. About 12 boats in, I guess, a lot of neutral. Cleaned up, suits are dirty. Had Kip for 2 hours. Much better now. Rolling like hell on the turn. Hey, figured it out. We drank 165 pints of beer, each! In 2 days! Good Gad, 45 gallons of beer. No wonder we are all to hell. Good thing it was weak beer. It was Castle beer. Home brewed, 9 pence for a quart off ice. Nice drink. We each had empty beer bottles. Looking for a jeweller's shop. Charlie rode the bike all over the city. Read Cassandra, pretty good. Went kip early.

SATURDAY, 22nd

Still rough, meeting breakers of East Atlantic. Good Gosh! I'm still dazed. Got hangover. It's still taking effect. I'm sweating it out now. Got to laugh when I think back on it, it's very funny. "Durban" on Monday. I've got 7 shillings left out of 40. Plenty of Albatross. Cruiser "Glasgow" sighted Raider north of Madagascar, headed our way. Must be our Cruiser Escort gone to "Glasgow's" help. We are still forging along. Rumour has it that we are to go to "Durban" quickly and await news of the cruisers. Might mean a few shore leaves at "Durban" and getting my films done there. I hope so.

SUNDAY, 23rd

Getting along ok. No news of Cruisers. But "Glasgow" engaged Raider at 4:30 yesterday. Reckon, we shall get into "Durban" tonight after 6:00. Inspection by Major, what a bloody fiasco. Gave us half hour notice. Jackets, Puttees, Tops. Holy smoke, what a sweat. Boots dirty, Buttons also, stains all over pants. Ah, to hell with em. Who cares. Passed Inspection, he didn't look at me. Land in sight at 3:00 (Natal County). 6:00 outside "Durban, " messing about, avoiding minefields, suddenly were full steam ahead out to sea. Orders from the Cruiser, I guess. Of all the blinding blasted luck. Dirty doodle, no shore leaves now. We weren't 2 miles off "Durban." Ah, nuts to it all. Same goes for all those guys that are wise or reckon they are. Went for pictures with Ozzy. Saw "Pride and Prejudice, " not bad. Almost succumbed in the heat, good gad, hot wow!

MONDAY, 24th

Still forging ahead. Headed due East now. Must be either "Mauritius" or "Singapore, " "Mombasa, " nobody knows. Grub is mighty good. Salad, fruit. Feeling damn fine. Where the hell is it going to end up? Another fire raid on "London". Damn, and blast it! We can't do anything about it. Dangerous territory behind us. The quicker we get away, the better. Where there's a Raider, there's something else. Took 2 snaps of our Boats and the Boys. Mighty hot, worse than ever. Went 1/6 with Charlie H.H. No good. Sweat ran off. Temperature 126 degrees, 156 degrees- Engine room. Eating oranges all day, Sea very calm. Headed N. East

TUESDAY, 25th

Not a bad night. Sleeping naked near C. Way, also the rest of the boys all around me. Some prize specimens, wow! Dickies of all sizes and calibers. Sea-like glass, half speed. Wonder why? Had a bath and salt water. Good gad! Eating is one sweat. Still, we all clamour and gorge like wolves, heat or not. Sleep on deck every day for an hour. Can't help it. Getting lazy as hell. All the boys are turning black. We are buying tinned fruits, ham, etc., from Canteen. Eating like lords, me and Charlie. Passed neutral Freighter today. Done only 210 miles today. Rifle inspection ok. Well, I guess I don't worry so much now. No, I shall drop it. Guts and hair, used to care, you know, but I think I'm getting past it now. Had a twinge of guts. Wonder if it's coming back. I guess so.

WEDNESDAY, 26ᵗʰ

Woke up with water pouring in through the deck above. Was alright. Just missed me, but Dolphin was right under the air chute. Soaked him. Tropical storm. Guys on deck came in like rats. Sea-like glass, I never saw it so calm. Good God, it's stifling. Something I've eaten makes me stink horribly. I laugh. All guns firing today; practice. Hell, of a racket. Cruisers and dive bombers practice on us, and it gives us an idea of what it'll be like. Passing through "Mozambique Channel" now. No land yet. Sailing N. East for "Mombasa." Eating like a horse. Hell, of an ordeal at meal times. Sweating like pigs. I'm burned up, too. Ah, we'll get plenty of that out here. Some guys are like pigs, bloody buckets of slop under em, spills all over the floor. Hell, it's awful after meals, grub, paper, slop, shit of all sorts. We walk in it. Not one of em will lift a hand to clean the floor. Dirty swine. But of course, I do it myself. They fling all they don't want, such as tea waste, on the floor. They shave, wash clothes, and wash their feet, bodies, and clothes all in the same pan that was meant for the dishes, which same are washed in each mealtime. Got paid 10/-

THURSDAY, 27ᵗʰ

Lousy night, too hot to sleep. Most boys are on deck, so I must do it tonight. I woke up a lot, everyone naked, plenty of good views yowsa! Sea very calm. We're now headed north through "Mozambique Channel, " "Indian Ocean." No land is sighted as yet. Our speed varies, so I don't know. Sometimes half or full ahead. Had the usual kip on deck under the motorboat. Hell, the plates were too hot to stand on. Had the usual slimy dream. That's a dozen now; it must be the grub or the heat. Lovely waste of my youth. Boys are still bickering. One of these days, there'll be trouble. They're like wolves. We're 6 degrees below the line, much hotter here.

FRIDAY, 28th

Last day of the month. Slept on the upper deck last night. Some laugh. Charlie saw a rat run up wire over my head. I was asleep. He couldn't stay. He went below. I got up and spotted the rat run up another wire. Slimy, bloody things. I move to the open deck. Boys were uneasy. Still, I slept ok. No rat is going to disturb me. Charlie and I got a bottle of drink between us on 1/9, which is okay, too. They cleared us off the deck, 5:00 scrub down. Had a usual nap. Slept till 2:30. Slightly cooler today. Flags at half-mast. Somebody dead on "Glasgow" being buried at Sea at 6:30. Poor sod. Hell of a place to die, at sea. Still, he may be better off than some of us, considering what's to come. Talking to a sailor, reckons these invasion barges might be used. We are all going to "Malta." There are nearly 1600 men in this convoy: signalers, infantry, and gunners. Bren Gunners. All complete for invasion. Sicily, I think, as gunners will lay barrage for the rest. These Barges aboard are armoured and hold about 200 men or more each. They are stocked and ready with food, fuel, etc. Flaps drop down for quick get-out. Twin engine, flat bottomed. Ideal for the job. We have men aboard that have been trained for it. They get nearly 3 quid a week for it. Suicide squad. Very valuable cargo. Aeroplane engines and parts, etc. I don't like the look of it. Why Malta? Smashes my plans. It's a bloody Island! What chance have I got there to make a break if I must. Bill Cross has 2 quid pinched from his shirt. Slept on the mess deck, ok. Getting blasted tired of this trip. Still, after a day, it won't take long. Can't get any news from home. Hell's delight will be a big change when I get back again if I get back. Geesh betcha!

MARCH

SATURDAY, 1ˢᵗ

Well, that's one month of it gone. Only about 23 more. It should be nearly finished, then. A bit cooler, but it will get warmer again. Seas choppy. Slept on mess deck ok. Had to move Tandy, though. He's ok. Think I'm putting on weight. Mustache is getting bushy; knew I could grow one. An Italian Raider, flying ensign, when ordered to stop, hoisted the Italian flag. Opened fire. They then scuttled her. 100 prisoners taken.

SUNDAY, 2ⁿᵈ

Still battling along. Took on another Destroyer. Off enemy territory still. Italian Somali near the point of "Aden." Mines spotted. Paravanes used. Shaky moments. Doing a lot of maneuvering. Inspection: missed it, fatigues, got rifle inspection, though. Must write Pop. Hells delight it gets hotter and hotter. Can't sleep below, can't do anything. We have our meals, and then we rush on deck for air. Gets you down too much. We're getting lazy and listless. Sweat pours off us with every movement, but we don't feel it run. There won't be much fat on me soon. The greyhound breed. Wilson at "Viera" the guy is a boar. All those East side guys are alike. Ignorant swine! Had a hard day. Cleaned socks, sewed buttons, and shorts. Washed uniforms and others. Hell, just like home. "Dorchester" left us, going back to the Antarctic. They say she's after that Raider. Our boats sent messages of thanks. Proved that "Glasgow" was a hit. Speed reduced 25 knots.

MONDAY, 3ʳᵈ

Land Ho! Island of "Socotra" off the starboard side. We are now well in "Gulf of Aden." Fairly calm, with no wind or breeze. Wow, is it hot, bloody sight better than the line? News has it 11, 000 Italians and C.O. surrendered in "Abyssinia." African troops were caught in snow and ice without warm clothing or adequate clothing. Rations of 4 biscuits and a tin of bully beef to 4 men. Still, they gained a valuable country. Mussolini's empire in Africa is cracked. "Bulgaria" sold over to Hitler's new social order. The guy gets stronger. Churchill needs to hurry! Order to wear life belts constantly is a dangerous area. Italian Somali off our port bow. Hanging on to a few bobs for "Alexandria." I think it's our destination. More beer! What I would give for a few of those Cape Town long beers on this trip, wow! A lot of bickering is still going on amongst boys.

TUESDAY, 4th
"At Sea"

"Glasgow," nice boat, light, modern, well armed. The "Dorchester" old fashioned, heavy. Very cloudy, lots of rain. Reminds me of the Bristol Chanel. Rain came through the deck again last night and woke us all up. Soaked my bed. Moved 3 times. Lousy night! Had a quarrel with Leiser. Like a wandering Jew, he got his blasted kit all over the deck and left a pail of washing on my post. The usual noise, blind and blast! Still, I won. Not calling at "Aden" now. Straight on for "Suez." Still in the Gulf. Had smack at H.H. No good, usual luck. Pictures tonight, must have a look, see.

WEDNESDAY, 5th

Very good pictures. The usual, singing and sweat. It was terrific. Passed through "Hells Gate" at about 9:30. "Arabia" on one side. Italian Somalia took on Red Sea Patrol, 2 Destroyers. Buoys mark Channel. In the Red Sea, very calm and cooler also. Some dopes wanted to know why the Sea wasn't red! Wrote 4 letters, hope they make it ok. Well, our trip is almost ended. I'm not sorry. You know I'd like to make a dash for freedom. Plenty of adventure, what? My thought, shall I go back? Do I want to? Yeah, I guess so. Have ye fling now. Is it worth it? I feel lonely without Joan. The Sea has no attraction now. . A lot of the boys are down with dysentery. Water is contaminated with oil. I don't drink it. Once is enough. It's thick with oil. I drink tea, on the safe side.

THURSDAY, 6th

Decent night. I'm the only one on the floor now. It's got a bit cooler, so they took to the hammocks. Got the screaming shits again. Hell's delight, what a gut ache with it, wow! I'm on the gallop to aft every minute, water or food. Orders to clean up mess deck and paint work, and also to get everything together. Be in by Saturday, I guess. I got all my stuff fixed up, did a bit of cleaning up, etc. Won't be sorry to get off this blasted boat. It palls too much of one thing: continuous bickering, strife, and enmity. The sooner, the better. German troops in "Bulgaria." Hell will the guy never stop! Well, they'll never stop him now. He'll have a stab at "Turkey." He will make it, too, if he tries. They can't stop him. Much cooler now. In the middle of the Red Sea. Enemy territory on one side still. Close to "Egyptian Sudan, " though. 6 years ago, since I was in the Red Sea last. Viera in hospital (dysentery) Poor sod. They called him back from sick leave. I don't know. I try to laugh. Forget it. I don't care. But I still think of Joan; can't help it. She's around me all the time. Drives me nuts. I can see I'll fail now. I wonder, I have a lousy make up, I guess. Ah well! The future will prove it for me. I always waited, and it came. The sun will always set for me. Got Paid.

FRIDAY, 7th

"At Sea"

Sighted outlying Isles of "Suez Bay." Egypt, on either side. One side, the mountainous coast, other side, low-lying sand hills and dunes. Very pretty. Yellow against the blue of the Sea. So, this again. The land of the Pharos and the ancient Egyptians. I had many curious thoughts as I gazed upon the hills, etc. I'm seeing it through older eyes now and won't forget easily. Getting along very fast. Finally, "Port Suez" 4:00. Dozens of ships here of every type. A few of the large ones were Britannic, Arundel Castle, Cameronia, Orbita. All over 20, 000 tons each, crammed with troops of all sorts. And have the appearance of these ships changed? Wow! I didn't know them. Port Suez on our port bow. Looks like a fairly big place. Plenty of oil and petrol tanks dotted about on the shore line. Big pipe lines along here. I guess we are anchored down now, opposite a freighter with a collapsible steamer on her in 3 parts for invasion purposes. There are dozens of big Liners around us. 2- 3 funnels, etc. This is where they get em, eh? Britain has plenty of boats anyway. Troops moving, Nurses, etc. Doubt if we'll get ashore.

SATURDAY, 8th
"At Anchor, Port Suez".

Pretty cold at night now. Slung Hammock last night. Perty kicked up a noise about me being in his light, and he whined. I soon shut him up. Had a good night. Still got screaming shits, 4 days now. Ah well! I didn't go to the hospital like most of them did. Opposite Castle Boat. Some big Liners, all right, here. No shore leaves. They had all the invasion barges out on trial today. They can move about, too. Carry about 150 men. Estimate about 400 Ships here, nearly all troops. Desert all around us, sand dunes, etc. No bum boys here. Some hawkers selling stuff at exorbitant prices. Charlie bought the chain for 5 bob, holy smoked mackerel, the guy's nuts. When we were in the Gulf of Suez, he asked me if it was the Canal. The Gulf is about 100 miles wide there.

SUNDAY, 9th
"At Sea".

Moved off at about 7:00. They say the Canal has been mined so we are going back to the Red Sea. We are headed in that direction anyway. Hell's delight one large pleasure cruise. 5 weeks now at Sea with one shore leave. About ½ tobacco – sailor -2 bob. I guess the letters got away anyway. Met convoy coming in. "Somersetshire" Red Cross ship left the Cape after us. Weighed anchor in a small Bay, all 3 ships, no escort. Can't figure out what they are here for. Rumour has it that a raid in "Suez" is expected. Cross came around for volunteers for invasion trials on barges. Charlie and I are okay; we are all dressed up. Beaches are just nice for it. Cancelled. Ah, nuts! And so, to bed.

MONDAY, 10th
"At Port Suez and in the Suez Canal."

Woke up to find ourselves in "Port Suez" again. She moved quietly. Big boats all around us. There are about 6 Castle boats here. Moved into "Suez Canal" at 8:00. Fine sight. Monument of lions, etc., at the mouth of the Canal. Sand, desert on either side, about 100 yards across, 90 feet deep, 90 miles long. Lots of houses, villages. Palm trees, camels, and native soldiers were on guard. Other boats are following us. I took 2 snaps. Bloody shame, that's all I have left. Some fine snaps, too, here. I can't remember much of it, though. Order through to pack everything. Boys feverish. Hell, to play. Order to change into a battle dress. God, what a mess they're in. Wrinkled, smelly, and dirty. Mine are awful. Still, we got into them. What a sight they are. It's cool up here, so I guess we need something warmer. I've got everything packed, it didn't take long.

The Suez Canal was taken from the aft of the Glenearn. In the distance, there was a large tug and one of our convoy ships. In between these lies the sunken wreckage of a cargo ship bombed, sunk by Italian planes. There were 3 more behind this one also sunk. They had to be pulled aside to let us pass.

The city of Port Suez was taken from the boat just after we entered the Suez Canal. Canal in the foreground. On the Canal bank are the tents and vehicles of the Egyptian Police and native troops guarding the Canal.

Lots of stuff is being pinched all around me: kit, shirt, etc. Some guys sold their clothes in "Freetown, " "Cape Town, " etc. Dopes! It'll be hell lugging all that kit again. Yeah! Balloon barges along Canal. Little ones like overgrown sausages. Saw Muslim women, covered, also ye natives in fantastic garb. Boys whistling and shouting. Passed an Italian cargo boat that escaped the Canal, got caught halfway, and sunk. Bloody ticklish getting past her. Passed 4 more barges and Tanker in a hell of a state. By aerodrome here, the mouth of "Bitter Lake". Also, Naval Base. They've had a raid here recently; some boats sank, and there were craters all around. Huge camps all about. Thousands of tents dotted all over the sand. It's very flat around here. We've dropped anchor now in "Bitter Lake"—a natural expanse of water between the canal. We are dropping Signals Corps. Here. There are several Italian Prison Camps on the shore of this lake. A Highway runs along the shore. I can see vehicles running along it. Boys went in swimming. Wasn't bad.

Chapter 5:
Egypt March 11, 1941 -
April 19, 1941

TUESDAY, 11th
"At Anchor. Bitter Bay Lake".

The other two boats are with us now. Came up in the night. They are trying the Invasion barges again, running back and forth to shore. The Signal Corps get off at 8:30. It seems we are going in still. Had a raid on "Port Suez" at night at 3:00. No damage done. Suffering Snake, I've still got screaming shits and gut ache. Must be cold in the gut. Get pretty melancholy at times. I think of Joan a lot. Do I miss her boy? I think of the times we quarreled. Very few, I know, but what time lost, where as we could have been expressing our feelings differently, yeah! It sure comes back now. I guess I love her more than I ever knew. Well, there will come the day of retribution. Will I ever forget this boat? Blimy, Vera Lynn on records, I guess not. Me, Ozzy and I have designs for escape. It's possible. It's been done before. Orders to get ready by 1:00. Done so. Swine lifted my side hat and I had to wear a steel helmet. Good God, it was awful! We were in full battle dress and full kit. Two kit bags. Sweat! Wow! We were detailed into barges, packed like Sardines. Driven to shore, got off and dumped our kit on the side. The natives were making a railroad, all chanting while working. The foreman standing over them with bull whips. All swathed in long robe sheets, like long night dresses and twisted turbans. All barefooted amongst the granite and stones. Feet like leather. All bums, calling for cigarettes in a sing-song voice. The heat was burning. They were selling oranges, tangerines for fags, one for one. Lovely oranges. There are military corps all around us. 20, 000 Italians, many Scott's Guards here, airdrome also. There are about 600 of us here on the key side waiting for a train. Fishing vessels along side. Natives smoking calabashes, all talking gibberish. Very funny. All lined up for tea. Tea and one cake. Hell's delight, I could have eaten 1000 cakes. Wish I had brought some bread. Oh well! I guess our troubles start again. Train comes in. The usual time and rush to get in, we had already put on and put off our kits five times in the usual army style. It was agony. Words can't describe it. This is Geneva Camp, by the way. Me and Charlie got in with Tiny and the gang. Coach like Yank ones, big, comfy, lots of room. Pulled out about 6:00. Lots of singing usual thumbs up bull. All wanting fags. Nice scenery, palms, orange groves, camels, and Arab people. Lovely kids, dusky, nice teeth, etc. We had many stops, various stations, natives along the ride with fruit, etc. 10 tangerines for piastre (2.5d), chocolate ordinary bar 1/-. Hell, of a noise, usual bargaining. Got rid of my African half-crown, 2/- change. 6d worth of delight. Got caught, though, only about 3 in a large box. Later on, I got ½ piastre in change change-off guy. Crafty sods! Slept on floor 2 hours. Moon shines lovely like the day. Camp fires, all our and Arab camps. Dave got caught, 2/6, for bread and eggs, laugh. He got 2 piastres in change for 2/6. Bread and eggs are 6d. He lost 2/- on the deal. I whipped up the loaf as the seller passed. Good bread and eggs. Train good speed. We won't touch "Cairo". We are going to the "Sidi Bishr" military camp.

WEDNESDAY, 12th
"In Camp Amrya".

Arrived at camp at 3:00. Usual dash to get out. Small siding, bugger all here. Line up, squads, etc. march off up the road, tents in the distance. Me and Charlie with Tiny and the gang still. Forgot to mention I passed over the Nile last night. Good bridge. Marched about 1 mile. This is a rest camp for men in action. Big green yard nearby. We were all detailed into tents. Me, Charlie, Tiny, and gang all in one tent. Fine big tents, square 3 ply canvas, very strong, sandy floor. Hell, of a laugh! All of us were tired, hungry, still we had our jokes. Nothing inside! Bamboo trestles from outside. What hellish things, no mattress, no blanket, no grub. Felt lousy. Staff Sarge came around with a box of grub. Huge slice of bread and some messy corned beef at 7:00. This was all we had for 10 hours. No tea or drink. Still, we felt good in that blasted tent. Well, it was nice and warm, so we lay down to sleep. Then, slowly, I began to freeze. Oh, it was horrible! We all had to get up finally to stamp and walk about. We were numb. Egypt, eh? Hot by day, freezing by night. Sand all over the place. Well, Dave and George had screaming shits. Poor sods rush out into the night, in open ground and wind. Well, got up at about 6:00, washed from a tap, awful. Lined up an hour for it. Lined up an hour again for grub. Packet of biscuits and corned beef, lovely. I'm writing this while sitting on my trestle in the tent, with the boys around me cursing, singing, etc. The sun shining, lovely, quite warm now. So, this is Egypt, just sand, nothing else. Charlie and I are off to visit an Italian prison camp nearby. Roll call 9:00. Whole draft is divided up into troops 1-6. About 40 troops under officers. We had some first drills. Bloody awful, just like "Deepcut" rookies. Still a laugh. Sand storm blowing up. Can't see a yard in front of us. Sand in our hair, mouth, ears, eyes, everywhere. Awful! Got 3 blankets, and fixed our beds up with bamboo. No shave yet. Tomorrow hooray! Old Blondie again. The twelve are here. They shipped out as ship gunners, were in the "Pantelleria" raid, and got torpedoed off there. They put in at "Athens, " had 6 weeks there, good time, then went back to "Alexandria" for 3 weeks So here now, waiting for the next move. No Officers, bloody fine time, he reckons. Lucky dog, it's good to see him. Had a long talk, we messed about, had a drill, went to the canteen. All crap games and housey housey. Filled with Aussies, New Zealanders, Canadians, everything. Had beer with Charlie and Blondie. Nasty smell of garlic. Bloody asses braying ceaselessly. Ok, in bed now.

THURSDAY, 13th
"Camp Amrya".

Good night, lots of fresh air. Shook sand, etc., out of everything. Had a wash and shave out of a billy can. Hah! Bit tight, cold water.

Wow! Some shave managed to leave the skin behind. Breakfast 7:30. Bacon, bread, tea. Not bad. Feel fine. Sun hot, no wind. Roll call 9:00. Inspection ok. No brass to be shined. Out on route march. Passed dwellings of natives. Horrible, dirty, squalid Goats and sheep live with them. Lots of Typhoid amongst them. God knows what they eat. Was told by Aussie that nearly all the fighting was done by British Forces. Yeah! And all that bloody noise about the Aussies winning the Libyan Campaign is bull, he said! British propaganda, huh! Blondie said Greeks got bugger all. No ammo or planes. If it wasn't for Britain, they'd be lost. So much for what we are told at home. Back from route march. Charlie, Aussie, and I have decided to go to "Alex" tonight. Got native to wash our clothes. I piastre per article. Ok. Pay today. Got paid 10/-, 50 piastres, free fags (50 woodbines), boxes of matches. Dinner 1:00. Aussie's here with us. Guy told me he just got Xmas mail, 3 months. We won't get any, I'm afraid. Natives come around selling fruit and chocolate. It all grows near by. Me, Charlie, and Ozz got a Red Cross van in "Alex". Hell! It's awful; houses are in ruin, dirty, there are flies, and it's hot ach! God knows how they live. Went to Fleet Club. Beer there is duty-free. Fine, big place. Café, Bar, Shops. All fixed prices. Holds 1, 000's. We had a good tea, 3 eggs, sausages, chips and tomato 1/-. Went into the city. They have Trams. Hellish affairs, like Rio, kids dash after one, to shine boots. All ask for fags, beggars all over. Went to Curio Shop. Ozz was looking at rings. Plenty of Bazars and mosques. Snake Charmers, Palm Trees all over. banana groves, orange, etc. Lots of dames. Damned dirty, flies every where. Lot of Rickshaws about. Had Beer and Cognac-Port. Met Tiny and gang, all going to Sister St. and Beer St., Went into bars. They give one plate of sandwiches, etc. with a drink. Guys come around with fruit, oysters, etc. We were finally semi-oiled. Got carriage to Sister Street. Ha! Holy smoked mackerel. It was terrific. There was at least 1000 men of all sorts all looking for it. We tried em all. Sightseeing. They wanted 20 ackers. Guys were lined up and waiting. They were Government houses, licensed and supplied with all necessities. Outside are washhouses, which are well used too. Behind this street was out of bounds district. Me and Ozz had open knives in our hands. It was mighty dark, stinking, and narrow in this quarter. We found an Aussie with his skull bashed in. Kids were guiding blokes to houses. We saw a Can Can Dance with Cigarettes. Went to dozens of Bars. Beer was 3 Piastres a glass. 6.5 a bottle. At Fleet Club it was 4-5 piastres, a bottle, and lousy beer. Oh, awful taste of garlic about it. Made me sick. Port was awful. Cognac was alright. All three of us ok. Usual cost, got a third back. Got watch mended and bought a roll of film. Get others tomorrow. Going in tonight for em. We missed the train, got a taxi to "Sidi Bahri". Missed fare, we all dashed off. Met Tiny. Waited 3 hours to move. Went for a drink, though we missed the train. Charlie dashed up track after it, but it was coming to him. Funny. Got it, Me, Sam Dave went the wrong way walking home. Retraced steps got in at 4:30.

FRIDAY, 14th

Bloody, great sandstorm, absolutely deep yellow, and can't see a yard before you. 60-mile-an-hour gale. Sand everywhere, our tent is filled with it. I'm writing through it. Fine, like dust. Men are going about shouting for guidance. 4 tents were torn up and blown away, and all the kit lost. Roof of the Cookhouse was blown off, all our rations spoiled, no grub today. All spoiled at Naafi also, go hungry. Our faces and cheeks yellow, our eyes bloodshot, everything covered, had to lay down with towels over our faces. Can't go out, you'll get lost. It's so fine it got into my fountain pen. Cleared up at about 5:00. Got the train into "Alex" in a compartment with Greeks. Nice Chaps. Went to Fleet Club. Got my watch, 6 Ackers, cheap. Had something to eat. Saw a fight between Aussies and native Police. Police used rifles. One Aussie was knocked out. Van took em away. Sat down in the park by myself. Egyptians strolling about, long dresses, fezzes. Strange! Lovely scenery, gardens, flowers, bananas, oranges, old stone pillars, etc. Walked into native quarters, and was warned to keep out. Got a train at 12:00. Got to Amrya at 4:00. Take 3 hours to mess about outside "Sidi Bahri." Blasted trains are awful, one a night to Cairo. British-made engines, etc.

SATURDAY, 15th.

Had 3 hours of sleep. Breakfast at 7:00 is usual of bread and tea and a spot of marmalade. Our day off. Me, Charlie, Tiny, and a gang of "Alex." Got train ok. 1 hour to "Alexandria." Went to Fleet Club and had clean up. Shave, 1 Piastre. Oh, he almost skinned me. Breakfast me, Charlie, George. I've only got 5 P.T. Borrowed 15 P.T. off Tiny. Blasted natives won't leave us alone. Shoeshine, hawking stuff, belts, watches all for 1-20 P.T. It's a lovely day. Walked about, looking in shops, etc. I notice very few women about, if any. They are office staff or veiled Mohammedis. I guess their faith keeps them in. After all, we are unbelievers. Some good, fine buildings here. Trams are awful, dirty, and noisy. Plenty of services here. I bought a belt, watch, etc. Lost Tiny and gang. Got tired of walking. Went to Fleet Club and met Tiny and the gang. Had a stroll again through the native quarter. It was terrible. Houses in ruins. Kids make water and others in the streets. Rubbish stinking in streets. Donkeys, Goats, and Chickens in houses and Streets. Garlic all over it. It literally stinks, all of it. It's a wonder they don't have Plague here. Saw remains of older city, temples, and pillars. Me and Charlie are broke. Just got the army van back. Feel damn sick, something I ate.

SUNDAY, 16th

Woke up at 12:00 and spewed all over the floor. I reckon there was garlic in the food. Boy, was I ill. Slept better after. Tiny and the gang came in at 4:00. Had a good time, they said. Sister Street, of course, not for me. Wouldn't touch it with a barge pole. They're nuts! Breakfast, the usual bread, jam. Hell, I'll go skinny like a rake. Oh, Joan, I'd love to see you again. Where the hell is it going to end? The African campaign is almost over. I guess it will start in Greece again. Detailed for fatigues. Clean up tables, etc. Had a talk with Blondie. Nothing doing today. Went to the canteen for tea. Sold tobacco to Aussie 20 P.T.

MONDAY, 17th

Up at 6:30, had a shave. Boy, did it drag. Me and Dave, the toughest beards in a tent, took 45 minutes in a petrol can of water. Breakfast, bread, bacon, tea. Lousy. No inspection. Chilly today. Dinner of tea and bread and jam. Hell's delight! 3:30 parade, revelation, guard. Night and day! Good god, and it's supposed to be a rest camp! Bloody Officer, rat, real British Army stuff. Don't do this, that, and the other. Swine started this gang business and this grub, too. One meal a day, a bowl of stew at 6:00. It's 3:00 now, and the next meal is at 6:00, and I'm starving like the rest. Bloody hole, this is sand, wind, and natives. They come around selling chocolate, 5 P.T. each, and they all chant. Also, English newspapers and Egyptian mail Cairo 1 P.T. They do our washing also- 1 P.T per article. Now we have to do guard and foot drills, and we're gunners. Also, pay for our stamps-1 P.T. We'll have bugger all left soon. What an army. Democracy heh! I laugh. Me, Wally, Perky got N.A.A.F.I van into "Alex." As far as "Hustaffa" Barracks. Got a tram into town. Passed huge tanning and hide plant. The stink was terrific, horrible. Laugh. We rode on a platform with the driver. Went to Fleet Club. Film's not ready until 8:00. Had a game of snooker with a sailor. Went to YWCA, ping pong with girls. Had 5 acker meal. Hell, did I enjoy it? I was starving. Only got 15 ackers left. Film's ok, cost 15 ackers. Not bad. I was broke, though. Walked to Seous St. and Looked in at Top Hat Club. Aussies playing hell, the gang was fighting, and others smashing chairs. 10 were trying to get 1 outside 2 were stretched out on the sidewalk. There were 12 dance girls, prostitutes rather. Aw, it was horrible, and that was lousy beer. I left without anything. It was the same all down that street. Got an army lorry. He got lost. I walked a mile, got in at 1:00

TUESDAY, 18th.

Aussies started a riot in N.A.A.F.I. 4 of em in clink. Their pals threatened to burn N.A.A.F.I down, so we are to guard it. I was detailed to guard prisoners: 4 Aussies, 1 German, 1 Italian, and an Arab. This Arab assaulted a Sgt. Major and an M.P. He's slightly mad and damned tough. Hell, and they put me to guard them. I've got 10 rounds anyway. Bloody, lousy system in camp here. They've got 52 men on guard with one tent between them. Had a row with it's Sgt. snotty sod, always sneering. I'd like to turn a Pom, Pom on him. Welsh Corporal gave me tea. What do you think? Cled Perry was out here and went to Crete just a few days before I came in. Holy Smoke of all the blasted luck. No wonder he didn't get any of my letters. Well, well.

WEDNESDAY, 19th

Had about 4 hours of sleep. I notice, though, that when I wake up, I feel fine, wide awake. I guess it's the tent and the fresh air. Dismount guard at 7:00. All's well. Day off today. Didn't do much; I had sleep. Boys doing P.T. of all things in the desert. Grub, as usual, by hell. Well, going into "Alex" tomorrow and gorge. Saw Blonde. I sold 2 bottles of beer and got 1 P.T. each. Bought tea and a sandwich. Felt much better. Hell, we're weak from hunger.

THURSDAY, 20th

Had a lousy night. Cold and gut ache. Blasted draft from tent doorway. Me and Mike avoided P.T. Sat in the lavatory for 1 hour. Air raid over "Alex." 9 Gerry's passed over. Fleet in action, heavy gunfire. Nothing much to do today. Had route march. Blondie and a crowd in it. Their bravado is cracking. Short march. Whole gang of us on the road. Got a big trailer into "Alex", about 50 of us, some ride! Tiny had a tattoo done, didn't care for it, too dirty, etc. Saw huge battleships in the dock, all sorts. Me, Blondie, and Charlie went to Forces Club. Had a lovely bath. Got weeks of sand out of us. Had a huge meal, cost 9 ackers. Boy, was it good. First good meal for a week, Met Ray. Philpot is here, along with Ozz, old Nelson, etc. Coastal Defence is already in units. In action yesterday, lucky dogs. Nice, easy time. In "Alex". Missed seeing Philpot. Try and see him soon. Came over weeks before us. Ozz in hospital (syphilis). Poor old Ozz. The times we had together. The London Road Hah. We bought some whiskey, wine, etc. Went to Cabaret's, etc. I bought a bottle of port 5 P.T (2/6) also half a bottle of whiskey 25 P.T (8 shillings). They wanted 10 P.T., a bottle of beer at a dance club. I tried to open a bottle of whiskey and pushed the cork down through my neck. It burst and went all over us. Lost half of it. Got a slight booze on. Went on, met Tiny, and the gang all fixed up. Segal is some laugh. We stood at "Seous Street" for 1 hour. Me, Charlie, and Georgeorge, got a van. Tiny and the gang missed it. They stayed in "Alex" and came back the next morn.

FRIDAY, 21st

Another day. Bored with the whole thing. Seems we are here for some time, bloody hole! It's alright in a sense, near town and all that, but I'd like a letter, etc. It's reported there are tons of mail in "Cairo, " but we can't get it. Blinding Army Corporation! Sand gets everywhere, too. Got off early today. Me, Blondie, Charlie, and George grabbed the lorry. Officer a bat man driving a lorry into town (Cairo). Very nice chap, but a blasted ride, wow! Rattle, bang, bump. Got along, 4 hours to go. Stopped at half way house (cup of tea, 6D a cup. River Nile in the distance also passed one of many pyramids in the distance. What a lot of desolate waste here. Nought but sand, sand, and more sand. Strikes me; this Egypt is no good to anyone except the country around the Nile. Got to "Cairo" after 4 hours of travel. Distance about 140 miles. Straight tarmac road, decent road too, level, sound. Saw a few Arab trains and Bedouins on the move. Lovely flats and modern buildings outside "Cairo." Passed over the Nile. Fine wide river, like the Thames. Plenty of pleasure boats and houseboats of all kinds. The usual things, of course, are people in fezzes and long gowns. The smell of garlic and Turkish tobacco and a thousand other rotten smells from a thousand different sources. Trains are very good, though. 1st and 3rd class. The officer dumped us in the suburbs and got a train in. Forgot to mention, a lorry was full of Kit bags. Managed to get a few things. Got a train to Y.M.C.A. Had feed, then to TOC.H. Got a bed, lovely, springy, clean sheets. We were like kids when we got into them.

SATURDAY, 22nd

Woke up at 6 as usual. Got up at 7:00. Natives bought us a lovely cup of tea. I had a hot bath. We set forth into town. I had 15 P.T. 3/- not much, hah! Had grub, 1 roll, and tea 3 P.T. Had a look around town. Fine city, big like "Buenos Aires", fine big stores, flats. Wide streets. Much better than "Alex.", although the beggars and hawkers worked us a lot. Shoe shine. They sell everything from laces to beer on the streets. One guy was selling women's sanitary towels, another, cigarettes and French letters. Calling out their wares also. No embarrassment. They are dirty, unkempt natives. Most of them have diseases of the eyes. The sand does it. The eyes are inflamed, bloodshot, and running matter most of the time. There are all types of black, half-caste, white, blonde, and black hair. Hell of a crowd. Saw a Mosque, the King's palace, and also a lot of architecture. Took a train out to the Pyramids and had to change trains once. Cost 1 P.T.- 2 1/2d. About 15 miles out. The pyramids were marvellous! Guide took us around for 3 P.T. each. Gave us a detailed account of everything. Took 4 snaps, one of Sphinx, hope they turn out. We went inside. Took 1 hour and a half to get through the lot. First came the one and only entrance on the south side, straight in, then up. We had to bend double all the time. The passages everywhere were about 4 ft. high by 4 ft. First, the Queen's tomb, a square chamber built out of solid granite blocks. Average size, 18ft. by 10 ft., 18.5 tons in weight. The outline of the Queen's sarcophagus is there, with chambers behind for Jewelry. It took 30 days to get the Queen's coffin into the tomb. The coffin weighed tons, so it took em a day to move it a few yards. The entrance was about 60 ft. long. Everywhere were these huge blocks of granite, all set on each other without cement. The same with the King's chamber, except it was larger. These Pyramids were built 5, 000 years ago. They are tombs of the Kings and Queens of the 4th dynasty of Egypt. At the burial hall, the granite and alabaster blocks were gigantic. It took my breath away! The size and perfect state they were in. Also, the alabaster was transparent. Most of these blocks were brought from 800 miles away, from a quarry. The Pyramids were built from sandstone, granite, alabaster, and black granite. The shape of the barge is where most of the blocks were brought. All the Pyramids were glazed with alabaster, but a Caliph 400 years ago stripped it off for a Mosque. The Sphynx was marvellous, just as one sees it in pictures. I couldn't credit most of it. It is too vast and old to think about. Height of the Pyramids was 280 ft high, covered 13 acres of ground, and the base took 30 years to build. We went to the Zoo. Great there, took a snap. Then back to town. Had great feed in Y.M.C.A. Sold box camera to Tiny for 25 P.T. Not bad, clear profit. Much happier with that. Eggs are cheap and plentiful, as well as coffee. We went out to Alex Road and caught an officer's small van. Boy! It was great. No noise or bumping. To cap it all he had a load of captured cigarettes and biscuits, Italian. We helped ourselves. When we got off, we were bulging with stuff. We made it in 3 hours. Fast going, hah!

A few of the lads and myself with the second largest Pyramid. Note that the top is still covered with alabaster plaster as it was originally. The rest was carried away for the mosque of Cairo 700 years ago. The Pyramids were built 6, 000 years ago and took 20 years to build.

The town Of Mena is in the background, with a few of the local lads with their Steeds (Arab horses), Donkeys & Camels.

The Zoological Gardens Cairo. Elephant-carrying Kiddies. Very beautiful Gardens

SUNDAY, 23rd

Had fine sleep last night. A bit cold, though. I've got 35 P.T. now so I'm not bad off. Must send a cablegram to Joan from "Alex." Got on parade, ok. Half the boys missing, Tiny and gang. Officer put em all on guard tomorrow. Also, me, night guard, not bad. Had sandstorm at camp yesterday. Everything was covered in dust when we got back. Bloody nuisance! Fixed my bamboo bed up in middle of floor away from door. Got a cold draft through door. London being badly bombed again. R.A.F. retaliating on Berlin. War in Africa ending. "Berbera" taken and many others. We are closing in on all sides. 1000's of tanks, lorries are coming back from the front. Captured stuff also, guns, armoured cars, supplies all passing through by road and rail. The blasted son of a bitch flies, and natives are getting me down. I booted one sod through the tent door, selling stinking chocolate, etc. Dirty sods. The tent stinks if they come inside. Hell, what a country to fight for or protect. Bloody worthless. Let's get back to England!

MONDAY, 24th

Cold again last night. After I moved like I did, I woke up several times. Shaving ok now. Up at 6:00. Breakfast of porridge and sausages. Meal's much better. P.T. a big laugh. I just watched it. Fag issue – 50 woods, 2 boxes of matches. Will do me the week, alright. Blondie was pulled for not being on parade. We're on guard tonight. Took some snaps of camp, tent, and boys. Sold singlet to Tiny for 5 P.T. Clear profit. On guard 2nd turn. Bombardier Loring, Me, Dave. Should be ok. Bob came and took the tea to the tent. I laugh. Done first shift, easy. Knocked off bottles-P.T. each. Finished guard 11:30. Next guard 3:30. Went to bed.

Empire builders & tent. Can just see the framework of bamboo beds in a tent. Me, Charlie & Blondie.

More empire builders. There were 10 of us in the tent. Small lad on the right is the baby of the family (Tiny)

Camp Amrya itself. Looks a bit desolate, and it is as you see it.
Sand & tents, that's all.

The lads in action. 6:00 in the morning. Note petrol tins,
newspapers, etc., are all modern conveniences. Camp Amrya

TUESDAY, 25th

Cold last night. Blasted cold nights here. Can't keep warm. Slept in the uniform overcoat. Always a lovely day, though. Flies are driving us nuts. Also, blasted goats. Braying incessantly. Prayer drums beating last night. Some racket. Trilling noise, like Africa.

Got a day off. Me and Blondie went, "Alex." Got a Major and Staff car. Some ride! Lovely. Sent a cable off to Joan, also one for Smith, and Charlie. Put films in, also Joan's watch. Lot of trouble, too, that watch! 2/- for glass, 4/- for cleaning. 1/9 ½ for a roll of film. 2/- and 1/2 for development. Had a cheap meal 4 P.T. very good- 4 eggs, tomatoes, chips, tea, bread, etc. Eggs are very plentiful here and coffee. Lovely coffee here. Dame's ok. Saw a native funeral. Very impressive. Huge ornamental hearse drawn by 8 horses. All decked in gold silver, with angels. Walked about in shorts and a shirt, lovely. Beat Blondie at ping pong. Got the van home. Aussie Capt., damned fine fellow, treated us well. Supper is at 7:30 now. It's better; soup is ok. All of British Somali is taken now. Gradually taking it. Had singsong in the tent. Alright. Talking to R.A.F. said no letters in 6 months. Hell's delight!

WEDNESDAY, 26th

Lovely day. Up at 6:00. Shave alright now. Use Vaseline for the face. Ok. Had a good haircut at Fleet Club yesterday. Done P.T. also foot drill. Blasted bombardiers are hopeless. Drill also useless. All to hell. Doing it in shorts and a shirt. Nice and free. Sun is very hot and glaring, though. Dinner at 1:00. Stew, orange, what a meal, hell, I'm starving after it. Natives lost my washing. No more, I'll do my own! Dave, silly sod, just let off 14 times in succession. He opens his bowels 3 times a day. He's rotten! Hell of a laugh, though. Tent inspection and a half day off. Passed it, ok. Laid about, and had a game of football. Kohl has been made B.Q.M.S. also Lt. Sgt to T.S.M. Some promotion that! Staff-B.S.M. not bad. We had a game of Kit Kat after tea. Some laugh. Till it got dark, then we had a sing-song. Fine. Missed our supper through it.

THURSDAY, 27th

Up at 6:00. I'm on 1st prisoner guard today. Guarding Italian, Arab, and other prisoners. Breakfast 6:30. 10 rounds and rifle. Prisoners ok. There are detachments of them, Italians under their own officers, working about camp, digging, etc. They are quite happy about it. They are easy to guard. Got paid 10/- and 50 P.T. Also, issue of fags, 50 Abdullas, Special Forces fags, they're lousy. Finished off a letter for Joan. Must post it tomorrow. Our day off was altered 5-5. Prevents us from staying out very long. Sods! Can't go to "Cairo" now. Must get watch out tomorrow. 2/- for glass (3rd one) and 4/- for cleaning, full of sand. Hell, it will break me. I'll have to leave it. Can't be done. Usual blasted grub. It gets me down. Lousy beans are half cooked, the meat tough as blazes, and the spuds have no salt whatsoever in them. Same with rice, no sugar in it. Bloody grub for a hungry man. This lousy draft it is. Won't get anywhere while we are on draft. Bloody shirt still missing from laundry. Had a violent quarrel with black about it. He finally gave me another. Finished the prison Guard, ok.

FRIDAY, 28th

I'm tent orderly today. Report 9:00. Nothing to it. Cleaned up the tent and put everything in order. Tiny said the truck was going to "Alex" at 3:00. We didn't get it, though. Went on the road and got a truck halfway to cross the roads. Bunch of Aussies waiting for lifts there. Finally, I got a native truck full of limestone. Tiny lost his hat and got off. We went without him. Blasted native wanted 5 P.T. each for a ride. Had an argument with Aussies about it. Blasted sand and dust were in the face and eyes everywhere. George and I went in and got my watch. Unbreakable glass 10 P.T. (2 shillings) They cleaned it also ok. Met gang on the street. Got films, all ok. Went to Maleesh Bar and had 5 P.T. for feed. Boy, did we enjoy it? First good meal in a week. Eggs, chips, etc. We were starving. Went to pictures "Spring Parade" with Deanna Derbin. Very good. Went to bed in the Asmara Hotel in Muhammed Ali Square. Me and Charlie in the bridal suite, what a laugh! Big canopy over beds. 8 of us together. Blasted natives shouting and laughing, I couldn't get to sleep for some time. Got up at 8:00. The lavatories are funny holes in the floor with footrests on either side and wooden shoes to put on for the event. Went to Maleesh Bar again. Breakfast, more eggs. Went Y.M.C.A nice hot shower for free. Lovely. Had a game of ping pong, etc., and beat most of the boys at it. Met a lot of the other lads in town. We walked around the sea promenade. Very nice. Big flats looking out to the Mediterranean. Walked to the Palace and catacombs. Also, Mosque. It was lovely art. Boy, what beautiful masonry. Saw Tombs of Kings and Queens, and also that of Cleopatra and Anthony. Big rooms carved and painted with Egyptian signs and frescos. Also, old pottery around. Big marble boxes were where the Mummies of Cleopatra and Anthony were laid. Went back to the city via the native quarter. It was horrible! Stinking, dirty squalor. Kids were making water in the streets, paddling in it. Flies by the millions. Garlic, frying stuff, buildings falling in through age. It was indescribable. Had Dinner. Eggs again. I'm down to 10 P.T. now 2/- went pictures. Cost 6 P.T. 1/3 had to borrow from Tiny. Good show, a fine modern cinema film, "Brigham Young." Went B.S.C. for tea and more eggs. Had to borrow. Got a truck home from Siesta St. We've eaten 25 eggs all told in a day. Found our tent in shambles. 4 others had moved in. They're going out tomorrow, though. Thousand more men. Half came into camp again. All sorts, R.E., R.A., R.A.S.C. There are literally bloody thousands here now. Takes an hour and a half to line up and get meals. All above includes Saturday the 29th.

SUNDAY, 30th

Got up late and felt lazy. On village guard tonight. Fine time to go on, just when natives are celebrating too. Usually, a lot of trouble. Oh well, I've got 10 rounds. Decent breakfast, sausages, marmalade. It's okay when there's no sand about. Postage is free now. Getting very warm now. The summer is coming and bloody mosquitoes with it. Flies are driving me mad while writing this. Getting our proficiency to pay today. I could do with it, but my wife gets it. Nothing doing today. Lay about. Wedding in village, native. Well, it's the most interesting and yet revolting sight I have yet seen. The drums I reported earlier, as well as the dancing and clapping, were the preceding celebrations. They were doing the "can-can". A crowd of male natives form a circle and chant and clap. A young native girl does the shimmies, hips, and bosom shaking with a cane and naked. She stops suddenly and points to one in particular. This is her future lover. Meanwhile, the bride and groom, all swathed in sheeting and the bride covered, were mounted together on one camel, riding around their future house. They finally stopped and were rushed into the tent, then all those in the tent came out, leaving the bride and groom alone. There were about 10 women attending. They stood guard at the door. Suddenly, there were screams and sobs. These subsided, and then a lot of shouting inside. A woman rushed out, waving a pair of nickers and handkerchiefs with blood all over them. They hung them on the tent in full view. I realized then what it meant. The screaming and blood-stained garments were the passing of the bride's virginity. Disgusting! This exhibition proved the bride's virginity. It was all accompanied by gunfire, shouting, and shrill noises made by the women. A goat was killed. All the woman dipped their hands in its blood. The gunfire was to scare the evil spirits off. Everywhere was filth and dirt, sheep, goats, and chickens in the tents. Their garments were filthy also. I reckon the bride is to be about 14, and the groom is about 30. I took 2 snaps of these scenes. Went off Village Guard ok. with Sam.

The wedding

94

Playing the drums

The Groom

MONDAY, 31st

Not much to do today. Had an afternoon off. Blasted life is getting boring. About 1600 men came in this morning. All massing together with us. Hell, the grub line is about a half-mile long. It's a 10-minute walk to our tent, so the whole meal operation takes 2 hours. In the meantime, there is sand and wind to put up with. Our grub is cold long before we eat it. It's bloody awful! Segal was down with a rash, so I took him to the hospital. About 100 men were down with sickness. They're not getting enough grub to keep them going. 2 bits of bread and jam at 4:00 to last till 7:30 next morning. We were going to kick, but they won't stand behind us. Had an argument with Sgt. Ah, it's no good. We haven't a chance. Wrote two letters to Pop and Vi. No mail as yet. I've been dead broke ever since Saturday. Hellish. The boys are all homesick and grumbling over the inactivity and the country in general. It is a blasted, desolate hole, though, without a doubt.

APRIL

TUESDAY, 1st

Lovely day, up at 6:00. Shave ok. Breakfast not bad. Done P.T. finish 10:30. Laid in. Dinner had a double lot; one whack was not enough. Stew and 4 oranges. A fight in the lineup, like hungry wolves. Afternoon off. Walked around the village. Shambles as usual. Dirty lot. A lot of men are moving off to Greece today. Yugoslavia stood firm against the Axis. Germany said to be marching in. British fleet sunk 5 Italian ships, 3 Cruisers and 2 Destroyers. All of Germany getting a bashing from R.A.F. One guy said no mail for 6 months, postage now free.

WEDNESDAY, 2nd

Night guard tonight, Naafi, it be alright if I miss 2nd shift. More troops coming in from the western desert. They tell hellish tales, so many prisoners they machine gun them out of the way. Our Bren guns are no good up there, get jammed, etc. I collected a few Italian badges, etc. Aussies are bringing in all sorts of trophies. Tons of material and stuff coming in. Their lorries are rotten affairs. But the Breda gun is a beauty. 45 of our boys are in hospital, Pox mostly. Well, they knew better. None of that for me. Too much respect for Joan.

THURSDAY, 3rd

Done shift guard. No second one, ok nutten to it. Blasted fast inspection of all the bloody stupid ideas. One guy was caught with dirty feet. In a blinding sandstorm, we had to sit down in the sand and display our feet. Well, did we look good? We got away and caught a lorry for "Alex." Went to pictures. "City of Conquest" damn good. We kicked up a din in there. Some laugh. Got a bed at U.S. Club, a big dormitory. Had a pillow fight. Old Blondie had screaming shits 7 times in 2 hours. I woke up at 6:00 with screaming shits, it was awful! Ok, later. 11 P.T for bed and breakfast, ok. Had billiards and ping pong with the gang. Went to

Y.M.C.A. for the bath. Down to native quarters, oh, that stinking hole was as terrible as usual. Egypt has lost its glamour. It's not worth seeing. Lifted cream with Sam, he got caught, I got away, and hid tub of cream in the lavatory. Sam was detained but won. Went to pictures, then B.F. Club. Went to dance. Ok. Caught a truck at Fleet Club right to Naafi door. So, to bed.

SATURDAY, 5th

Friday with the above. Had a damn good kip. The old bamboo bed is all right. I've got it fixed fine. Went on day guard, ok. Had a big boil on shoulder. George got it out. Hell, I nearly keeled over. 50 of our boys detailed for guard on roads. That lessens the draft. "Benghazi" retaken by Italian and German troops. 9 ships altogether sunk by British Navy. Heavy raids on western English cities. 14 nights of quiet over London, thank God. Yugoslavia still standing fast. Greeks driving on. British forces capture "Keren, " "Massawa, " and "Asmara, " driving on to "Addis Ababa." Closing in on all sides. The R.A.F. batter hell out of em first. It's all British forces doing it there. U.S.A. takes all enemy shipping that's docked there. Trouble in "Syria". This blasted war will go on forever. When will it end? I'm sick and tired of it! It's getting us nowhere. We're stuck in this camp doing nothing, useless. We get so far and stop. If we start retreating in "Libya, " we may go in, training or not. Done a lot of washing today.

SUNDAY, 6th

Damned hot today. Egyptian summer. Done nothing all day, just lay about. Fixed up my shorts, etc., and had sleep. Hell, there are millions of sandflies now. The heat has brought them out. Can't do a thing. I can feel myself go mad now and then. Blasted black cooks cook the grub and the tea in the same pot. The tea tastes like onions. It's lousy. Killed a huge snake today outside the tent. Sam and Blondie are down with the screaming shits. There are about 50 in the hospital. I've got a huge boil on my shoulder. Waldock had dysentery. Blood, Night crabs, if they don't change our diet soon, we'll all be in hospital. Bread and cheese and jam without stopping, no greens, etc. It's no wonder we are all ill. What a lousy country this is, if only people could see it in the raw as we do. It's not worth it.

MONDAY, 7th

Tent orderly today, ok. Paper says Germany declared war on Yugoslavia and Greece. Already bombed Belgrade. Nazis push through from Bulgaria. Italy declares war on Yugoslavia also. British forces take Addis Ababa. 200 miles in 2 days, good going. All quiet around Libya. Quiet around London, damned good job. In my opinion Yugoslavia won't last a week nor will Greece. There will be hell to pay soon. Bloody great sandstorm just blew up. Oh, it's awful. We lay on our beds with a damp towel over our faces. We can't see each other; it's so thick. Although we'll shut the tent up tight, we are choked with it. There's an R.A.S.C. dump here with 500 or more cars going to rot. Trucks of every sort just lack repairs, that's all. Bloody shame, what a war. There are tons of rations lying about, as well as petrol and all sorts of stuff. When a dump moves off, it's never used.

TUESDAY, 8th

Hell, of a sandstorm blowing still. Lasted 2 days now. It's torture getting meals, etc. Confined to tents. I'm tent orderly again today. Laying about rotting. Bugger all to do. Getting us down. Flies by day, mosquitos by night. Getting hotter also. Grub is bloody lousy. Running out of bread. They are giving us hard biscuits. Boys are grumbling. Caught cook house wallahs giving natives bread. Dirty sods! It can't last. We've had stew, spuds, or hard beans and an orange for meals. This for 4 weeks, no change. And bread and cheese or jam and tea with a taste of onions for our tea at 4:00. Then we go hungry till breakfast at 7:30 in the morning. Cold bacon and spuds with onion tea.

WEDNESDAY, 9th

Greeks and Yugo are holding Gerry on all fronts, although they withdraw on one. 10-1 in strength. 60 Gerry divisions attacked from Bulgaria, Austria, Romania, and Hungarian borders. British bombed Belgrade and Syria. Turkey neutral. Thousands of British troops leaving here for Greece. We are withdrawing in Libya. Derna taken. German and Italian troops were used. British advance beyond Addis Ababa. 300, 000 Italian prisoners were taken in all campaigns. 6, 000 British dead. British are training parachute troops for France, I guess. London raided again after 18 nights free. Thousands of men moving through this camp, all sorts. There are tanks, lories, armored cars, and tons of material here. They come and go, but R.C.S. stays on. I doubt if we'll ever move. They don't know what we are for, I think. Aussies have all gone over to Greece. Most boys are down with screaming shits and dysentery. Mike is very bad. Gut ache. Some of the boys buy stuff from the village, very dangerous. We got nothing to do now. Boys are restless. Blasted Segal and Mac, arguing all day and night. Segal's sex mad, I think. Queer sod. Tich and Greyer a quite a pair. Tich hasn't changed or bathed for weeks. We threatened to strip him, so he bathed and changed. Couldn't sleep last night, blasted sand flies, mosquitoes, and heat almost drove us mad. Not to mention the bed, hah! Tough eh! I laugh. This bloody Egypt. To hell with it. I've had enough.

THURSDAY, 10th

Well, here it is, April 10. I'm 23. This is the 9th birthday I've celebrated abroad. Yessir, from 14-17, etc. Say, I've sure had em in some strange places. "Quebec" the strangest of all. Then, on a freight train and so on, and one in a logging camp, My 16th in "B.C." on a farm in the "Fraser Valley." Some are on the Prairies, and now this is Egypt, "Alexandria." I wonder if I'll see another one out here or anywhere. Well, it's in the hands of God. I feel I will, although it won't be long before we go into action. It's not far off. We will move soon. I'm not afraid of death, but I am afraid of dying for a useless cause such as this. Hell, no one will gain either way. I'll be forgotten like thousands of others, and I'll leave broken hearts behind me. I'm young, and I love my wife. That's all I care about: my wife and my people. I prefer them alive than dead by bombs, etc.; anything's better than that. Let's have peace to that of this slaughter. It will end up nowhere. I'd willingly give everything I possess now to go home and settle down with my wife. I've had enough, and I'm sure every man I know thinks alike. If Hitler had taken and dominated the world, I'm sure he couldn't have made it worse than what we suffer now, or to that of death, dying for nothing in particular. Holy smoked haddock!

FRIDAY, 11th

Kicked up stink about grub. No breakfast for us, no ration. I got the Orderly Officer, and said my piece, but no good. The men are yellow gutted, and won't stand behind us. Gave it up and went hungry on Parade. Detailed for guarding of empty tents the Aussies just evacuated. Me and Mac, about 8 of us, about 2 miles away. Got there, scrounged about, got much loot. These Aussies are wasteful sods. Ammo lying about clothes, boots, all sorts. They don't care. There were millions of bottle caps. Boy, do these guys drink! Fixed up tent, grub brought to us. Ok. Nothing to do all day lay about. No guard, good grub. Y.M.C.A. nearby. Played Ping Pong, etc., with Mac.

SATURDAY, 12th

  Doing ok. There are about 1, 000 empty tents here. What waste. Blankets, clothes, petrol, paraffin, and gallons of it are going to be wasted. We are using it for cooking. Tons of food lying about. Good God. And some people go without. Pounds of sugar and tea and tinned milk. Tiny and George came over on a bike. We went out shooting and used about 50 rounds. Aussies gave us machine guns to play with. I couldn't hold it at first. Hudson fixed up breakfast in the morning: eggs, bacon, and tomatoes. 1.5 P.T. is not bad. Saw Mike and Sam. They're some distance away in another camp. Used Italian Breda and Bombs. Found several badges one Italian medal for the Abyssinian War. Dissention in camp. Boys quarrel over who does the washing up. Well, bend my torso. Are they a lot of lazy sods? Won't even wash a dixie out. Sponder is fed up; and says he wants relief. That's how it is. Someone always messes things up.

SUNDAY, 13th

Me and Mac went to Y.M.C.A. Our men were gone when we got back. New relief was in. Sponder had fixed it alright; they had taken our Kits. We walked over, got Kit, met Mike on the Ration truck, and got lifted into "Alex." Had a meal in B.F.C., Met Pattsy, went to pictures, very good, 4 Sons. Went to B.F.C. got 2 rolls of film. Got an Army truck from Fleet Club. Boy, was it cold! Had only a shirt and shorts. Some wind! Truck full of drunken Aussies. Say, are these guys tough? Yeah! In my loot, I picked up boots, leather coat, ammo, a haversack, belts, hats, and so on. Germans got "Salonika". They're about half ways into Yugoslavia and half ways into Greece. 80 Gerry tanks were destroyed. Night fighters beat the night bombers while the moon shines. 40 raiders were brought down over March. We're using a Yank fighter Havoc Douglas plane. They have advanced in Libya, as far as "Tobruk." We can't hold them, it seems. They're coming in, about 200 miles away now. We were raided yesterday. 50 bombers, some racket. We got 5. Cleaning up in "Abyssinia, " nearly over there. "Bristol" and "Coventry" hit badly in England.

MONDAY, 14th

Got back last night at 1:00 and went right to Naafi. Ok. There has been a sandstorm blowing for the last 3 days. It's bloody maddening! Sand everywhere. In your hair, mouth, eyes, ears, clothes, blankets. It's driving us nuts. No sooner we get our grub, then it's unfit to eat. It's clogged with sand. By hell, this bloody lousy country. It's Easter Monday. Here I am, laying in my bamboo bed, completely covered, to keep loads of sand out. I can hardly breathe. You remember Joan, how I used to hate being muffled up or having my head covered. Say, dear, I sure must get used to that now. I'm mighty lonesome for you, honey! Let's hope it is God's will that we meet again for good. This war has taught me a mighty big lesson, yes, and I'll adhere to it after. It's not too late.

TUESDAY, 15th

Sandstorm has let up, a relief too. I'm tent orderly today. Nothing happening, no Parade at 2:30. a Bit of digging and machine gun nests around the tent, to stem Nazi advance, I presume, laugh. We have a rifle and 50 rounds. The Nazis are at "Sallum" on the Egypt border, 200 miles away, using cruiser tanks. What a hope of stopping em'. Although I think Wavell has something up his sleeve yet. Nazi's enter "Belgrade". All of Germany getting terrific battering by R.A.F. Cruiser Bonaventure sunk, our best A.A. Ship. U.S. sends Flying Fortresses over. Also, ships through the Red Sea. Greeks and Yugos holding Gerry back. However, Gerry is halfway into Yugo.thousands of our troops leaving here for Greece. We are now fighting Gerry. Our leave cut down to 12 hours. We're on short notice for Malta. Hell, what a joint to go to. They have 10 raids a day there. Me and Mac on guard duty, got out of it.

WEDNESDAY, 16th

Went to "Alex" yesterday. Took us 2 hours to get in. Dumped off at Polish Camp. We knocked about went to various clubs. Had a shower, wrote letters in Y.M.C.A. bought films. Aussies beat up Native Police. Went down to Sister Street. Hell! What a shamble. Very brisk business. Don't worry, Joan I'll have to be mighty low to try that and lose your respect. My love is stronger than that for you. 100's of sweating, swearing men going in and out. Awful. They have the Red Cross Station for them, out of bounds and orders plastered all over. Thank God I have good control of myself. You know me, Joan, my control. I can exercise that; never fear. Got back by lorry. The driver was drunk. Hell, what a nerve-wracking experience. Got in about 12:00. No breakfast this morning, got up at 8:00. I've overslept, so no grub. Still, that's nothing. We're used to going hungry in this man's army. The lovely grub the Aussies and other camps get around here, and yet we live on cold bacon, biscuits, and stew. Also, 10/- a week, and the Aussies get 35/-. The poor British Tommy, the lowest of animal life.

THURSDAY, 17th

Payday. Guard duty last night, security patrol, 40 men. Blacks have been knocking things off. Nuts to it. The guy woke us up but we turned over and went back to sleep. Got paid 11/50. 10/- for 50 fags, 2 boxes matches. Me and Gang got a big R.A.F. wagon into "Alex." Hell of a sandstorm on, worst yet. Couldn't see the hand in front of us. Played ping pong. Beat the boys. I'm not bad at it now. Sand falling in clouds on "Alex." M.P.'s out for all R.A.'s from "Amrya." All are being recalled. Well, I guess we move. Nuts to it, we didn't go back. Went to Pictures, 2 Girls on Broadway. Very good. Had tea at Y.M.C.A. very good. Caught a lorry home. Orders, reveille 3:30 wow! It was 12:00 then. We packed everything and had tea. It was too bad that we were just organizing our tea. Primus milk and tea, all buckshee. Still, we must leave it. I'm not sorry to be leaving "Amrya" and its blasted sandstorms. Got to bed at 2:00 and up at 3:30. Got grub and handed in blankets, but I had to rush it. Left all tea and sugar behind, boots, coats, and ground sheets too bad. My Kit bags both were crammed. Hell, we thought we'd collapse. Moved off, swine made us march to the Station.

FRIDAY, 18th

As I stated, we marched with a full kit, two kit bags, and a rifle. We almost died. Got train. Goodbye "Amrya" and good riddance. We've had enough of you. Blondie and others left behind. We'll meet again. Too bad. Got to the docks and parked on key. All Glen boats are still in, also another new Glen boat. Same old ships all over. Had tea biscuits and cheese. Hell, short rations again. The gang is all together. Had the order to take off the kit. We had a walk around. I took some snaps. Got native to give us a tour of the bay for 2.5 P.T. Went all around. There were about 5 capital ships,

2 cruisers, and about 5 destroyers, all French. Lovely ships bristling with guns, etc., and a lot of our boats are in also. Got back in time for the boys to move aboard the ship. Another scramble then for the kit. Hell of a struggle up the gangplank. Aboard another Glen boat. Similar to Glenearn. We were put on a deck hold, about 150 of us, tightly packed like sardines. We are walking on each other. Then our C.O. told us we were not to smoke between decks at all, nor on deck at night. Reason - we are carrying a load of high explosives and Cordite, also tons of petrol. We are going to Malta. The toughest waters are going. Well, I guess we've struck lucky for another soft berth. Where we are put, there are 4 wooden ladders up to the hatch hole. So, one can use one's imagination to determine what would happen in the event of torpedoing, etc., 150 men in a hold of about 35 feet by 35 feet. Ah, well, why worry? I'll come through it. I have faith in myself with the help of God. If it is his will, so be it. Lined up for two hours for tea. A tin of corned beef and chunk of bread between 2 men. Also, tea is very substantial. Yes! Then, the farce of farces, we had to line up and cheer the Glenearn as we passed her. Bloody lot of bull. Left Alex at 6:00.

Having tea on the key side just before moving onto the Breconshire. Note lineups and billy cans. Alexandria docks.

The harbour, Navy, Interned French Battleships, and Merchantmen. Alexandria. From native dingy whilst on a sail around the harbour.

Heavy Cruisers Perth & Aussie. Also ships in harbour. Alex in the background. Taken from native dingy.

Chapter 6: At Sea April 19, 1941 - April 21, 1941

SATURDAY, 19th

"In Mediterranean".

This is the "Breckon". About 12, 000 tons. Sister ship to the Glen boats. Coincidence, we should have another Glen boat. We are making a dash across the Mediterranean to Malta, 900 miles. We are doing 18 knots, have 6 pom-poms, and 4-3inch naval guns. Escort- 1 Cruiser and 2 Destroyers. All Australian. The cruiser is "Perth." This ship has done 16 trips to Malta, some to Greece. Has been bombed and raided each trip. So what! It was hell sleeping last night. We were closed in and sleeping cheek-by-jowl. It literally stunk of feet etc. hells delight it was awful, sickening. Still, it must be done. We're up on deck for one hour or so for meals. Corn dog, biscuits, tea. For dinner, we had a chance to have soup and tea. I hate the bloody sight of corn dogs now. Who wouldn't after 4 times a day? Slept the best part of the day. Had raid, 20 Stukas. Got through ok. No casualties or bombs dropped. Cruiser kept them high. A bit nervous, but it passed. Boys in the M.M. draft were scared stiff, running around like sheep. Me Sam, Mac started a bank and lost everything. 6 bob in debt. Got mad, though. Tiny and Charlie are fooling about. Oh well, one pays for the experience. Still bashing along ok. If we get tonight over with it will be ok. I won't mind getting torpedoed by day. At least you can see where you are. If it must come, it will. I would like to hang on to my diary and snaps, though, and I'd love to see you again, Babe, too, above all. I think one day I will look at this and laugh. 28 Raiders brought down over Britain last night. Heavy raid on London. 1, 000 planes used. The raid on Berlin was also the heaviest of the war. That's the idea: lay each other in ruins.

Somebody will quit, then. Raid on Malta. Convoy torpedoed off Crete. We lost transport and 200 men. This happened this morning, just behind us. I'll tell you! This draft is charmed. 1, 000 Gerry killed in Greece, 60 planes down. Yugos caused unified resistance. Germans are too much for them. I guess Greece will fall soon. It's hell again tonight. Stinking feet, sweaty bodies, snores, groans, grunts, some talking in sleep, swearing. I'm writing this at 1:00 at night. Can't sleep, were right aft.

Pretty rough seas. En route to Greece, Malta. This destroyer was later hit and sunk in the raid by Gerry a day later. Didn't realize what we would go through at this time, aboard ship Breconshire.

En route through Greece. Aboard ship Breconshire while making a mad dash for Greece & Malta. The convoy was attacked by a

force of 35 Bombers, Gerry & Italian, Stukas & Savoias. 4
Merchantmen were hit (2 sunk), plus 3 of the fleet, 2 Destroyers
& 1 Cruiser. 7 Bombers were shot down in the foreground.

The destroyer laying a smoke screen, also smoking from afar.
She was hit by the bomb. Merchantman sinking to the right.
Another was on fire and smoke was pouring overhead from all
the ships that were hit.

SUNDAY, 20ᵗʰ.
"At Sea in Med."

Aboard "MV Breconshire." Had a good night but woke at 4:00, a
bit cold. Amusing to see the attitude of men sleeping, and boy, did
it stink. Up at 7:00, breakfast. Corn dog and tea, hellish!
Mediterranean Fleet joined us. Boy, some Fleet, about 30 of em.
Capitol ships, cruisers, and about 15 destroyers. Ajax and Barham,
Formidable, Warspite, Perth, Valiant and others. Made a fine sight
as they steamed up and closed in around us. They are not an escort
because this boat is part of the Med fleet. I guess they are going to
Malta to refuel. Pretty smooth going, a bit chilly. We're still in
shorts. Air raid, action stations, 5 bombers passed over. We opened
up, but they were very high. Later on, sounded like a Sub. The
Destroyers dropping depth charges. They almost lifted the ship out
of the water. Well, we are certainly lucky so far. Thank God for
his mercy. I didn't expect to get through this far so easily. Got grub
from Maltese lads going home after 12 months in "Alex." They
were very happy and excited. Say! Wouldn't I be too? Got a good
dinner cooked, changed from bully beef and biscuits. Got tea, etc.
It's good to see the Galley in full swing again. It is very
reminiscent. Had roll call and inspection. Told to be ready to
disembark tomorrow. We got in early. Certainly, it's good to be out
of the sand/stink of "Alex."

Courcigeaus & a few more. 32 ships altogether. Some fleet!

Boys looking overside at the fleet.

Warspite & Formidable, Carrier & Capital ships. Part of the Mediterranean Fleet that escorted us to Malta. Taken from the Breconshire.

A parachute mine hit in mid-air by a Bofor shell just over the Grand Harbour. This was dropped like many others by Junkers

88-87 over Malta, particularly Valletta & Grand Harbour. The blast was terrific (note the fire on the docks). I was within 500 yards of this. 8 were brought down.

The Grand Harbour, Valletta. Showing Docks, Piers, etc. Pretty deserted at this time due to heavy raids. Whenever a convoy came in, there would be hell to pay. The Italians would spot, or Gerry and then the blitz at night of mines & H.E.

Bombs would start

She kept a good watch on us, just like a mother.

Chapter 7: Malta April 21, 1941 - June 10, 1943

MONDAY, 21st
"Malta, St. George's Barracks"

Woke up to find the ship slowly moving into Malta Bay. Had screaming shits bad. Was amazed at the size and beauty of Malta Harbour and the town "Valletta" spread out all around it. Reminded me of Sydney Harbour. People were all out cheering us, the first ship from "Alex" in 13 weeks, although they come from England fairly often. Learned that four U-boats followed us in the Med yesterday. They got one, and that was when the fleet dropped charges on her previous trip. This boat had been torpedoed twice but missed, although they got the "Bonaventure" behind and were escorting her. So, I gave up a prayer of thanksgiving to God for the mercy and protection in sparing us. Fortunately, we were spared by God. We gathered our kit on deck, and all the gang got together as usual. We were anchored in the harbour. A paddle boat took us from the ship to the quayside. We had three air raids. No planes. Got on the quay, lined up, and marched off to the barracks. The bloody kit bags almost killed me, but I still managed. Much evidence of bombs with wreckage all over. People cheering us. Very small shops, old-fashioned, old stone walls, very strong, winding narrow streets. Smell of the East. Very religious people. Icons and statues all over. Got to the barracks at about 1:00. Barracks, about 100 feet down, look something like "Woolwich, " balconies, etc. Had good grub. Put into rooms, gang together again. Another air raid. Guns firing, very brief, no bombs. Went to town and had the first beer in 3 months, Simmonds beer. It was lovely, 7D for a large ½. Narrow streets, hardly any cars or traffic, of course. It's only an island of

90 square miles, but it is densely populated and has marvelous scenery. Had a walk around and got back by 7:00 as ordered. Another raid passed off. Muster parade. At last, we are detailed for units. Me and Charlie (still together) and about 30 of us. Tiny, also on Light A.A. on Bofors, open sights. Our Colonel is a very nice chap. George by himself. Mac, Mike, and Sam are on GL, so we are all on something different. We are split up, but we won't be far from each other. We move off tomorrow afternoon. Went to bed fairly early. Guns and bombs woke us up. Holy mackerel, what a din, unholy. Got to sleep and woke again for another raid at about 3:00. It was Hell! Still, it passed.

TUESDAY, APRIL 22nd
"St. George's Barracks"

Got breakfast, ok. Packed everything. Me and Tiny went to town. Had a walk about. Considering the bombs dropped, there is very little damage. A couple of boats sunk in the dock. The population of the island is 250, 000, 64 miles around. Lovely weather now. Very little traffic, petrol 2/10. Very few women about. The Maltese are small in stature. The language is more Arabic than anything. Very religious, Roman Catholic. The island is nothing but huge walls, forts, and towers. Marvelous structures. The shelters are built into them, and they are fine, strong shelters. Things are dear. 1 shilling for a cheap meal. Clothes are also dear, shirts 15/6. The pubs have beer only twice a week. They soon run out, and then they wait for the next shipment. Went back for dinner, etc. Parade at 2:00, into lorries and away. Of course, the usual procedure, kit bags first. Air raid on the way. Gerry dropped land mines; you could see them floating down. The whole island shook when they exploded. Got to our HQ - 74th Light AAA. No room, so we were in tents. Had to put them up, then our first meal since dinner. Piece of cheese, bread, and tea. Isn't life sweet? Hell's delight, I got a Sgt. Major, very regimental (git up thar), oh nuts. I met the rest of Light AA. There are 69 of us now, so we are better off. Our tents are on a grassy plot behind the barrack and overlooking the sea. Very nice views until they start dropping mines in the sea. Field kitchen, and so on. Officers ok. We were about to have a beer in the house when the raiders came. It was dusk. Well! I have never seen anything like it in my life. There are nearly 200 A.A. guns on Malta, and they were all blasting, also about 50 searchlights, Bofors, 3.7, 4.5, 9, " 3, " Lewis, Bren, Pom poms. Holy smoked bacon, it was Hell on earth. They got them in the searchlights and brought two down. Boy, some sight, dead center, they went to pieces. The pilot bailed out and fell into the sea. Well, I felt shaky. We all did. London's nothing on this, even Tiny says so, and he spent six months on a gun sight in London. It finished at 10:00, an hour of it. It was like years. Well, we went to bed finally after one hour and had a peaceful night.

WEDNESDAY, 23rd
"Racasoli Barracks, Malta"

Up at 6:00. Breakfast—sausages, lovely, cold, and greasy, that's all. Air raid passed off, dropped bombs. Blasted Air Force doesn't seem to do anything out here. On Parade, swing your arms. Hell, like "Deepcut." Roll call, talk by Colonel. MII inspection. Another raid over. We're in battle dress now, with tin hats and respirators. Kit inspection. Everything is laid out. Fag issue, 50 woods. Water was rationed here, and I had a mug full to shave in. Cold, great! Charlie and other Lieutenant bombardiers stripped raw deal after 9 months. Lot of Kits missing, list made. Get our old Kit bags soon. Contents will be our own. Ordinance not to know. They came out to Malta on the "Otranto." We were bombed in the dock here, and some Kits were destroyed. I guess this will be our last issue, damn good job. I'm sick of Army Kit. Another raid. A huge bomber passed over, about 25, 000 ft. The heavy A.A didn't get near it. Lousy shooting! He dropped a few parachute mines. Saw them float off. Boy, do they kick up a dust? Done some washing, etc., went to Naafi, here very dear, Polish 6d a tin. New call-up of Maltese, 22-23 years old, about 2-3, 000 of them. They get 14/a week.

THURSDAY, 24th

"Racasoli Barracks, Malta"

Marvelous, a quiet night. Had a good kip. They've brought down six planes this week here. On Parade 9:00, marched over to the Battery Office by Bombardier Cross. BSS M waiting for us. The inspection was very strict, but it passed okay. The usual brawling, etc., and blasted officers—lot of sods. Had shocked. Our Sgt. yesterday is an officer today. Then they split us up into squads and gave us a Buffs Sgt. each. Well, well, after nine months, we are in our R.A's. They gave us marching drills and turns at the halt. 1-2-3. Hell, we went mad, of all the blinding cheek. We told 'em so. They said we were good at it, and that was all we'd ever done. Short arm. Ok. Dinner, ½ day. Cleaned up. Charlie and I went out for a walk. Marvelous with the old walls and forts, gates, and drawbridges, there are also thousands of statues. Lovely sculptures are everywhere. Very narrow streets, very hilly. Had a look at the shelters the people have burrowed into the rock. Sandstone under cliffs, they have, at places, a good 50 feet of solid rock above or about them. Absolutely bomb-proof. The Civil casualty list is very small, considering the bombs dropped and the large population. Raid on, so we went in one of them. They were all tunnels, small rooms, and large families. A lot of children about. I guess that's all they must do here. Most of the men are out of work. The Government pays very little. They are much cleaner than the Egyptian people, though. Few of the lads were drinking the usual wine, and hellish stuff drove one mad. They ended up fighting each other. Got back. Raid got into the shelter. I think there were about 50 raiders up, and everything was in action. They dropped everything from mines to aerial torpedoes. Could see the mines float down. I counted 30 flares burning at once. Twenty-six were brought down (Raiders). They were coming down in all directions, into the sea, a lot. One of our Bofors and crew was wiped out, which was a direct hit. We buried them today, six together. About 200 bombs were dropped. It finished in an hour.

FRIDAY, 25th

Had a good night. Tiny on MTT at HQQ, 12 of our boys taken for Bofors to make up for those killed last night. Got paid. Rifle inspection. March drill. What an army. Mine sweepers out for mines. They shake the Island. Finally, quiet over England and London. Yugo's still fighting. Greeks and Imperial Troops holding out. And still, it goes on. Well, we've seen plenty of action to date. It's about ten times worse than London during a raid. Thank God they don't get it like this. And still, we live again, thank God! Had a lecture by an officer. Theory of Bofor, etc., okay too. Detailed for water carrying. Bloody cheek! Water supply blown out. Took about 200 petrol tins and filled them up in a village 5 miles away. The locals turn out to watch. Feel like Storm Troopers, all looking at my belt of badges. Men from the desert, they said, hah! Got back late.

SATURDAY, 26th

Giving us a day off. Got issue of chocolate, Cadbury's plain. Me and Charlie got a dinghy over to Valletta. 12-inch boat 2d each. Lovely going across. Best and prettiest harbour I have ever seen. Similar to Sydney Harbour. 2 ships sunk by mines, so they were careful. Had a walk about, sightseeing, etc. I met Sam, Mike, Mac, and Dave. Not in action yet. Will be soon, though. Went to the pictures "Vagabond." Violinist was an Aussie, very good. Very small theater that holds about 200. Had to stop halfway through for an interval. Raid on during the film. Dropped a roll of film off and bought a fresh one. Went down into the Honky Tonks. Hell, what a street! Like Sister Street in Alex. Bars with a bit of music and girls. Beer 8d a bottle, about ½ a pint. Girls expect to drink for a dance. Aw nuts, I said. And the star, Dirty Dina, boy, was she horrible. We got the hell out of there. Went up to the bridge. Bought native wine 1/- bottle. Weak port, wow, it knocked us over. Spewed in the street, Charlie fell down and couldn't get up. I had to carry him into the shelter, and then we all fell down in a corner, almost smothering Mike. The shelter was empty and had lights. We slept there until 2:00. It was so damned cold we moved into a public shelter, got slung out by cops. Broke into a bus. We lay in there. Then I discovered somebody lying alongside me. It was a girl. The bus was used for sleeping by a whole family. We got out without them knowing. What a night. Ended up in a shelter again.

SUNDAY, 27th

"Racasoli Barracks"

Woke up feeling horrible—head, sick stomach. Holy smoke, that stuff is killer. No more! Mike was sick again. Sam couldn't see for a while. Went to Vernon Club for a wash, etc., and felt horrible. People coming out of shelters. The girls are very skinny, with legs like spindles. Joan, you have lovely legs compared to the majority of those here. They're not bad-looking, but I know somebody better. Got the boat back to the other side. That took my last 4d. Got back, bread and treacle for breakfast—don't they treat us well! Packed Kit and tents, ready to move off at 1:30. Going to "Ta Qali, " near the aerodrome here. Germans 30 miles from "Athens." Part of the Greek Army capitulated, and Imperial Troops withdrew. Yugoslavia finished, now German territory. Heavy raid on "Manchester" and "Plymouth." We've had three raids already, all in one hour. We've had 500-odd raids on Malta so far. Our battery has brought down 33. That's 12 guns, not bad. Moved off in buses. 24 of us for Ta Qali and 40 for "Luqa." Good ride, with lovely views. Got there, not bad, in the middle of the Island. Fighter Drome, alongside battery (ours)—4 guns on the hill. About 20 Hurricanes here. Put up tents. BSMSM with us, fussy old sod, like an old woman. Captain a surly bugger, Sgt. okay. Villages all around and Holy City, a huge fortress all walled in. A fine place.

MONDAY, 28th

"Ta Qali Drome" Training Course

Up at 6:00. Grub is good. George Scully is cooking. Inspection, Bofor Training, FAA Sights, vertical and lateral zero. Easy, of course, but we had the usual dopes with us. Four raids today. Blasted fighters do nothing here. They take off and keep away when a raid is on. The GLL and Heavies do the work. They stay very high, though; I can't reach them. Had a dive bomb attack today. Lost a seaplane. "Athens" occupied, that's Greece finished, and I guess, of course, Russia and Turkey do nothing. Ah, why the Hell don't they call an armistice? No, they can't stop him. Gerry's broken through into Egypt (Sollum). We got out just in time again. The luck of our draft as usual. Bloody BSMSM fusspot wants all kit rolled up, etc., like a lot of Boy Scouts we are. Blokes are getting mail, etc., but not us. Oh no, do we ever? Went down to the village, not much there. I had a drink, Blue Label, okay. Walked about—a street very similar to "Amrya." Not so dirty, though. Maltese old dress is similar to that of women in Egypt, and it is very warm. Lovely churches and statues, etc. Women okay. Developed well at 10-13, got kids, and are usually carrying another. Goats and sheep on the streets. People staring at us as usual. Walked back. Raid at 10:00. Hell to play. About 50 bombs on the drome, land mines, etc. Big convoy in and part of Fleet. Heavy raid on Docks. A lot of new Hurricanes came in. About 15 on the Drome here. Raid passed off and I couldn't sleep. Raid again at 2:00. Cookhouse blown out. Boy, was it heavy stuff, and how! All in shelter.

Couple of Police Patrols. Malta police. Fine horses. Musta Drome in the background. Main road Rabat-Valletta, and our air raid shelter on the left. It could tell a tale.

TUESDAY, 29th

"Ta Qali"

Up bright and early. Find shaving fairly easy, etc. Lovely weather. Had a fairly good breakfast. We're all on fatigue today. Helped move Battery HQQ out to a safer place. Went there by truck and shifted furniture out of private houses to make room for HQQ staff. Had a good day, lots of fun, etc. Had a raid. Got back early. Good dinner. So endeth the day. Bar fag issue and one letter for Shulman, posted in December, none for me yet.

WEDNESDAY, 30th

Holy smoke, what a night! 6 raids, we got up at 10:00, 11:00, 1:00, 2:30, and 4:00. Seventy bombers came over first and about 200 in another. Good God, we were crushed into the shelter, every man on their faces. Men next to me were trembling. I was the last man nearest the door of the shelter. I counted 33 flares right over us and the drome. I could see mines swinging on their parachutes. Could hear the whistle and thud of DAA Heavies, 1, 000 lb. bombs. We waited until they went off. Hell's delight, the explosion was terrific. Wham! I thought my ears were coming out. I prayed and shook. We couldn't speak. Never in all my life have I ever been so scared. The raids in all lasted 6 hours. 6 Hurricanes were smashed up on the field. A hangar and Naafi were destroyed. A gun crew was wiped out. They flew down a searchlight beam and killed the crew by machine gun fire. We finally got to bed at 4:30. By hell, we were all buggered up. It was a concentrated attack on the Heavies, alright. 34 Raiders were brought down. The Bofors got about 12. Heavies got the rest. The fighters here are not allowed to fight owing to the small number of fighters we have. The Convoy brought 16 new ones in. That makes about 60 here now.

MAY

THURSDAY, 1st
"Ta Qali"

Got up at about 9:00. I had about 3 hours kip. Felt lousy. Found a couple of parachutes, flare ones. Huge craters and wreckage about. About 26 DAs about, one in the hangar. A mine nearby wrecked 4 planes. 2 Buffs killed guards. Valletta is badly smashed up. Last night was hellish again. They were on the docks this time, using mines and torpedoes, and stayed for about 2 hours. Used 50 planes, brought about 10 down. Night Fighters are in action again. Saw engines drop out of Junkers. Boy! Are they smart pilots—they came down within 200 feet and machine-gunned positions. Slept in the shelter till the cold drove us out. 4 raids today. 30 Me's. Mixed it with our Hurricanes. 1 Me and Hurricane lost. Some mail today, 12 letters. Some posted in April, some Xmas. None for me. What lousy organization is this so-called British Army? Our grub is just as bad, and only 20 of us. Can't get the rations, they say. Bully Beef, biscuits, bloody blasted stuff. Makes me mad. Can't do anything about it.

FRIDAY, 2nd
On gun today. Had a quiet night last night. Damn, nice too. First good night's rest for a week. On the gun, all about it. In theory, should go on the sights next week. Getting on okay with the course. Picking up what we had forgotten. Of course, it's all static, and there is no predictor. Our training was mobile and Predictor. Blasted BSM is getting quite tough; he roars and shrieks at us. Hell's delight, we left that behind at Deepcut! You have to eat here, shave and wash there, do this, and do that. The guy is like a schoolmaster. As we are all Cockneys, I suppose we can take it. 4 raids so far. 2 Hurricanes knocked out by me. Boy, are those Me's good—they dive like rockets. Our pilots are dead scared of them. They wait in the sun, get 2-3 Capronis as decoys, then wait until our lads get at the Italians. 3 Junkers came down today and picked

up 12 pilots. About 12 Hurricanes lost so far in 2 weeks. Hurricanes are hopeless against the Me's. Lost the Destroyer "Essex" today. Gerry dropped a mine on her. She blew up and turned over in the Grand Harbour. Smashed up Valletta badly. Got paid 10/-, spent 2/-, and I already owed Tom 1/-. I'll soon get rid of it. I'm damned, it's hellish being short of money.

View of our camp just below gun positions. Ta Qali

Ta Qali fighter Drome. Wrecked Swordfish in the foreground, Hurricanes in the background.

SATURDAY, 3rd
"Ta Qali"

Quiet again last night. It's marvelous. Had a good kip. As a result, got up late and couldn't finish cleaning up. Left a bowl of water on the bed, all kit hanging about. BSMSM played Hell. He roared like a bull. Still, I got away with it. 13 Yank Beaufort Fighters came in today. A 2-engine Fighter Bomber. Pretty fast. I guess they'll use them soon. Nice-looking plane, but I reckon it's no match for the Me's. Had a lecture and gun drill on FASAS, etc. Got our laundry and a half day for rest. Another air raid. BSM is as scared as Hell and makes a dash for shelter right away. Aw, nuts to that. If I get it now, I do. Nothing will prevent it. 6, 000 Imperial Troops evacuated from Greece. A nice brave withdrawal again. Well! I'll be glad when the last withdrawal comes. Went to "Rabat"—a damned nice place. It's built on a high hill on solid rock. Called the Holy City, also the open city. There are about 3, 000 evacuees here from Valletta. No guns there or below it, so Gerry doesn't bomb. Some lovely women there. It would be impossible to get in if the gates were closed. Put a roll of film in.

The Holy City "Rabat" 5 miles from Valletta. About 1000 feet up. Entirely encircled by solid stone walls, bastions, etc. Contains the brotherhood of Roman Catholic Priests, etc& a Cathedral.

SUNDAY, 4th

Hell of a raid again last night. Ten mines dropped on Valletta and the docks. We had to get in and out of tents three times to take shelter. I counted 35 flares. Night Fighters were up. They (the AAA) got 2 Junkers (Bofors again). They had it in the lights. It couldn't get out, so it machine-gunned them, but they filled it with shells. Went to Valletta. Hell's delight, what a mess. Four mines dropped right in the main street. It's ruined. I've seen nothing like it; it's absolutely smashed. They're digging bodies out wholesale. My roll of film is gone. Bloody shame, it was all of "Amrya" too. Ah well, if that is all I'll lose in this war, I'll be lucky. Nice ride by bus. REE Camp mistook a mine for a flare. It wiped the camp out. Killed 8. 2 Junkers were brought down this morning. A mine at Rabat didn't go off. It was 8 ft x 4 ft. That's a nice article. People of Valletta were all nervous. They're running around in circles. All moving like ants. 130 Bombers were used last Saturday night, according to GLL. 16 Bombers were brought down over Britain. Blitz on Liverpool. Quiet in London. Trouble in Iraq. They're shelling our bases and oil lines. Adolph, again, is the right smart Army for that. All troops off Greece. Gerry advances in Egypt. African troops were sent up to Egypt. Fire in Abyssinia. 26 ships, Yanks in Suez.

Section of Kingsway, the main street of Valletta, after the blitz period. Four mines did this in one night. This is only a very small part of the damage. Hundreds of buildings were smashed. In fact, the whole street was rendered useless.

MONDAY, 5th

3 raids today. Bit of one last night, but it was not bad. Had a good night's sleep. Gun drills all day, mostly FAsA and Deflectors. Blasted officer got us confused; he was too quick. Still, as usual, I followed ok. Good average, etc. I'm wise to this Army now. Boys in action say no sights are used hardly unless you have a good constant course. Blasted rations again. Bit of cheese and bread for tea, a few spuds for dinner, etc. Bloody starving, all of us. Big convoy in, all ammo, etc. Can't get natives to work. They offered them 27/- a day. They refused. They made the Manchesters do it at 2/- a day. Went up to Rabat. Walked around the native quarter. Dirty, smelly, narrow streets. They dump the swill in the streets. Goats, etc., running about. The east as usual. The raid came on. Hell, did the people scatter. Holy smoke and how. A big mine landed nearby and didn't go off. Ugly damned thing. The dames

are ok. Some laugh. Of all the Monkey walks I've seen, Malta beats them all. All the dames, everyone, up and down, about turn, well, well! Good night!

TUESDAY, 6th

Good night's rest.

Very damp at night, though. Bed boards are blasted hard. Ah, nuts to it all! Still trouble in Iraq. Troops at grips there. The oil line is in danger. On gun today, FASAS #4 laying, etc., I did ok. Raid on. 25 Me's, escort, and 10 bombers. 1 Me down, 1 Hurricane. Boy, the Hurricane hit the ground with a bash. Machine gun fire all over. Bombs on Luqa Drome. Grub is still scarce. Got fag issue, not bad. Some of the boys received mail dated April 21st, and others received it from Xmas. Their people haven't received their cables from Cape Town and Alex yet. Well, Joan, I hope you get yours, ok? Well, we're posted Charlie, Fred, Tom, myself, and a few others. 8 of us are going to a site on the Base, sea base, and petrol dump. Nice place. We are off tomorrow at 6:30. Well, here we are. Now, I shall see what I am made of. I wonder if I can stand it. The Bofor is the suicide gun. They are taking the Maltese off because they leave the guns. They won't stick in and face. Went to "Rabat" with Charlie. Ok. Got films, very good too. Had a stroll about. Saw B.Sgt. and Sgt's, well canned on spiders' blood (Ambique). Some example for a BSM drives me nuts. Had an alarm. Got a good view of Gerry caught in the searchlights. By Hell, the Malts are smart in lights. Counted 9 in beams over docks near "Luqa" and "Valletta." The Bofors barrage was terrific. There were a good 50 Bofors bashing away. Wow! They got a "Dornier" 4-engine. Smack, he came down like a stone. All crew were killed. It blew up and burnt. Big oil dump hit by a bomb; some fire! Night fighters got 2 Junkers. 3 Hurricanes brought down yesterday and 1 Me. Raid finished at 11:00, lasted 1 ½ hours. He dropped a lot of stuff on us.

WEDNESDAY, 7th
Gun sight, "Marsa Scirocco"

Had a good sleep, up at 6:00. Breakfast was one sausage, bread, and tea, nice what? Got into full kit. Lorry came and away we went. Glad to see the back of the BSMSM. Nice ride to the above site. Maltese were manning the guns and we took over. We're in tents, 8 of us, with Sgt. and Bdr. So that makes 10 of us. Mason is cook. So far, we've got 3 tins of bully beef and 1 loaf of bread for 10 men. Not bad, eh? They look after us as usual. Decent gun and pit, etc. Had an alarm; we manned, and nothing happened. We're taking any number on guns as we get there. Rations came. Sack of spuds, a few loaves, and some meat. Works out to about 4 slices of bread a day, 1 lb of spuds, and 3 cups of tea. So, we buy a few eggs from the natives, 2 ½ D. each. Just shows, well! We've unpacked about 300 rounds of ammo already. Had dinner, bread, corned beef, and a cup of tea. I'm putting on weight. 8 of us have shifts of 1 ½ hrs. on the telephone for orders, plots, and bearings. Had an alarm. Manned 4 plus on GL. Saw about 40 then. Very bad visibility, low clouds. High-level bombing. A stick dropped about 200 yards away. We just about shit ourselves. Heavy AK fired on Hurricane. Hurricane got Gerry (night fighter). Big Sunderlands coming in.

THURSDAY, 8th
Lousy night last night. Raid finished at 11:00. I was on guard at 11:30, came off at 1:00. Stand until 5:00. Raining and blowing. Got to have 3 crew stand to on guns because of Sunderlands anchored here in the bay. Taking mail tomorrow. Must write to Joan for it. Some more of the LAAAA came in. They're in our battery. Still stand to, went to sleep on telephones. Hell, was I tired? Erected 3 tents for boys coming in. Charlie and I on leave today at 1:00, but we can't go anywhere though. It's a lousy rainy day with no money. So, all we can do is lay in and get some sleep and stink. What a life. And I used to grumble in civilian life. Got blasted wet on the tent job. Cook spoiled our dinner. Hell! No raids today. Bad visibility. Doubt if he'll come over tonight. There are

23, 000 British Troops on this island. Wow! A good many infantry regiments. Picked up fleas from somewhere. Bloody things itch like Hell. I'll be alright for sleep tonight though; I have no duties. I'm doing ammo numbers now, safest and easiest.

View of our tents and Naval G.L. equipment, as well as terraces of ground rising from the sea.

A few goats, etc., but too far to be any good

FRIDAY, 9th
"Gun Sight, Marsa Scirocco"

All quiet last night, had a good sleep. Still raining and foggy. Got up late. Breakfast, fishcake. Cleaned a bit. The "Breconshire" anchored in the bay here. Also, 6 Destroyers. The "Brecon" has troops aboard, etc., and they are unloading as fast as they can. 26-ship convoy came in. We expect some heavy stuff tonight. "Sunderland" is still in. "Brecon" moved off and also Destroyers. Damned good job. We were expecting Stukas. I walked to the village. Hell, there was nothing there! Came back. It's lovely around here. From the water up, it's all in terraces. Little plots of ground walled in. Clover, grain, spuds, beans, figs, and lemons. Watched men plowing. Very primitive. 1 horse and a curved trunk of wood with a shear on it, goes in about 3 inches and makes a furrow about a foot wide. Lovely bays and inlets. We are right on the cliffs. Monk got 2 postcards today. I've got nothing so far. Said his wife got mail from Cape Town, ok. Cleaned up gun, etc. Had alarm. 12 plus Me's and Ju's 88. No action. Got paid 8/9. Blast them. They took off a third this week. It's getting less each week. 30 Raiders were brought down over England by Night Fighters and AAA. Bit easier in Prague. "Darlan" of France selling his country. Granting ports in Syria to Hitler. All English AA are here together. Naafi here sells cakes 2d. Hellish.

SATURDAY, 10th
"Sight Searchlight, Marsa Scirocco"

Had no alarm last night. Had a good kip. Lovely day. "Sunder" is still at anchor. I guess he'll have a smack at her today. Grub is much better now. George is cooking. 11 ships in Grand Harbour. There should be some fun soon. Buffs coming off guns at docks, taking 5 men from each site here. Blasted luck we get another move now, I expect. We're never settled, always on the move. Yeah! As I thought, Charlie, Mant, Hudson, Johnson, and Ram are leaving. I, Donald, Bombardier, and Jim, four of us left. The rest are going to the docks. Tiny came for them. Had a chat with Tiny. He's still at BHQ, although he's moved twice. A DAA fell about 100 yards from him. He fell flat. He just escaped. We said goodbye. So now there are only 4 men on each gun around here. Alarm, plus 10 Me's. Boy! This is it. I took #2, Don #3, Jim #4, and Bombardier #1- ammo. Our fighters took them on. Could hardly see anything, just flashes of them. Spotted an Me about 4000 ft up. Bdr. gave a shout, then I saw another sod come straight out of the sun. He was on us before we could move. I thought it was a Hurricane hit because he was smoking, but it was an Me 109. Machine-gunning as he came. We got 6 rounds off, but he was down and gone. The walls prevented us from firing further. A Bofor further on got him. He dropped into the sea. The Sunderland was blazing. She sank in about 5 minutes. Incendiaries. Nice shooting, but goodbye mail! Bloody, lousy organization. She's been there 2 ½ days! We've been manning continually because of that. A lot because visibility was bad. But on the first nice day, they take 5 men off each gun for the docks. So, when Gerry came over, we were short 5 men. Well, what a fiasco! Hopeless! It was easygoing for Gerry. The sod came down within 50 ft. No Hurricanes about. So, 75, 000 pounds worth was gone. 2 weeks ago, the same thing happened. Before that, 10 Wellingtons he got 'em the same way. The Wellingtons were lined up nicely for him. What a war. Our Major is like a fool. A Lt. General came around; the stupid questions he asked. If a gun went up to 90 degrees, would the shells fall out, etc.? He was like a doddering old grandfather. Full moonlight tonight.

Here I am again on the blower. Raid in progress. Just before the attack on the Sunderland

The Sunderland burned and sank after a Me 109 had come down 50 ft. above her and filled her full of lead. Taken just after the action.

SUNDAY, 11th
"Sight Searchlight"

Surprisingly, he didn't come over last night. Lovely full moon. Done 1-hour guard from 11:15-12:15. Wellingtons and Beaus out on raids, I guess. Had a good kip, no alarm. Stand to 4:45. I took snaps yesterday of the site, gun, Sunderland's, etc. Two alarms so far (Recco). Our fighters got a Ju 88 good. Some heavy shit went up. Otherwise, quiet. Nothing unusual today. It was fairly quiet. Ah! Here he is, alarm 9:00. Plus 40. Wow, that means about 60. Policy tonight. Searchlights. 2 Fighters, no Heavies. Lights engage at 3000 ft. Well! He came over in relays. The GLL was crowded. Coming in from Italy in a continuous stream. They each dropped about 15 bombs each. Bash! "Luqa, " the airdrome and the Docks. Poor Charlie. The first night, too. They got one in the lights, but Fighters were miles away. He came down, diving right over us. Hell's delight, I thought our last moment had come. He was about 50 ft over us, a Ju 87 Stuka. The lights got him. We opened up 15 rounds. He dropped bombs and mines. Hell, what blasts. We almost went nuts! And so, it went on. Mines, bombs, guns, and machine guns right up to 4:30. We were deadbeat. He knocked hell out of the Island. It was terrific. And the defense was hopeless. They didn't get one. Four times, he dive-bombed us, but we couldn't see them. Well! We had about 1 ½ hours' sleep. Had another alert at 6:00, so we stood for about 1 hour. George cooked a damned good meal today, Sunday; Yorkshire pudding was not bad.

The Bofor is at rest with Bdr. "Slats" Slater, Smudge, and Die Hard Don on the blower

MONDAY, 12th

"Sight Wolseley, Marsa Scirocco"

Tried to get some more kip. Slept for about ½ hour, and the Sgt. advised us to pack up. Hell, another move. What a war. What a lousy Battery. We'll all go nuts between them. We have now to move over to the above site, where we are to take a course on gunner and signals. Imagine it, as though we haven't had enough, the dopes. The Buffs are taking up the sites here. They came from the docks. So, this is a rest actually for them. They have split up and messed about here and there. Everything is a shambles. We took our gear over, erected two tents, and dashed about. We were almost dead from fatigue. I'm sure there are 5th columnists on this bloody Island. He knows all about our convoys coming in when our fighters have landed for fuel. He knows about our defense policies at night. He knows the layout of this Island. He's a dead shot with his bombs. And so it goes on. He does what he likes here. Alarm. Plus 40 coming in now. He used 700 planes last night over Britain, London mostly. Bloody awful. Poor people. As yet, they can't count the dead. Oh God! Have mercy on them. Why don't they quit? It's of no use. 400 British bombers raided

Hamburg. That's what causes it: retaliation. 130 Night Raiders were brought down in a week over England. But what good is that? He is turning out that amount each week. Infiltration of Syria now. I can see all of the East going under. Suez, Syria, Palestine. The States won't come in, not while there is money to be made. Oh no! Just a few lousy politicians caused all this bloodshed. 75, 000 British were captured in Egypt. Churchill said we can't stop him from supplying Libya. He's superior to us in arms in Egypt. He's got a stronger air force. If he can send 150 over here and 700 over London, I guess he's got plenty of stuff. Another raid. Heavies. Passed off.

TUESDAY, 13th
"Sight Wolseley"

Actually, I am sick at heart and worried for poor old Joan and the family. They are right in it, and that bloody great raid on Saturday. I pray to God for their safety. No news or letters of any sort. Please, God, watch over them. Hell, last night again. Just got into bed. I was expecting it, though. Heard the whistles. I was dressed by the time the sirens went off. Couldn't wake Shilos and Herring, so we left them there. 15 plus came in. Beau fighters and Hurricanes went up. They dropped about 20 on Luqa and 100 on the Harbour. Stukas came down. Wow! Their engines don't synchronize. Like a motor revving up all the time. Suddenly silence. Down she comes, whaaaaaa whop. They dropped about 200 yards away. Hell, it was frightful. Thank God they won't get it in "Southall." Finished at 11:00. Up again at 12:00, then up again at 2:00. No sleep. It's wearing us down! One guy is going nuts. Some more can't stand it and can't go on sight. Well, my nerves are getting worse. Gun drills all day. Sgt. Guest. Ok. I'm ok at laying. Got fags and, of all things, 2 letters from Joan dated February and April. She's ok. Hardly any news in it, though. Her brother Kenny's in the hospital for something, but she didn't say what. He expects to be called up in August. It's all quiet so far. 3 raids today. High-level bombing. Me's and so forth.

WEDNESDAY, 14th

Lousy night again last night. He came over at 12:00 and again at 3:00. Still, we had a few hours of sleep. Took shelter in ammo dump. Dropped a lot of stuff on "Luqa." Dive-bombed a few times. On-guard drill all day, easy. Getting the Bofors off pretty good now. BSM with us, old sod. Barks and roars like Hell. Played Hell with me because I read Joan's first letters on Parade. Ah! Who the Hell cares? Me's came over this morning, about 15 of them. High-level bombing attack in the afternoon. More Me's, they came over at about 30, 000 feet. Hurry Birds are messing about. Down they came, got 3 of ours. They fell like stones. Bloody Hurricanes are useless. The Me's are too good for us. This occurs every day. What the people of England don't know, ah! The lousy organization of the Army on this Island! We are being messed about now. Changing sites, moving, etc. Hess deserted Adolf. Came over to Scotland by Me, took personnel. I wonder what's behind this move! More dope, I suppose. Something stinks in Denmark. Feeling great these days, damned healthy, thank God. No gut pains, etc. Nice climate here.

THURSDAY, 15th

Hell again last night. He came over at 12:00, 3:00, 4:30. Bombed "Luqa" and Docks. Used Ju 88-87 Stukas. About 50 plus in all. Some fell near "Pigsty." As usual, hardly any opposition. Heavy AAA, no results. Hell, we were in and out of bed like jack-in-the-boxes. We sleep fully dressed. By Hell, are we getting a bashing? My nerves are all to Hell. Came over today 3 times, Me's carrying 2 bombs each. 60 came over first. We were manning Wolseley. They came in at 20, 000 feet, couldn't see 'em, but they hit "Luqa" Drome every time. They shot one of our Hurry Birds down. Poor Pilot didn't have a chance. He came straight down from 15, 000 feet. It's suicide to send our fighters up. They're no match for the Me's. Their cannons open up at 400 yards. That's the 6th fighter this week. Total loss. Got letters from Joan and Vi, Feb. and March. Nice to get them.

FRIDAY, 16th
"Wolseley - Sight and School"

He came over about 3:30, not bad, got to shelter. Slept through the raid. There are about 100 tons of ammo stacked in this shelter. So, we wouldn't have to worry much if hit. Some of the lads wouldn't leave the tent, but the guns opened up. Well, they came out of there like greyhounds. Curses, howls, groans, looking for their kits. Ha! On fatigues, up at 6:00. Went to Luqa to move ammo from place to place in the huge underground store. What a place! 80 feet beneath solid rock. Ton upon ton of ammo, petrol, etc. Say! Some money's worth. A raid was on, 75 Me's, 110 came over. We didn't hear a thing. Saw the Wimpys, 10 of them that got dived and smashed flat. Also, Hurry Birds and Beau's. Boy! Is Luqa Drome a mess. A direct hit on B. H. Q., which exists no more. Those boxes of ammo (Light AA) weigh 150 lbs. each. We had to carry them on our backs 200 yards. Hell! For dinner, we had bread, corned beef, and tea. Some dinner, hellish delight, the grub is lousy now. 2 pieces of bread and jam at 4:00, that's all. Dinner-stew, and a very small portion. Breakfast- sausage and bread. Boy, we starve most of the time. Cakes at Naafi 2d each. The boys buy eggs at 2 ½ d a time. No sleep at night just shows we are in bloody fine condition. Can't get enough or safe enough to send Joan a cable. Blast it! I asked for 60/- credit and might get it. Flies are hellish here. Not so many as Egypt, but they sting like wasps.

SATURDAY, 17th
Not too bad last night. Fairly quiet. A bit of gun drill. On leave today from 1:00 to 9:00 tomorrow. Got 18/9 and 10/- on credit. Me and Don went to the Sliema dance. Lousy. From 3:00-7:00. They were all paired up. Lousy lot of dames. Had a dance, went to Valletta, to Vernon's Club. Got a bed there for 1/-. Valletta still bad, hardly cleared anything yet. Tons of wreckage about.

SUNDAY, 18ᵗʰ

Damned good sleep. No raids. Bad weather. Boy, was it good in a soft bed with sheets. Wow! Had breakfast, a game of snooker. Went to Sliema for a bath. I used all the water. Don had a half bath with about a bowl full of hot water. Hah! Slid out of it for free. Back to Vernon's Club for dinner. Pork chop, first one in months. Sure was good. Had a shave. Sent a cable to Joan. Put in a roll of film. I guess the Egypt roll is a dead loss. Dance at Vernon's. A fine hall, Army band, stone floor. Hell's delight, what women, all shapes, some decent though. Had a dance, a bit slippery with boots. One dame had her hair smothered with lard. Cripes! What a stench. Got back by bus. Few of the boys pissed, and how, ambique (whiskey). Well, I've kept off it so far. Malt told me it's made from leather water. Wow! Poor guts! Not for me.

MONDAY, 19th

"Sight Wolseley"

No raids last night, boy, what a kip, great. We packed up, ready to go to Luqa sight. One of the hottest sights in Malta. It's the bomber drome, and he hits it the hardest of all. All the heaviest bombers are there. We've lost 20 there on the ground. An RAF chap told me Command wouldn't let the hurry birds go in; they were only cruising. He said Hurry's are equal to Me's. Duke of Aosta in Abyssinia seeks terms. I guess he's shot his load. Spain allows Gerry troops free passage to Gibraltar, and the same applies to Syria. It's my bet he closes the Mediterranean in 2 months. Took a lorry to Luqa. As usual, they have 12 men and about 5 tons of stuff in one lorry. Hell's delight. #1 site is the worst of them all. There are about 10 Wimpys, 6 Beaus, and Glen Martens about 50 yards off. There are craters all around the site. Huge chunks of bombs, shrapnel, and wreckage of at least 12 bombers where they have been machine-gunned and bombed on the field. Ah well! We might as well have the worst as anything. There are ten of us: Scully cooking, Sgt. Guest, Bdr. Slater, Bachelor, me, Gurin, Don, and others. The Pit is pretty strong. The guns do I in every 3 actions here. It's too much of a strain otherwise. We are

"Stoneheap, " and one can imagine why. We got fixed up, had tea. Grub's better already. Scully sees to that. No action tonight. An hour each pocket by day, one man on all night. No manning during the raid. Shelter is about 400 yards off. All's well.

TUESDAY, 20th

"Sight Stoneheap, Luqa Drome"

Raid about 4:00. Bombs on Docks. 4 Plus, finished in ½ hour. Ok. Stand to 4:45. Tea. Stand down, ok. 2 on leave today. Aosta gives in. Abyssinia under Union Jack. That ends that. Few more troops for Egypt. 6 raids so far today. One, I thought we would never come through alive. Me's 110 (25 of them) dived, 2 bombs each, hit 2 Beaus and a Wellington. They all caught fire, complete loss. We were in a gun pit. Terrific barrage put up. We are helpless. Too high for us, 15, 000 ft. We had to crouch down. I got under the loading plate. Hell! I shook like a leaf. I couldn't help it. Shrapnel whistling and whining all around us. 2-500 lb. bombs fell 50 yards away. Destroyed reservoir, killed Maltese chap. Again, we live. How much longer? No rations come, bugger all for tea. They expect us to go through this hell and starve at the same time. The swine! I'm on guard all night. Wire cut, so the phone is out of order. Nuts to it. I'm in the tent tonight.

Our sleeping quarters at sight. In the background, Valletta & Grand Harbour

138

Inside of Tent

The Gunsight "Stoneheap" Luqa Drome

WEDNESDAY, 21st

All clear last night. Thank God. We had a good sleep. I'm off guard today. Early recon raid. Ok. 8 new Hurry birds came in. They carry extra tanks for the trip from Blighty, 10 Wimpys, and some Dormers. Hell! The Island's rotten with planes, all coming in just when he was overhead, looking around. Well, we can expect another dive-bombing attack. I was right! 30 plus coming in; now we're for it. Order over the phone to take cover. Well, we got no shelter, so it's into the ammo dump. It's full of ammo and cocktails. Nice place, eh! Down he came. Hell's delight! About 50 heavy bombs on the drome. Our fighters got the hell out of the way, you bet! I said a few prayers. Don couldn't stand the noise, so he put wool in his ears. He machine-gunned, we manned, bashed away, no good. All clear. 3 planes burning on the drome. Again, he scores. None of his are hit. Isn't it bloody sweet? Every day, he comes over and gets 2 to 3 of our bombers on the ground. Our fighters are not allowed to go in. They just cruise about and watch. The heavies bash away without effect. Away he goes, happy as hell. Fighter pilots at Hal Far Drome on strike. They don't like the policy. They want a crack at the Me's. Crete was invaded by German parachutists dressed in new "3" battle dress. Came over by gliders and troop carriers. Hell of a fight going on there. Poor old Cled Parry is right in the thick of it. The battle still rages there. Invasion trials tomorrow, up at 4:30.

4 of our bombers burning after Me's bombed Luqa Drome. Taken during the raid

Some of the remains of Wellingtons and others that had been hit by bombs and burnt out on drome. About 20 planes in all.

THURSDAY, 22nd
"Stoneheap"

The alarm at 4:00. A few Ju 88s came over the docks. Dropped HE bombs. Had to man outposts with rifles. Cycle troops (evasive party) passed through. Finished at 8:00. 2 alarms today. Nothing developed. 3 Wimpys and 2 Hurry Birds went out today. East, I guess. Glen Martins out on recon, etc. Gerry invaded Crete again and used 5, 000 men by parachute, gliders, and troop carriers. They bombed and machine-gunned all day to begin with. Poor AAA went through it. Hell, we know what it's like. Ground strafing, wow! They captured 3, 000 men in 2 hours. A lot of confusion, though. One can expect that. I wonder if they'll hold out. Poor sods, it must be hell. No wonder it's a bit quiet here, except for the dive attacks by day. Although there is no moon, I guess he will try flares again soon. George is sure turning out good grub these days. Yeah, man! Had jam tart and duff today. Cheese pie, etc., and macaroni done in milk, which is mighty good. It can be done. He traded some corned beef for eggs with the Maltese. Fresh eggs for breakfast. The boys drank a lot of ambique, 3d a pint bottle here. Leather water! I'm still off it. I respect my guts too much for that! Bloody crawling things in bed at night: earwigs, glow worms, spiders, mosquitoes. It's hell trying to sleep. Did some washing today. Weather lovely now, getting hotter every day. Quiet over London. Thank God. I guess he's busy in Greece. Free French are fighting in Syria. Turkey to intervene if Gerry goes into Syria.

The Lewis-son of Bofor comes in very handy at times. Note the gunner

Couple of tough gunners! Our friend Bofor and the man on stage in the background. Note the attitude.

143

FRIDAY, 23rd
"Stoneheap"

Good kip last night. I guess he's using his stuff at Crete now. Stand to. Raining like Hell. Dam, good job. Me and Bach detailed to move Bofors to new site #5. West and south of the drome. The old pit got a direct hit. Luckily, the crew was in the shelter. Got the last crossing. Pretty big drome, about 100 acres of it. By Hell, there's some wreckage about. I counted 4 Wimpys, 3 Beau fighters, some Blenheims and Hurricanes burnt, smashed, and so forth. The hangars are in ruins. DAsA are all over the place. They exploded 5. Messed about putting in the foundation, sandbags, etc. No grub. Had to work from 11:00-4:00. Raining also. Buffs take over at 5:00.

SATURDAY, 24th

All is quiet again, not bad, and it makes a good change for us. Got our old Kit Bags (after 10 months). They withheld some stuff. Got my best battle dress. The last time I wore it, I was on seven days of emergency leave, hah! Got dressed up and left at 1:00. Got a bus from Luqa to Valletta. Went to Sliema and got snaps. Given 10 shillings change too much, not bad! Met Tiny, Sam, Mike, and Charlie. Damn nice to meet again. Charlie on Docks. Mike and Sam are on GL heavy battery, 4.5s. Tiny- dispatch at Castille and made a Lance Jack, too, hah! Went to pictures (Rio), it was ok. Got razor blades after asking at 15 shops. Couldn't get the film, fags are scarce. Had a drink at Vernon Club, 5 1/2d a blue. Kingsway hit again. Hell of a mess, 6 killed. Got back at 7:00. Had grub at Mr. Zammits, eggs, chips, and beer at 7d. Not bad. And so to bed.

SUNDAY, 25th

Had a good lay in. All quiet last night. George brought grub around. Tea in bed, hah! Bit chilly last night. H.M.S. Hood sank. The German Bismarck got her. Hit her magazine off Greenland. Too bad! Hell is going on at Crete. 1, 000s of men (Gerry's) lost. Navy smashed up a convoy of 40. Sunk the bloody lot. Sunk 4 destroyers. Gerry almost driven out of Crete. It's costing him something. Wow! They're being bombed continuously there. And still, it goes on. I wonder how it will end. He's making a bloody good effort. If he gets Crete, they are sunk out east. 17 quiet nights in London. Damn good job. On course tomorrow. Signaling and Morse.

MONDAY, 26th

"Stoneheap"

Stand to 4:45. All well, had a bloody long walk to BHQ. Through the valley, etc. Sgt. Bradley took 4 of us, Wiring and Theory of the Telephone. It was ok. Had 2 alarms, but nothing developed. Lovely weather, very hot. Gerry bombs Crete all day. Our Navy fighting like Hell. Shows Gerry's using his stuff. No raids over there. He must take Crete or lose this war. By Hell, some battle going on. The RAFA and Navy are destroying tons of his stuff. They are not picking survivors up. No time. We shall see. The uprising in Iraq is quelled. The leader flees the country. Reports of the "Bismarck" sunk. Just shows the English were led to believe that Gerry had no fleet! He still has. Having mock invasions here, just in case. The United States kicking up stink. I guess they're getting around to it. What a war. The blokes are fed up. They've had enough. Who hasn't? We're sick of the whole damned thing.

TUESDAY, 27th

Over twice last night, 10:00-3:30. Policy. Blind A.A. He floated in; engines cut off. Down he came, whomp! About 10-20 Ju 88. Bombs on the Docks. We weren't Duty Gun, so we took shelter, 40 ft. down. Alarm again at 9:00 and 3:00. Me's and Recco. Not too bad. Yankee volunteer Pilots here with Beau Fighters for night fighting. Blenheims doing good work, 5 go out twice a day. I crossed the drome today. There are stacks of 500lb bombs. Boy! I got out of there. Crete still Hell. Gerry holds a Drome still. More men dropped by parachute. Our Navy doing well. I'm with Sgt. Bradley on wiring today. Done some Practical work on Lines. Also, cause and remedy, not bad. Had dinner at BHQH. Pretty good. I'm on Picket tonight. Blasted phone doesn't ring. Ah, nuts! Who cares! Bismarck definitely sank. Revenge is sweet.

WEDNESDAY, 28th

Came over again three times last night. I was on the phone. Bell wouldn't ring. When I awoke, the bombs were already down. Flares over "Luqa." Didn't get much sleep. Blinding fleas kept me awake and snakes nested in sandbags. Could hear them hissing. On phone lines today, not bad. Nothing unusual to report. The "Dorsetshire" got the Bismarck. Torpedo. Gerry penetrated Egypt, and Syria is now in his hands. 3 Cruisers and 4 Destroyers of ours sunk around Crete. We think the Italians are operating over there now. Gerry's too busy over Malta.

THURSDAY, 29th

"Stoneheap"

Good night. No raids. Didn't go to school. On leave today. Nuts to the school. 4 days now, and I know, sweet bugger all. Went to Sliema, took pictures, and walked about. Bought a film for 2/6pence, quite dear. They've run out. No convoy. Put the roll in. The bed at THH is pretty good. Had breakfast there, had to work it. Slid out. Went to Valletta by ferry. Clearing up bombed Kingsway. Ok now. Boy, was there some damage, wow! It's scorching hot out. Got back at 5:00, had tea, and washed 4 shirts, 1 towel, and 2 pairs of socks. Not bad, eh Joan! Scrubbed them too in boiling water. Heated it in our cookhouse boiler outside the cookhouse. Washed the torso down. Washed my hair in greasy water. Well! Well! It was awful. Couldn't do anything about it, gave up. Alarm! Nothing doing. Couldn't make bed. Boy! Was I in a mess? Imagine greasy water! Will I ever forget?

SATURDAY, 31st

No stand to. Duty Gun. George brought tea. I took the teapot back, got hot water, and washed my head again, then under a cold tap. And that's how I finally removed the grease. Still fighting hard in Crete. Hand to hand, bayonets. 30, 000 German parachutists dropped and brought in by 1-200 Ju 52 troop carriers. They landed at a rate of 1 per minute. The Germans are now in possession of two drones. They have been dive bombing continuously with Stukas, Ju 87s, ground strafing, etc. 11 days now. Both sides have had enormous losses. The Navy is stopping sea landings. We've lost five cruisers and four destroyers. More British troops have landed, but Gerry is pouring them in. The German parachutists come down with Tommy guns firing. They have Trench Mortars, Machine Guns, Rifles, Food, Bikes, Tents, First Aid, Bombs, Grenades, Receivers, Transmitters, Ammo, Petrol. In fact, everything that is wanted comes over and is dropped. What a brain and organization. I don't suppose it can hold out much longer. But by Hell, what a stand! He's losing 20-30 planes almost hourly. The RAFA hit a drome and destroyed 100-52s. Poor old Cled, what of him! Syria now German. British advance in Iraq. Stalemate in Egypt. They're holding out there anyway (until he gets more stuff over). 50, 000 Italians surrendered in Abyssinia. I guess they're sunk. Roosevelt gives a speech. More support for Britain. He put the country in a state of emergency. Yank patrol for "Dutch East Indies." RAF personnel to be trained in the States. Fairly quiet in Britain, thank God. No more mail, so no more boat mail to go home either. Too risky. The States takes over 98 foreign ships, including French "Normandie." Big Italian liner, which sank in the Mediterranean. 18, 000 tons. Blenheims based here are doing it. They are fine bombers, also Glen Martins.

JUNE

SUNDAY, 1st
"Stoneheap"

Quiet last night. Doing 1 ½ hours guard each now. Telephone out of order. Had an order to camouflage the sight. Got to pile stones around it. They've only just thought of it, of course. This site is too large and square; it's easily identified, and they've just thought of it now. Well. Well. Major King came around. Sgt. got Hell. Dirty gun. Sgt. doesn't give a damn, like all of us. We have no enthusiasm or spirit for it. Why should we? When we can see the administration around us. Crete had over 15, 000 troops evacuated to Egypt. They couldn't hang on. No air support. Our aircraft was coming in from Egypt, 400 miles away. Also, inadequate AAA defense. Just shows. The British knew it was coming off yet made no attempt to fortify it or get planes there. It lasted 14 days. 1600 German planes destroyed in and around.

MONDAY, 2nd
Good night again. Telephone school finished. Came back to the site. Nothing much happening. No raids so far. News of Crete. Some troops were isolated there. Planes dropping food for them. Aussie press blames Britain for not fortifying it, but Britain excuses itself by saying Crete was Greek 6 months ago. Pretty poor that. Iraqi armistice. Regent takes over. They're allowing our troops to pass through Iraq. Germans getting hold of Syria. Admiral Darlan siding with Nazis. I can see Hitler getting a stranglehold on France. I predict Hitler will take Suez and Egypt in time. Our defense is lousy. The Empire has been going to pieces for years. We were not prepared.

TUESDAY, 3rd
Raid last night. Searchlights got him 3 times. No cooperation by fighters, though. When they lit him up, the fighter was miles away, firing at sea. I guess the fleet was mixed up somehow. Our Hurry birds had an excellent chance to get him, but the cooperation was

lousy, as ever. On leave today. It's coming around pretty quickly, every 5 days. Actually, it's not worth having, bar leave for a rest. There are only a few dances, and the drink is dear, all the girls are partnered. Most girls can't afford to go. So, dances (2 of them) are ruled out. So that leaves pictures. Very old films. There are about ten cinemas, and as a rule, I've seen 8 of them. So, I have an orgy of pictures and food. I don't drink, so I don't go on the booze like most of them. Our boys are drunk on Ambique continually. Slats and Len, hell, they are getting to drink bottles at a time. In the morning, they look horrible, their eyes puffed out and their faces bloated. They look and feel terrible, but still, they go on it every night. If they can't get a beer, then Ambique (leather & lotus water). Their excuse is they've got to keep their nerve up. I admit it's pretty bad, nerve-wracking, alright, but the damn stuff makes you worse the next day!

WEDNESDAY, 4th
"Stoneheap"

Came back off leave early. Had a good sleep. Raid for 2 hours during the night. Troop carrier shot down. I stayed in bed. Ah, nuts to it! It's a thing you can't run away from. Boy, oh boy, is it warm now. Our dress is full KD, not bad, but too clean though, and also has too many buttons. Things are almost normal in Valletta now. They're getting the debris cleaned up. They're selling the salvaged stuff. Our fighters on different policies are now engaging, and we should see some fun. No news of importance today. Evacuating officers' wives from here to Malta by Sub.

THURSDAY, 5th
Raid about 10:00 last night. A few Italian bombers came over with escort. Nothing occurred, so I went to bed early. Most of the boys went to "Zammits" on the booze. Blues and Ambique. George is over there after tea, as a rule. The boys are grumbling that others get in early and drink all the beer. There is only one brewery here, and each seller is rationed. They sell out in a few hours. George buys them all. He gets a pound wage and usually is broke the same night. Hell's delight! Our blankets were steamed today to kill

fleas, lice, and other crawling things. In bed last night, it was Hell. It was very sultry. Mosquitoes by the hundreds, fleas, and earwigs biting, crawling, and hopping everywhere. By Hell, Joan, you'd laugh to hear me. I groan, roar, scream, laugh like a madman. But my enemies are merciless. I got up and finally put my pants on. Went to sleep about 1:00. Say that ain't nothing. A few letters came in by Sunderland. Quinn had a few airmail postcards. Don had a letter. But not for me. I guess Joan wouldn't think of airmail or postcards. Damn, and blast it. Why the Hell don't they inform them? Still, Joan should know somehow. Ah well! Absence, no news, good news. Rumors of us, the 59th battery, leaving in August. Some dopes got hold of a yarn. Lots of hooey! Germany is still getting into Syria. It won't be long now. He'll have the East, then maybe we'll quit. Why don't they get wise to it? They cannot beat him now. Still taking prisoners in Abyssinia. Hell of a lot of good that will do.

FRIDAY, 6th

Raid last night. 10 plus, bombs on docks, etc. I was on the phone. Didn't drop anything on Luqa, though. Nothing much today. Exam of equipment. I got paid, but there was no credit. I must go easy. I don't want to go into debt. Might get our colonial pay yet. 40 new Hurricanes came in Mark 111. All got special tanks. They do it from Blighty in 5 hours. 2000 miles not bad. 5 Blenheims and 2 Wimpys also. All going East. Stopped here for fuel. Received a letter from Joan. Must have come with 3 Sunderlands that came in. No news in the letter dated May 20th, 2 weeks, good going. The letter was a tirade of moans and misery. Apparently, old Nabsy, in his loyalty to me, misconstrued a harmless tête-à-tête. Had it out with her. Can't understand it. Must remember this for future reference. Can't believe Joan would do anything funny, nor can I blame Nabsy entirely. But the letter maddened me. Here I am out here, wasting my youth and omitting all the points that would worry her in my letter, and yet she sends a letter of woe such as that. Ah well! It remains to be seen who the Hell cares!

SATURDAY, 7th

Went to Zammits. Had a few blues, eggs, chips. Ok too. He's got some lovely peaches, lemons, pomegranates, and grapes in his garden. All sorts, figs, apricots, oranges. Some garden! There's wild mint growing all around our tent here; lovely smell. Also, beautiful lilies, poppies, and others. Cactus and lotus. Zammit has a shelter, private. What a beauty. Electric light, beds, stove, water, and so on. 30 feet into solid rock. Had a Hell of a night, a record number of raids. 7 in 5 hours. Started at 11:30 and finished at 5:00. About 50 heavy bombers in all. He dive-bombed, high level, machine gunned, mined, every conceivable blasted method. He dropped 25-250 lb bombs across Luqa. 6 fell 50 yards away. Debris, splinters, and stuff of all sorts heaped around us. He got a bomber on the drome. It burned. Hell, what a night! Not a wink of sleep. 4 fighters up, and they went in several times. Gerry didn't come down low enough for us. Well, we finally turned in at about 6:00. Up at 8:00. Wrote a letter to Harry. Lovely weather now. But we are feeling the strain of ceaseless bombing. It's wrecking my nerves. All of us. The boys are drinking more Ambique. So far, I've kept off it. We're preparing for invasion now, like Crete. Ah! Well, nuts to it, let it come. I expect I'll fold up. Anyway, I can't run away from it. It will follow me. Gerry has all the dromes in Syria; we have all in Iraq. We occupy Mosul. He's shoving men and materials into Syria still. Why won't Churchill quit? He's finished. They'll have the East. Let's quit now while we are intact. Our Army's bungling and disorganization can't beat him. The bloody, hopeless, blinding stupidity of it all. What a country. The damned daft things that are done here. The things that they expect of us.

SUNDAY, 8th

"Stoneheap"

2 raids last night, 3:00 and 4:00. Lasted till stand. So, we had about 3 hours of kip last night. The fleas and mosquitoes wouldn't let me sleep. We are all literally covered in bites, lumps, and scratches. The mosquitoes here don't buzz, so the sods take a chunk out of you before you know it. Our Hurry Birds got 2 Breda 120 bombers. The lights held 'em, while Hurricanes went in and

filled 'em full of lead. They came down burning. He dropped his load on us first, though. 12 bombs, the nearest one 10 yards away. Blew our sandbag wall down and flung lots of stuff over us. We had just time to flatten out. We saw the bombs leave the plane. All the pilots bailed out; God knows where they landed. I don't suppose our people worry about that. I'm damned if I do! Didn't do much today, the usual thing, on leave at 1:00.

MONDAY, 9th

Went to the pictures, etc. Holy smoked mackerel, it's getting me down. Oh, for Southampton and other places I am familiar with. Saw Charlie at St. Angelo. Damned nice sight. Good grub. All Naval. Good site and billets. We are still in louse-bound tents and still partake of lousy rations. Bad cheese and salmon. We are short of everything. Bloody maddening. Got a tin of tobacco from Charlie. Good stuff. Slept at Vernon's, not bad. Messed about in general. Money gave out (naturally). Came back. Allies and Free French enter Syria. Guess it's too late. They usually are, hah! Who cares? Nuts to it all. I'm in a torpor these days, can't interest myself in nothing.

TUESDAY, 10th

Fairly quiet last night. Our reco's report the Gerries moved out of Sicily. I guess he's busy in Greece and Crete. Only Italians left, and they haven't the guts of the Gerry. So far this week, we have shot down 3 Breda 120s and 1 Caproni, not bad! The Italians drop small-caliber bombs too. Nothing of importance today. Our troops advance into Syria. Free French come over to us. Controversy over Free and Vichy Forces. Douglas has as good as sold France to Germany. So, it's one hell of a state now. Don't know who's right or wrong. George is flogging our rations for beer and Ambique. Going short, he and Manly drink like fish. Received cable from Joan. All is well. And still, it goes on. Boy, are we browned off from it all. We're going nuts here. The fleas and flies are still making life miserable for us. We're covered in bites, etc.

WEDNESDAY, 11th

Quiet last night. Good kip. Well! From about 2:00 on, first the sand flies, then mosquitoes, finally fleas. They vied with each other for first place on me. They bit, buzzed, padded, crawled. Good God, on top of that, it was stifling. Me and Quinn got up and had a walk. We finally went to sleep at about 12:00 or 1:00. No stand-to; the guard was asleep. No tea. George sold the rations for beer. Inspection and Medical (Slatts) covered in bites, me with sand fly bites. 6 raids today. Caproni brought down. One of our fighters lost. The raids weren't much, passed over high. Britain advances in Syria. Reports of picking up Gerry parachutists as they march. Free French still coming over to Britain. Hell of a lot of arguing, threats, and notes between nations. Ah! It's a mess. 15, 000 British alone were lost at Crete. 17, 000 Gerry. 150 troop carriers and 110 fighters to our 100 in all. We lost about 10 naval craft. The Gerry did not use Imperial uniforms. They drove the British wounded and captured before them as they advanced. Poor sods. Our men in the trenches had to kill 'em off before they could fire at Gerry. Reports from British pilots that every drome in Britain was crammed with aircraft. Very quiet these days in England. They think he's short of planes. I don't think so. He's got plenty. He's resting, I reckon. That guy hasn't started yet.

THURSDAY, 12th

"Stoneheap Luqa Bomber Drome"

Sentry last night. Eaten up by fleas and mosquitoes as usual. Had 3 alarms, but nothing of importance happened. Stand-to 4:30. Day dawned bright and clear as usual. Alarm at 8:00. Recco and 10 Fighters. Our Fighters shot the Recco down, a Caproni. Another raid at 12:00. Recco and Escort, 23 MEs. Our Fighters shot down 5 MEs. One of our fighters was lost, but the pilot was safe. Boy, some barrage went up. There was shrapnel clinking and buzzing all around us. I don't mind bombs, but the bloody shrapnel unmans me. I picked up 16 pieces, red hot, each as big as a teapot. We have different pilots now. A Canadian squadron and some London Fighters. Allies still push on in Syria. Heavy raid on Alexandria,

250 killed, poor blasted Arabs in those rotten houses. We've lost 15 Blenheims in a month here and about 12 Hurry Birds. 700th alert today on Malta since Italy entered the war. Airmail went out. I got a letter off. Had to disinfect tents. Bloody great rat holes under my bed boards. Literally crawling with insects. Got a new issue of books and a game of draughts of all bloody things. The books are poor, also all crime—cheap stuff. Recon, I know the reason for my gut pains now. Rushed meals, yeah! Don't get any of that now, as I take time over my meals. I'm in perfect health now, thank God.

FRIDAY, 13th

Nothing done last night. All quiet. Had a good rest. Had the usual eggs and chips at Zammits. The boys bought a bottle of old Port between them on 2/6. I didn't partake of it, my usual aversion against Port. It was damned fine stuff, though. The boys were canned. Nothing doing today. No alarms. 23 new Hurricanes came in. Me and Frank on leave. Got paid and got a bus to Valletta. Stayed at Vernon's. Went to the pictures, no good. Had bed among 30 others, the predominant stink of feet naturally. Heard the program from Windmill London. Hah!

SATURDAY, 14th

Had a good sleep, took shaving gear in the gas mask. Had grub. Had photos taken and so on through to the afternoon. Went to the pictures again. Saw a good many of the boys from heavies (Ozzy). It's warm now, all the Army in shirts and shorts. Women in light frocks. Enough to drive a guy nuts. Had a dish of macaroni for dinner. Plenty of plums, apricots, and peaches about now. Sent a letter off to Joan. And so back again. 52 Hurry birds and 4 Lockheed Hudsons came in. Boy, the old band is turning 'em out now. 1 Hurricane crashed on landing. 1 ran out of petrol and fell into the sea. Hah! 4 Hurries reported missing now. 2 out of petrol fell into the sea, another fell near us from 1100 feet. Pilot killed. Another overran itself on landing and was smashed up.

SUNDAY, 15th

Couldn't sleep for hours, blasted fleas and mosquitoes! Pretty warm, too. No alert. Nothing much today. Went on the drome and had a look at Hudsons and new Hurricanes. The Hurries seemed tiny, bad construction. Hudsons are fine birds, carrying 4-500lb bombs and smaller ones. Built in California. There are lots of Glenmartens here too. All yank. Blasted rations short again. I rather think they're still going on beer. Always the food question. What an existence! The tinned stuff (all our grub is tinned) comes rotten—rotten bacon and salmon. Spending 1 shilling a night on food doesn't leave a lot for leave. Quinn got registered mail tonight. Lucky dog, money, but nothing regarding the war. I don't like the lull!

MONDAY, 16th

Quiet last night. Stand-to. Very bad visibility. 4 Wimpies couldn't find their bearings. One crashed, too bad. I guess a few of our letters went west on her. The others just made it. Had one alarm today. This silence is very ominous. Don't like it! A Colonel back from Crete said the tactics used were machine-gunning first, 10 Me's every morning. 750 Troop Carriers and 250 Gliders with about 100 Fighters—1 a minute. We had 10 Bofors on Crete. Hell's delight! 17, 000 Gerrie's were killed, 15, 000 British. Our Captain kicked up Hell, as usual. Sight is very bad, he said; men have no enthusiasm. Ah! If they treated us well, they might get it. It's bloody hopeless! Grub is rotten when you get it, lousy books, tents, and billets crawling, underpaid. I don't give 2 hoots. Sent a letter and snaps to Joan. Camouflage tents tomorrow and move their sights. No news of import. There will be a bash soon, I expect.

TUESDAY, 17th

Fairly quiet last night. Had a hard day. Moved tents and kit. Camouflaged them. Moved them under trees about 200 yards off. Makes them even further away now. Bloody foolish! So far from gun and cookhouse. And they want speed. Why? The AAA are in action before us men. It was literally boiling hot! Some job! The figs are ripe now. Big garden near, with tomatoes, peaches, and marrows, etc. Went to Zammits, had the usual. His lemons are ripe. Big ones, 1d each. Also, oranges. A big field of onions near here too. We are surrounded by fig trees, cactus, and lotus trees. The women work the fields by day. Very primitive methods. All hand work.

WEDNESDAY, 18th

Big raid last night. Me and Frank didn't get up. Nuts! 1 plane dropped 60 small bombs on the drome. I slept through it. Boy! Am I browned off, utterly dejected. This is getting me down. New orders every day. Maneuvers in gas masks, rifle drills, camouflage, gun drills, special periods of dress. And air sentry on top of that. And all in this bloody heat! The stupid bloody orders. All the boys are complaining. They're fed up. No heart for it. Today, all the MV rations (tinned) were rotten. So, we had a few spuds and a cup of tea for dinner. A sausage for breakfast. A slice of bread and jam for tea. We are starving. I am broke and on leave. I've spent my dough on food at Zammits, so I've none to go on leave with now. As I said, 10 tins of meat and vegetables were rotten. 18 months old, no wonder. I've seen it being canned (at P. Knowles). It's one hell of a life. On top of this, Me's came in and machine-gunned. Our nerves were shot. So far this week, we've had a tin of salmon, 5 tins of corned beef, and a tin of bacon—bad. All rotten, can't be eaten. They won't renew them, we will go short. This is how we fare. I'm bloody well sick of it. No mail. I miss Joan and home. I don't give a damn how this war ends up. He can have it all. Let's go home and finish. We are deteriorating here. Everyone agrees on that. It's a waste of life and youth.

THURSDAY, 19th

"Luqa"

Raid during the night, not much. We've got our nets at last for the fleas. Had a good night last night. It was a pleasure without the mosquitoes and sand fleas. I was on leave from 5:00 yesterday. Had no money, so I went nowhere. It was a sod of a day today, we couldn't go anywhere, and the books we had were not worth reading. The heat was terrific, and also the flies. On top of that, a kit inspection. I got out of it. I slid off while they went through it. A new order compels cooks to have one cold meal a day a week. What a huge joke, considering they give us nothing cold to have. Result, we had to buy tomatoes and cucumbers out of the village. That's how the money goes, and they call for efficiency and enthusiasm, by Hell! I'm utterly browned off today. Got a violent headache. Could eat a bloody good meal. On night guard tonight. The same old thing. What an outlook. "Amrya Egypt" isn't as bad as this. Hell's delight! I could go nuts if I thought it would do any good.

The RW Kents getting their grub

It's brought around by bike & trailer. Some mess, besides being cold. It comes about 5 miles. R. W. Kents are rifle guards, etc., of the drome.

FRIDAY, 20th

Lousy night. Raging headache, sick stomach. Must be the sun or bad food. It's 110 degrees of heat, and we are in it all day. They won't allow us to wear topees, but sod them, we will in the future. Woke up about 6:00. Still bad, pretty weak also. Limbs and eyes ache like hell. I spewed my heart out. Couldn't eat breakfast. Took 6 aspirins, but they had no effect. Had to lay down but did stag. If I went sick, I would have to be at THQ at 7:00 in the morning. Then, they would probably turn me away, saying I was "swinging the lead." I know, I've seen some of this blasted Army. Everything is done to make the soldier's life miserable. Good God. It's agony these days. Nothing of importance today. Fighting in Damascus. French warships in action off Syria. Turkey and Germany sign the "Friendship Pact." Nerve war by Germany to Russia. We lost 3 Blenheims out of 13 coming from England. Makes a total of 11 lost this week. Grub still short. Blasted hard cheese and onions for tea. No wonder we're weak, no decent grub. 50 in hospital (12 gone home) with Sand Fly Fever, sunburn, stroke, scabies, etc. Ah, nuts to this! 110 degrees of heat, 113 degrees in Egypt. Just shows.

SATURDAY, 21st
"Stoneheap"

Went to bed early last night, about 7:00. I had to; I was too weak to stand up. My eyes were closing. God! I felt terrible—sweat, cold, a lousy night. Didn't sleep all night. I was sick about 3:00. Sgt. reported me sick. They came for me by ambulance. I was delirious. Taken to A.D.C. Luqa. Sand Fly Fever and a touch of Malaria from Egypt. My temperature is 102. Wow! What a headache! Small receiving hospital this. About 20 men here. All down with fever, sun, stomach issues, and bad food. MO okay. They put me on a liquid diet. For 4 days, I've had nothing but tea, bread, and some oxo. I feel as weak as a kitten and starving also. But if I had a meal, I couldn't eat it. Stomach refuses. Two guys in here from a bomb blast; shocked. Had a raid at night. We had to get into the shelter, not too good for sick men. I didn't expect to go down like this. What can one expect? Bad food, hot sun, and all those flies and fleas. Bloody horrible.

SUNDAY, 22nd
"Luqa A.D.C. Hospital"

Had a good night. Made good friends with Welsh orderly. I was on a liquid diet (tea and bread), but he secured some decent grub for me. He comes from "Barry, " decent chap. Nothing of importance today. Germany invaded Russia at 4:00 this morning. Turkish-German Pact squashed. Now we shall have some fun. A good many people will be disappointed, though; Russia is not what they were led to believe. "Flint" brought in with the fever. He was pretty bad. That is 2 from Stoneheap.

MONDAY, 23rd
"Luqa A.D.C. Hospital"

Fighting on the entire Russian front. Finns on Gerry's side, pushing in from there. No accurate accounts as yet. 30 Me's destroyed over Channel and France by Fighter Squadrons, R.A.F. Damascus occupied by us. Not much activity over here. A sub was close by last night. Coastal Batteries opened up. I'm okay now. Expect I shall be out tomorrow. I got over the worst myself in the tent. All sorts of craft coming here from England. Bring mail also. Nothing from Joan as yet. Bad distribution.

59th Light A.A. 74th Regiment R.A Malta. I was in the hospital, when this was taken.

TUESDAY, 24th
"Luqa"

Left the hospital at 11:00. Felt fine and walked back to sight. Manly was arrested by Sgt.—absent without leave. In Clink RAFAF, well, he deserves it. Guess he'll miss his Ambique now. Hot as hell, 115 degrees. The white buildings and roads glare, damn painful to the eyes. 25 Gerry's shot down by fighter sweep over France again. 65 by Russians. Hitler's Panzer divisions are slicing their way through. News is obscure as yet. Macchi Italian fighter shot down over here today.

WEDNESDAY, 25th

Good sleep last night. Recco and 19 fighters came over. Hurry Birds went in. 4 shot down. Lot of rumors about the new Sgt and officers on the Island. Rumors say the 100th and 64th LA A Batteries are coming out by sub to relieve us. Coming out in batches. They all think we're going home. Well, I'm rather skeptical about all this. I don't like being disappointed. We shall see. Another 20 Gerry were shot down over Channel and France by fighters. Our bombers over industrial Germany for the 10th consecutive night, apart from the bashings by day. I rather think these sweeps are a preliminary to an offensive on France by us. We shall see. Russian H.Q. reports 5, 000 Gerry prisoners. About 60 Gerry planes were destroyed. Battles are raging on all fronts. Hitler is trying to get in from Finland and Romania. His pincer movement again. I shouldn't be surprised if he succeeds. He's taken Brest-Litovsk and half a dozen smaller towns. We lost 60-odd ships last month, which is serious. We're spending 10.5 million per day in actual cash. The US and Britain are all helping Russia. The US is bringing stuff over to us, alright. Blenheims, Martins, Hudsons, Hurry Birds, and Wimpies are all stopping here, refueling, and going on to the East. We're using 50 fighters on Channel sweeps per day. Our crack squadron here is doing well. There are British, Canadian, and Yankee pilots. Smart kids, they are knocking 'em down like hell. Haven't had a decent night's raid for a couple of weeks. Italians are afraid to come over. 12 Glen Martins went out this morning to dive-bomb Sicily; 10 came back. I'm sick of this bloody site. I was glad of the change at the hospital. Onions and cheese are for the 4th time for tea this week, and it's Wednesday. The grub is bloody horrible and gives one no heart. I've no interest in anything. I'm browned off. Doug got made up (rank). He deserves it. Somebody must have it. Frank came out today. Manly is up before tribunal today. Guess he'll get a few months. Blasted kit inspection tomorrow. One every week. Everything must be rolled, placed, and folded just so. Oh yes, must be absolutely pat. Lot of dopes. Had a short arm inspection this morning in an open field. Strip naked, hands-on head, turn around, bend over, ha! For the whole world to see. And so ends this day, I'm damned!

THURSDAY, 26th

What a night! The Italians were over from 10:00 till 4:30 the next morning. The GLL were all to hell, and so was GOROR. Still, what can one expect? 5 Marylands, 7 Swordfish, and 5 Blenheims were coming in from operations and 5 Wimpies from here. So, the drome was all lit up. The Italian bombers came over and saw it all. Our sites didn't know who was who. They dropped very small sticks of 12. Didn't hit the drome once. Lousy bombing, considering they had the light to guide them. Had it been Gerry, he would have smashed the joint up. About 20-30 bombs dropped close by. We got no sleep. Prepared everything for inspection, and then it was cancelled. It's only natural, isn't it? Hot as hell, blinding. Brigadier came around. Ok. Got a letter from Joan dated June 13th, not bad. Russians have taken a town in Romania. They wiped out a mechanized division. A lot of planes were lost on either side.

FRIDAY, 27th

Quiet last night. Up bright and early as usual. Tea, stand to. Blazing hot, wow! The heat is terrific at 120 degrees and getting hotter. Had an alarm, recco with 20 fighters, dead overhead, heavies engaged, and also our fighters. 7 Macchis were shot down. One came down near us, machine-gunned us as he came. The whole thing blew up and burned. Not much left of him. The Italian fighters and pilots are lousy. Went reconnoitering on parachutist's trail. Found an orchard with limes, oranges, lemons, etc. You can bet we did well. Got paid 6.00. Me and Frank on leave. Valletta. Booked at TOC.H., messed about. Raid. He dropped his eggs and beat it.

SATURDAY, 28th

Raid in the night. The whole building shook with the noise of bombs. They fell about a hundred yards off. I didn't bother to get up. Up at 8:00, I had my shaving kit in a gas mask. Had a damn good breakfast, 1/- damn good. Went around bazaars and stalls. Went to Sliema for a swim. Lovely in the sea. Lots of people in too. Damn hot, wow! Better off this week, had 15/-. Saved a few bob from last week. Had a few good meals. Lots of English women in Sliema, officers' wives and daughters. Big dance at Vernon's, looked in. There were too many officers for my liking. Plenty of women, poor dressers, can't do make-up either. Joan could teach them that gentle art. Went to the pictures, lousy, and so to home. Letter from Joan dated February 3rd, just after I left Glasgow. 6 months ago, hell bells! They know how to sling them about here. Still, I can't grumble. I've had one from her dated June 3rd and 16th respectively. Her brother Wally is home on 7 days of leave, she said. He also has a stripe (no comment). Everybody's ok, and so on. Well, that's all fine. News up to date is not much. Sweden allows 20-30 Gerry divisions through. Russians fall back. Russians bomb Romania. Some tough air battles going on. Each claiming more than the other naturally. Britain is well established in Syria. Vichy forces trying to evacuate. Peace feelers were made by the German Ambassador at the British embassy. Nothing doing, says Churchill. On to the last Russian! All aid to Russia. USA has a program for 2, 560 vessels of all types. Their usual ballyhoo. Japan says a lot but doesn't know what she wants to do. Quiet comparatively over England. Another sweep of France and Channel. 15 Gerry destroyed. The heaviest bombs of war were dropped on Germany in the 20th British raid, successively, and so on and so on. Ah, balls to it all. Let's get off this bloody mud heap and go home. Jack told us the 16th of next month is coming, we hope. It's been coming for the last two months.

SUNDAY, 29th

Blasted ants in blankets last night. Hell, they were tearing chunks out of me. 9 Blenheims went to Tripoli this morning. 1 lost. They went out again later. Then 7 Wimpies, 5 Glens, and 5 Swordfish went out. All came back. They're knocking hell out of Sicily and Libya, not much like a Sunday. Makes no odds to us. We carry on as usual. Not even a bit of meat.

MONDAY, 30th
"Luqa"

About 40 new canon-carrying Hurricanes with 3 Wimpies and 5 Blenheim's came in. Hell, that's about 300 planes here now. The Wellingtons and Blenheim's are to operate from here. Good thing Gerry is occupied elsewhere, or we would have a nasty time of it. His Me's would soon fix these Drome's. They don't give a damn for the Italians. Much the same today. Grub is lousy. Still pretty lousy Short rations. Equipment exam 9:00-10:00, Inspector Blockford. Had to rush to change and fold and bullshit in the usual manner. Gun must be painted all white now after all that scraping and camouflage. Well, well! They don't know what they want. Change of dress 9:00-10:00. Overalls, onwards, shorts, they'll get it right soon. Frank turned his stripe in. I should think so. No pay. Guy is a dope to do it without pay. Had a decent meal at Zammits. Tea 8d. Pretty good. Bloody good thing we can get this. Sgt. back from leave canned. Eh! What a crew we are. Cook flogs our grub and Bdr. does nothing. Blokes are grumbling. Russians wipe out Panzer Corps. Gerry says they've shot 4, 000-odd Russian planes down. If they had said 4 million, it would have been all the same, and still, it goes on.

JULY

TUESDAY, 1st.

Order to lay Kits out different now. Also, must wear Topees. Yesterday, anyone wearing them would be put on charge, and now, one can get arrested for not wearing one. So help me! 2 new men today. Manly goes to B.H.Q. and makes 11 men on sight. One has been on the Island 3 weeks and came over from Alexandria by Sub. Says 180 are coming over the same way. Replacement Draft. Order came through to squash rumour of Battery leaving Island. I wonder! By hell, would I like to get the hell out of this Island? The heat is terrific. Can't stay in the gun pit for 5 minutes. We sweat like bulls yet we have 1, 500 sandbags to fill for alternative sight. 30 more coils of wire to lay down and numerous other jobs. The grub doesn't improve. The boys are grumbling like hell. We have had an invasion of small ants in our tent. So, we have them, besides fleas, now. Sweet life. Went on leave, put up at Toc H., wandered about, and had 5/-, so can't do much. Went to bed early. Listened to the wireless dance music. Boy! What memories Hah!

WEDNESDAY, 2nd.

Very warm. Up at 8:00. Good breakfast. Had 2/- left boy! Holy ole doodle, it's sweltering. Women going about with hardly anything on, believe me, they're something to see. Yeah, man! Went to Sliema and got snaps, ok. Left me with 6d. I was parched. Guess I'll have to go hungry, too. Went in swimming. Ok, swell. 100, 000 Russian prisoners, Gerry claims. Well into Russia. Hell of a battle going on. I reckon there is a big surprise coming. The German army is invincible. They'll beat Russia to her knees. If Britain doesn't take the offensive in France now, she'll never have another chance. Get Gerry on two fronts, but no, Britain is always 2 jumps behind. They are playing into Hitler's hands. He's using the same methods in Russia. Pincer movement, already his tanks are through and attacking from Russia's rear.

THURSDAY, 3rd.

Hell of a night. Bloody ants in blankets. We have nets for flies, etc., but they are useless against ants. Well! Nothing unusual today. Hot as hell. Blistering. Lot of work to be done. New alternative position, etc., etc. Got another letter dated Feb 3rd from Joan. Very nice letter. She's a good kid. Thank God for a good wife. I pray to God she is well and safe. Wimpies operating continually from Drome.

FRIDAY, 4th

"Luqa"

Ants are still at their dirty work. Even hotter today. Can't get any news of War. Last we heard, Russians were retreating, destroying crops and oil wells as they go. Nothing definite, though. In Joan's letter, Norrie is in the Home Guard, Jack has gone to the Leeds factory, and Harry is in the Training Center. Vi is engaged, and Pop looking well. So, they are all more or less branching out. And I stuck out here defender of a garrison, hm! Wrote a letter to Joan. Went this morning to Troop Carrier and Sunderland. Mock invasion (more trouble). We got to live on Iron rations for 6 days. Bully Beef and Biscuits. 6 days! Still, it won't make much difference; we are living on bugger all now, so we can fast, ok. Meanwhile, we must be ready to move. Everything was packed, gun ready to move. Entails a lot of sweat on the grub we get. Our agony never ceases. Am I sick of it all, gee, and how? No news of the Russian War.

SATURDAY, 5th

Had about 4 raids. Italians drop bombs anywhere and anyhow, and shoving off as fast as possible. They are dead scared of us and our A.A. and our fighters. Didn't get much sleep and stayed in bed, but the tent was no protection against shrapnel. Burning hot. Nothing much was done, a bit of camouflage. One of our Blenheims crashed after taking off. Reckon it was sabotage. Lot of Maltese Airmen. All leave stopped. Exercises started at 4:00.

I've gotta stay on the gun. I can't leave it. Must stay in a state of mobility, everything packed.

SUNDAY, 6th

Lousy night. Italians over 7 times. We were action guns, machine-gunning, etc. Bombs are fairly close. Blew the ammo pit in. Hah. Got no sleep, up as usual. Sargent, don't give 2 hoots about us. Nuts! What a life! Lousy rations still, square inch of bacon for breakfast. It's costing us half our wages to eat! Russians are being pushed back. Heavy losses for Gerry. Reckon 75, 000 died. He's finding it difficult no doubt, eh? Well, we shall see. I guess he'll batter himself out of it. My complex temperament is coming to the fore again. It's of no use. I cannot mix. It's dam difficult, but their company is useless to me. It's the same thing all over again. It's followed me all my life. I'm not unhappy, oh no! I prefer it, yes, by far the better of the two. Life has taught me a few lessons, but by hell, some things of a man's nature will never benefit or change. I am glad. I know where I stand. I believe I am a bit cynical and bitter about it all. Well, I know what I want after much groping. I certainly don't want this. I shall still wait. It will come to me. Vague, yes. Silly, yes. But there it is.

MONDAY, 7th.

Some night again. They came over one at a time at intervals of an hour. Their usual tactics. About 20 Capronis dropped bombs. 5 fell close by. I stayed in the tent. A bit nerve-wracking though. So near the Drome. Hell of a strain on this. About an average of 3 hours sleep a night, then on all day. Rations short again. Biscuits and cheese for tea. Bought tomatoes etc., our money doesn't last. We all chipped in. No good, Sargent won't do anything. No bread. Hell's delight, now they want us to build slip trenches. 8 feet deep, and it's solid rock around here! Bloody heat's awful. We don't know what to do with ourselves. Russians holding Gerry. Peace feelers "Eden" rejects them. Report by Gerry: 52, 000 Russians desert to them, also 300, 000 prisoners, hmm! Got to thinking of Canada, hell what memories. Wild geese went over today and brought things back to me.

TUESDAY, 8th

They made a mistake last night. Heavy A.A. put up a barrage, scared him off. Nothing otherwise. Had a little more sleep. A little cooler today, much better. Russians holding Gerry using 15, 60-ton tanks. 1000's killed. Russians destroying everything behind them. Peace feelers. The Syria episode is almost over. The agreement is there soon. 10 Generals give up in Abyssinia. A wimpy crashed while taking off. Looks like sabotage alright. It is the third in a week. Had a laugh this morning while making tea for stand to. I dropped a dirty towel in boiling water. Made tea and waited for the 1st comment. Lovely was the verdict. Well! I'm damned, had he known, I expect he wouldn't have drunk it, none of them. A dirty, wet towel. Same as in the early days, while getting breakfast for the guard, I dropped a plate of kippers in a dixie of tea. Whipped them out. Tea is lovely, they said. And so, the days go by. I dream constantly of Joan now. Hell, my heart aches for her. I'm downright sick of it all. Gee, do I miss her? Never realized how much she meant. So near in a dream, yet so far. I was quite disappointed on waking.

WEDNESDAY, 9th

Lots of plums about and tomatoes also figs and pears. It's an offence to touch them though. The grub is very bad still. Buying tea for the morning now. 3 shillings for a pouch of sugar, 3.5 shillings for a loaf of bread, milk 9 pence a tin. By hell, the chief principle here is self and self only. Well, I know something of that and how. On rations for 3 days, corned beef and biscuits 3 times a day. The boys are buying their own. They buy eggs and flour and make pancakes, etc., hah! A bit rough last night again. 2 sticks of 9 bombs each fell across the drome. Wimpy hit, burned out. Our fighters shot down 2 Caproni 100 in flames. Some sight. Nothing out of the ordinary today.

THURSDAY, 10th

Nothing last night, all quiet. I guess he's licking his wounds. Hurry birds went out machine gunning Sicily drome today. 20 of them. I guess we will get a reprisal for this yet. Nothing much today.

Wiring etc., expecting convoy, though. Paper reports 27 ships passed through Gibraltar. Syria asks for peace., or General Deutz has. About time, too. French killing French.

FRIDAY, 11th.

2 alerts last night. Bombs dropped at sea. The Italian has no guts it seems. Afraid to come in. Our fighters are pretty deadly with cannons now. Invasion exercise finished. Normal rations again (about an ounce more of each article). Wiring today. Boys bickering a hell of a lot over grub etc. Sargent and Bombardier bugger off all the time. No authority, it's hellish. Lads are quarreling with each other. I guess we've been together too long. Want a move? Well! I thought we would get a reprisal. 12 Macchis 20 came down and machine-gunned Drome and guns. I thought I would be eating dumdums, but luckily, they turned off at the crucial moment. The bullets cut a swath 10 yards from us. I got 16 rounds off, had a hit, and blasted camouflage net got in the way. Couple of the boys funked it. Nerves, poor sods. 6 were shot down. Nice plane, the Macchi. They riddled a Wimpy on the Drome and others but Wimpy burned out. Ah well! They might come back again. We'll have 'em then. Payday. On leave tomorrow. Dam change from this. Russians wipe out a couple of mechanized divisions. Fight going on well. All quiet in England. No letters so far. U.S.A. takes over the Island and relieves our men. Cargo convoys coming in. And so on.

SATURDAY, 12th

Bit cooler the last few days, breezy, and clouds. Lovely change. Done some wiring. Our bombers from here over Naples again, much damage. Lull on the Russian front. Reports of 8, 000 extra Russian troops moving up to the front. German claims of 4, 000 Russian tanks destroyed and 3, 000 odd aircraft. Russian claims of whole divisions wiped out, and so on. No convoy as of yet. On leave at 8:00

SUNDAY, 13th.

Went to Valletta, TOC. H. Pictures, lousy show "Green Hell" some lousy bloody pictures here, considering the price ½- and in this heat, 120 degrees, holy smokes it terrific again. In the cinema, smells of garlic, onions, sweaty bodies, oily hair, and heat. Wow! We had 3 alarms, but nothing happened. Our Hurry birds are on the alert now, with as many as 23 up at once. Bit warm in Kip. Had damned good breakfast, tried to buy some hair creams, and all I could get was a bottle of muck - 3 shillings, blue blades 1/6, soap toilet 6d, beer 8d-9d. Cakes 2d each. Hell, the prices are terrific. One is lucky to be able to get anything. Cigarettes 1/3. If the convoy doesn't come soon, there will be a hell of a shortage. Had a damned nice swim. Sliema Sea was lovely. Cut foot on rocks and got stung by a jellyfish (and they sting too!) Pictures again. Had to go without dinner, though. Must economise on 10 shillings and these bloody prices. Hell, this heat's awful! Bloody great fleas crawling around a bloke's shoulder in a cinema. Got back. Sargent says rumors of 10, 000 troops leaving the Island. The Chesters and Manchesters told to pack spare kits and under 2 hours' notice. A bit of salt is wanted here. The Battery is working itself to a fever pitch in the belief of going home. Not me! I don't like disappointments.

Nice swimming here. The water is always warm. There is no beach of any sort here or sand. That shown is stone.

This is typical of the many shelters all over the Island. Some have 150ft of solid rock above them. In nearly all, the people are established in them and live in them entirely. Such as this. Valletta

Whilst on leave. Taken in gardens of Valletta.

Ye old Ghari. There are no trains or underground here in Valletta.

It's either Omnibus or the Ghari.

MONDAY, 14th

Bad night again. 3 raids, so that means 6 times awakened, apart from falling bombs and shrapnel, also heavy barrage. No fighter policy last night. Very nerve-wracking. Can't get a good night's sleep and feel lousy in the morning. Nothing much today. Hot as hell, boy! Picked up the magazine of "Life of Bronte." Damned tragic reading, felt troubled, what a tragedy. Bill is down with a fever.

TUESDAY, 15th

Couple of raids last night. Indiscriminate bombing hell, the Italians don't seem to have any objective at all. Slept through most of it. New Glen's and Blenheim's came in. and also 2 Sunderland's. Wimpy broke its back on landing also a Glen. Lost about 10 planes in 2 weeks this way. The Blenheims and Wimpies are operating from here continually night and day. About 15 planes in each raid. Tripoli, Benghazi, Derna, Tobruk, Sicily, Naples, and also convoys from Italy trying to get through. The heat is terrific. Not so many fleas now. Sand flies don't bother us so much. I guess our blood is pretty rotten by now, considering the grub. So, I guess they don't fancy us. Lots of blasted horse flies, though. Sods! Got stingers like swords. We sleep absolutely naked now, just the net around us. Wake up wet, what with sweating and the dew. I close the flaps of the tent because of shrapnel. Picked tomatoes from the field nearby as well as oranges, marrows, and grapes. Ok. It's necessary to wash every other day now because of sweat. Shirts get saturated. Still, we have good facilities. Soft water well nearby, good sun, etc. we scrub everything.

WEDNESDAY, 16th.
"Luqa"

2 alerts last night. Stood pat. Bombs dropped, no damage. Don't get much sleep, though. The heavy barrage and bombs dropping keep me awake. Pretty hot all day. Drinking gallons of tea and water. Had 20 plus come in up to 5 miles. Thought we were in for a machine gun attack. The fighters drove them off, though. 21 hurry birds go up now. The latest cannon fitted Mark 4. Nothing of importance today. I write this diary in the evening, it's much cooler, and the flies are not so many, just before the sand flies come out, about 9:00 in the evening. All is quiet except for the Wimpies going out on operations. The tent is wide open. I write with this book placed on my folded blankets. Even this causes me to sweat. All around are the fig and lotus trees. The figs give off a sweet odor and are ripe. The lotus is ripening fast. A huge grape vine covers a wall nearby. Hard by is a pigeon house with about 20 cooing pigeons. Not far off is a tomato field with more grapes. Also, nearby is an orange, lemon, lime, and almond grove. Plenty of goats with tinkling bells. Picturesque Maltese, white trousers, shirt and cape. It paints a lovely picture, doesn't it? But live in it under these conditions, I now under one then would see that picture from a different angle. Very nice for the leisured tourist, though. Yes!

THURSDAY, 17th
Alert at about 4:00. Nothing much. Very hot again. Recco, with 20 fighters, came over. Hurry birds took 'em on. Shot down 3. Our Hurries attacked a convoy of coast here. Destroyed 5 ships. Stukas attacked the convoy coming in, 12 were brought down. Nothing of import today

FRIDAY, 18th

Anniversary today. A year ago, I joined up. Wonder if I shall be writing this still a year from now, still in the army? Horrible thought. I doubt it. I feel as though I've been in it 10 years. This bloody heat is awful. Had an order to complete the wiring. All day in this heat, everything glares white. Our clothes become saturated. Can't rest or lay down. Oh, for some rain or cool weather. To hell with this climate. Hell of a night last night. Was on guard. Raids started at 1:00, finished at 4:00. Didn't get any sleep. Couldn't sleep in the afternoon owing to the heat. Get a guy down. Boys are all complaining. Food is a bit better. We still buy, though. Flogged a pair of slippers 3/- handy. Flat broke. It's hell. Means you can't go to Zammits and eat. Long time from 4:00-8:00 the next morning. Convoy in 8 ships well loaded. Should be some letters and parcels etc. Hell of a lot of rats around the tent. Tried to get into the kit last night bit of shrapnel went through the roof of the tent. Didn't wake me up, though. Got paid 10 smackers.

SATURDAY, 19th

No convoy! Somebody spreading the bull. I guess that convoy will arrive next year sometime. Very warm again. Recco over. Hurry birds chased them away. Everything is normal in Syria. Russians holding Gerry. Russia is our backbone, if they give way then God help Britain. They'll receive the fury of his Luftwaffe in earnest. She would pay for this. Terrific bombing going on now. Neutral observers say Dusseldorf, Bremen, Kiel, Cologne, and the Ruhr are in a terrible state. A smoking ruin. 7, 000 incendiaries on each. The largest possible bombs, 2, 500 lbs. from morning to night. The British bombed France and industrial Germany.

SUNDAY, 20th.

Sent a letter off to Joan, also snap. It's well over a month now since I heard from her, and nothing at all from the family. Perhaps the convoy will bring them in. Had a good dinner today, and George exerted himself. All the fruit is ripe now. Tons of tomatoes out, also watermelons, and almonds. On leave at 5:00.

MONDAY, 21st.

Blasted busses full up. Finally got in. Too late for pictures "Bandwagon". Messed about and read at TOC H. Early to bed. 2 alarms. Didn't bother us, though. Had a good breakfast. Went to Sliema for a swim. Lovely water is magnificent these days. Good crowd there, too. It's amusing to watch the girls. The styles, the getup boy! If some of the English dames could see them. Old fashioned shoes, stockings, handbags well! Joan, I guess you'd have a laugh over it. Poor dames, they can't help it; they can't buy them, let alone afford them. They don't wear body belts or brassieres most of them. So, one can imagine the state of them. Yeah, man! Saw the film "Pinocchio" damned good. Suited me, blasted sentimentalist that I am. Some good music on, too. Memories again. Hell, I am sick of it all.

TUEDAY, 22nd.

Early raids last night. Bombs were dropped near the windmill. 10 of them, no damage. The other night, he came in with the Wimpies. Came in low. Lights were all on, on the Drome and even then, he missed the Drome. What a lousy bombing. It scared the lads a bit, no warning. The tents were riddled with splinters, and we were sleeping. It fell like rain. Bit of wiring P.P. also sandbagging A.P., stand by for convoy coming in. I expect she'll slide in in the dark. Nothing much today, bit cooler. Grapes are ripening. Russians holding Gerry, cutting them off. Jack's birthday, I believe.

WEDNESDAY, 23rd.

The usual. Standing to for convoy. 2 on stag. 6 miles off Delimara Point. It's already been dive-bombed 3 plus. We can't spare them, I guess. No damage. 12 Beau fighters came in. Wimpies went west for servicing. Beau fighters are the equivalents of the Me 110. Underslung engines, 4 cannons, 6 machine guns, 400 M.P.H. Some crates. There are 15 on Luqa now. They are operating continually. Blenheim's, Beau fighters, Glen martens, Hurricanes.

THURSDAY, 24th.

Quiet last night. Old boats gone out (10). New convoy coming in. 6 Merchantmen, about 6 Destroyers, 4 Battleships, and 3 Cruisers. It's like Robinson Caruso all over again. Certainly, nice to see the ships coming in. Sure to be some troops and mail, etc. So far, all is quiet. It's a wonder the enemy will allow this to come in without a raid. On leave tonight. No dough, so no go!

FRIDAY, 25th.

Raid last night. 3 dropped close. I was in bed. They dropped about 100 yards away. Hell, I hadn't heard the sirens. I simply fell out of bed net got tangled up. Bricks, stones, and splinters came whining overhead. 500 lbs, missed the Drome. Hellish hot today. Had a look at boats, old tramps, well-loaded, all sorts. Could gather much from them. One was torpedoed outside. A few Cruisers lost. 8 boats all together. Tons of ammo aboard. Went swimming. Sliema was great! Women ok, what a contrast to the dames of Glasgow. Some experience. Got back okay. Started with 5 shillings and came back with 2 shillings. Am I a miser? Well, it forces one to be. Got to. On guard tonight.

SATURDAY, 26th.

M.T. B's and Subs attacked the Island at 4:00 and 6:00 this morning. What a display and racket. They appeared within 100 yards of the harbour. Bofors and coastal defence opened up. Like a Blackpool display. Tracer is very light. Harbour spotlights. They dropped a few nuts. The Bofor boys shot them up. Got 3 M.T. B's and a sub. The M.T.B. broke in half and went down like a stone. Crews lost. The Sub? All I saw was a fountain of water and oil. They tried to get into the harbour and torpedo Merchantmen. What a hope. Big naval battle out at sea. Planes thumping like hell, the Beau fighters got 2 M.T.Bs. Mine went off and shook the whole Island. Wow! The noise was colossal. Captain Blackford, inspection. Got me for dirty boots, hmm! Passed off. Asked a few awkward questions, put my foot in it, oh well. This heat is terrible, no sleep last night. Can't sleep in the afternoon. "Rostrium, "said 200 L.A.A at Tina Barracks, 3 batteries. Wonder what that means?

Russians holding Gerry. Moscow bombed again. Japan still agitating. Italian convoy destroyed. The Blenheims and Beau Fighters from here did that. The Beaus are fitted with radio detection. We have been warned not to talk about it. It's secret and vital. Letter from Joan, she's ok, legs getting fatter. Not much in it as usual. No news at all. Blast it, the kid doesn't realize I suppose.

SUNDAY, 27th
"Stoneheap Luqa"

1 raid last night from 10:00-12:00. About 7 Savoia's dropped some heavy stuff near "Ta'Qali" 500 lbs. I bet Charlie enjoyed it. Still, I had a good sleep from 12:00 on. Official report says 12 M.T.B's, 1 U-boat, 3 Stukas, 3 Fighters Macchi's 200, 2 Recco's, 2 Bombers Savoia's. This is the first Sea attempt by combined forces of Italian and German craft. The convoy had a 2-day battle coming through, losing 1 Destroyer. The battle continued with the M.T.B. trying to get into the Harbour (they didn't get in). Although they smashed the boom and the Bridge, at a hell of a loss to themselves. I saw the U-boats and a couple of M.T.B.s"s destroyed. We engaged the Stuka's. They dropped 6 - 1000 lb each to no avail. The Italian communique claims enormous damage, which is entirely untrue. Russians destroyed the 5th Army, destroying everything behind them. Doing well, I pray to God, they can hold them. 4 engined bombers used by Britain over Berlin. Japanese affair getting worse. I guess it will come to open war yet. There will be a big moral effect if the U.S.A. comes in. I guess so! I still believe Gerry will batter himself out on Russia. England lost 17 planes in one day (some number). Australia will supply 1000 by October. Boy! What an output. Warm today, 125 degrees, yessir! To move causes a flood of sweat. Grapes are lovely now, and watermelon.

MONDAY, 28th.
The raid last night. Went down to Zammit's shelter. Bloody, great cockroaches and slugs, 6 inches long, ugh! And damp. Passed off and got back. Went to bed. Raid again at 11:00. Heavy barrage, no fighters. Tons of shrapnel. Too lazy to get out of bed though. A

piece of shrapnel went through the tent and just missed Frankie. Some heavy bombs dropped. Some blast. About 10 Savoia's took part. Bed full of small ants, well! I went mad and had to get out and shake blankets. All in a night's work. Sweat like hell in bed. 125 degrees, the heat is fiendish. The breezes are like blasts from a furnace. I can hardly breathe. Didn't do anything today. 14 Blenheims came in and 6 Glens. Got 2 more letters from Joan. 5th and 6th of July. She's ok. Thank God. She had 36 stitches in her face. Poor kid. She says she's fine though. Not much news, unfortunately. Russians holding Gerry 130 miles from Leningrad, and 250 miles from Moscow. British planes were used over Moscow. The U.S.A froze all Japanese assets. Getting serious there.

TUESDAY, 29th.

On leave. Got 1st bus ok. Strolled about Valetta. Went to Sliema. Had a glorious swim. Met dame, took me home dinner, quite a surprise, fine family, generous kids, very patriotic. Some dinner, chicken by heck, of all things after army fare. Lovely soup, yes, a very enjoyable day. Got back ok. Bill Cross and the gang take over at Windmill. Good to see them again. Unloading new Bofors and lorries. Rumours of the 59th being made mobile and going east. Well, I wouldn't mind. Can't get home so might as well have a move. Tobruk or India, I guess. Russia's doing well playing the Gerry out. Our boys strafing Sicily again. 4 Drome's. Results- no raids at night here. Saw a new crowd in Valletta. White long shirts, eager for action.

WEDNESDAY, 30th

Quiet last night. Had a good sleep. Some Wimpies came in. Bit cooler today, breeze. Grapes are nice now. 3 searchlights were killed in a raid the other night. I saw the light go out. They're dropping blast bombs. Received more letters, 3 from Joan and 1 from Harry. Harry finished training. On water machine. Nice work, I didn't know. They say everybody is ok. Joan sent a photo. She's got much fatter. She's ok. Beer shortage she says. Coupons for everything. No raids, well that's not too bad. We've hardly any beer here, and at 9 pence a half pint, well! They're a bloody sight better off than we are, I know. With our margarine-like axle grease, 1 sausage per man, our lousy biscuits, and 5-year-old cheeses. Our M and V rations. Some bacon, hardly any sugar. Some people should know about it. Ah well! We're hardened now. Jacky Hughes made an officer.

THURSDAY, 31st

1st stag ok. Nice breeze today. No raid. They've been over to Cyprus instead. Air arm raided. Sardinia and Sicily. Destroyed 36 Gerry planes altogether. Beau fighters again. Russians counter-attacking strongly. Japanese bombed the Yank ship. Hell to pay (apologies etc) Their troop and warships also air fleet over and occupied Saigon. Vichy has consented to ports and bases etc. for Japan in Indo-China. Britain and America together and strengthening the defences. C.R.A coming Saturday must get cleared up. Captain Blackford was reduced to Lt. King now Captain. Emergency ranks. New Major from the new regiment. New mobile Bofors coming in from the convoy.

AUGUST

FRIDAY, 1st

Raid last night. 4 bombers. Lights got them but Hurry Birds is too late. They were CRs, 4 engined. Boy, do they scram out quickly when lights get on them? Drop bombs anywhere, mostly in the Sea. They tried for the docks. Been bull shit all day. Cripes what a battery and a war on too! Scrub belts, rifle slings, container slings, topples and straps, billets, guns. Boots clean, in this dust. Sweat, sweat continuously. It's hell. C.R.A coming after and Saturday. That means about 12:00-2:00. On guard tonight. Nice and windy. Keep flies away etc. Boys are knifing each other while backs are turned. Grumbling and moaning. What a life.

SATURDAY, 2nd

What a kip last night. While on guard too! Except for huge bugs crawling about it was fine. George woke me with gunfire. 5:00. Beau fighters were just coming in, 6 of them. One with half a wing missing. They had been ground strafing over Sicily Drones. 400 miles per hour, 4 cannons, 6 machine guns wow! Poor A.A they are playing hell with them. And the Italians are helpless. They dare not come over here. We send 21 Hurry Birds up now. C.R.A didn't turn up! There we were, done up in our best, after working on it all yesterday and today and they didn't come. Besides stopping leave. The swine! They passed up the road in 5 cars. What an army. This bloody heat also. Signs of the battery moving. 80 fresh guns ashore. 3 new batteries. A New Major came around. OK. Found fault. Lot of naval craft about today, brought R.A.F personnel, etc. Russians counterattack on 1–800-mile front. Vichy and Thailand concede a lot to Japan. Britain and the U.S.A watch closely. Large convoy crosses Atlantic. Brings 3 Canadian divisions over. Wish they'd relieve us. Wimpies operating from Luqa again.

SUNDAY, 3rd.

3 alerts last night. New policy, barrage only. Scared them off. Dropped stuff anywhere, but they kept messing about till 1:00. Didn't get much sleep. Stand to. Felt mighty tired. Some Sunday! August though. 1 alarm, no development. Fairly breezy today. Rations cut down again. No breakfast this morning, the bacon was bad. We're paying 2 shillings a week now to get our own grub and cook it. Otherwise, we'd starve. Had a tussle with hair today, washed it in greasy water. Hell did I swear (memories) sand- sun etc. and so on. Russians still counter-attacking. On leave tonight, I'll go in the morning, I think.

MONDAY, 4th.

2 Alarms last night. I slept through them. It was very hot in Kip wow! The paillasse was soaked through. Had a game of netball, and we literally dripped. No bread so no breakfast. Got 1st bus ok. Walked around Valletta, and went swimming. It was glorious. Plenty of troops about. New drafts, also R.A.F personnel. Can't buy a damned thing. No hair cream, boot polish, or blades. It's hell. And prices! 2/- small mirror. 9/- boot polish, 2/6 for hair oil. Could get for 6 pence at home. Boy! Are they making good use of us out here? Russians claim to have wiped out 1, 500, 000 Germans. Hell of a battle still. New Whitley's coming in they say. Everything points to us going further east. Recalling rubber boots. Asked about A.G. wallets. Somethings up. I can't get credit. I guess that compassionate leave to mine, also Joan's money. 10/- a month what a struggle on the prices here.

TUESDAY, 5th.

No raid last night. Had good sleep, although I feel damned-sight more tired. Nothing unusual today, routine. It's cloudier these days and a breeze. Still very warm though. Had some fine grapes today. Communique reports Gerry bogged down in Russia. Penetrated slightly. Raid on Moscow. A few were brought down. Slight activity over England. R.A.F bombing Germany like hell, using 2, 000 lb bombs and short Sterling 4 engine bombers. Japan occupied all bases and territory in Indo-China. It seems as though they are anxious to keep on good terms with Britain and U.S.A. Raids on Suez, Cairo, and Alexandria, give Micha in the 2nd H. A something to do. Hah! They think they had it cushy. Our Beau's and Blenheim's operate from here day and night. Ground strafing Sicily and Italy. Poor A.A. gunners. Calamity! Lost wallet containing Joan's photos, letters, etc. Sorry, Joan. Still, I have the new one. Some kind sod pinched it while I was swimming. Have a few bob left over. It's handy and saves me supper at night also.

WEDNESDAY, 6Th.

2 raids last night. 4 Savoia's shot down, one 4 engine Cant. Boy! What a sight, A full moon, and light got em, they dropped their bombs quickly and tried to get away, but the Hurricanes could see them easily. Filled them full of lead and they all burst into flames, and crashed headlong into the sea, burning all the time. The crew didn't have a chance. This happened to all four. Guns didn't engage at all. Worth seeing! The people came out of the shelter all cheering. Give Mussolini something to think about. Had 4 hours of kip. Blasted rations were cut down again. What in hell do they think we are, canaries? 1 sausage for breakfast, a spoonful of m.v. and spuds for dinner. 1 cheese and a piece of bread for tea. Hell, if it wasn't for what we buy we would starve. Lousy sods. Cross applied for Colonel. Don't blame him. Between their dive bomb Merchants it's enough to drive anyone off. Old hands! None of them have any guts. More like rabbits during raids. They take cover, dash about and the bombs drop miles away. I was in bed in the tent when bombs fell 100 yards away. Can't run away from it. I guess Cross will get his other stripe. Don also trying for one. Hell, it's easy, but I couldn't put myself out for it. Nuts to 9 pence a day. It's not worth it to be a tool for a Sargent and Bombardier. No sir! We lost 3 planes during activities over Germany. Russian, and German battles still going strong. British cruisers attack Italian harbours. Hardly a defence there eh?

THURSDAY, 7th.

"Stoneheap"

1 raid. 2 plus. 1 shot down. They can't stomach it, I guess. We are going to "Lea" rest camp on Thursday next 3 days of complete leave with ration money. 3 days rest, am I glad to get off this site? It gets us down. Especially these old cronies. Guinn gave them a shock; they couldn't understand it. Nice breeze today. 12 Wimpies came in circling for hours. 5 Beauforts and 3 more Wimpies today. The Drome is rotten with planes. Hell, if we should have a machine gun attack or high-level bombing, they'd get any amount. Boat mail going out, I wrote 3 letters. Take months perhaps to get there. Received 4 letters, 2 from Joan, 1 each from Pop and Harry. All is ok. Harry waiting to be placed in a job after the course. Joan is out of the hospital and doing well, and so is Pop. Thank God they are all well. Frank, Har, and I all went graphing. Boy did we get some beauties?

FRIDAY, 8th

Raids again last night didn't hear a thing. I slept like a log. A lovely breeze blowing. Had a hell of a gutache. The grapes, I guess. Had the screaming shits. Did me good, cleared me out. Got some nice little boils etc., coming. Hmm! On leave, got bus ok, went to Sliema. Still no films. Met a lot of the boys, they're on 3 days' leave, not bad. We'll have ours soon. Mussolini's son was killed in a crash, Bruno. The guy that machine-gunned and gas sprayed, helpless. Abyssinians, by the sword, eh? These things are not forgotten, it's a start anyway. R.A.F. playing hell all over the place. Smashing Italy to pieces. Long queues and lines for grub in England. They're pretty short, although stuff is being held back, the best way. I doubt that England will ever go short of grub.

Sliema front. The monkey walk. Damn nice town this. Sister to Valletta. One of my stomping

grounds

SATURDAY, 9th.

No raids. Pay came very late, 8:00. No credit still. Not too bad today. Quite a bit cooler. Not many events either. Russian planes over Berlin, a lot of damage, etc.

SUNDAY, 10th.

"Stoneheap Luqa"

Sargent went today on the "Pred" course. Buqi, Buqi. We go on Thursday for rest etc. Leaves 5 on-site now, the details going to pieces. A Glen Marten in from Recco crashed, crew was killed. Happened very close. Bloody awful sight. Wind caught it, and went out of control. All recco stuff was lost from Italy. She burnt in a few minutes. Squadron of Blenheim's were taking off. One dropped all its bombs (8) by accident 15 yards from "Tal Hardack" our B.H.Q. and near the gun site. Hell, the blast nearly knocked me down. Hell, it must have scared the lads there. Nothing much to report these days.

MONDAY, 11th.

No raid last night. Had a good kip. Flies, fleas, and ants aren't too bad now. Much cooler. I've put lime down that'll keep em away. Nothing much today. A new gun came. Seems to be a cheaper job altogether. Girders are detachable, light gun stay, and very small hard wheels. Seems more adaptable for static work and the old one for mobile. That's my contention, that they are taking the old ones out and forming a mobile Battery. Went on leave to Sliema for a change. booked up at T.H. Bed and Breakfast 2 shillings. Lovely evening.

TUESDAY, 12th.

Lousy night. Hot, mosquitoes and sandflies biting like hell. Hard springs, couldn't sleep. Raid about 2:00. Italians dropped M.B. baskets and incendiaries. Fell pretty close. Most of the boys dashed out for shelter. Fighters shot 2 down. Had a fine swim, oh boy! Great! Have I got a tan? Yowsa! And so back home. They had the gun is ok.

WEDNESDAY, 13th

Good night again. Only 6 of u on site. We are definitely going tomorrow on rest. Put in for 3 quid credit. We are getting rations money, 2 shillings 10 pence per day. We shall eat at Tini Barracks. Russians bomb Berlin, also the British together. Mass raids 2-500 lb bombs dropped. Germany getting a terrific hammering now. 18 British planes were lost, and Tomahawks and Havocs used Yank fighters. Also flying Fortresses. Russians holding Gerry although Gerry has advanced in Ukraine. They are putting their weight there now, for a breakthrough. Hardly any enemy activity over England. 6 new Wimpies have come in here. Beau fighters have gone somewhere, farther east I expect. Planes are operating continually night and day from this Drome. Blenheim's by day and Hurricane and Beau fighter sweeps. Wimpies and Beaufort's by night with the fleet air arm. They are playing havoc with Italy, Sicily, and Libya. The Italians dare not come near here by day. Received a letter from Joan on July 25. All is well thank God. There are approximately 100 Bofors on this island now and a couple thousand L.A.A. men. Something on in the future. Japan is fairly quiet although she has occupied every place conceded to her. "Darlan" seems to be ousting "Petain" for power in France. Trouble in Norway. Insurrection in Yugoslavia. Reports say 4, 000 are fighting guerilla warfare. 2 million French join "De Gaulle". The U.S.A. supplying Russia as fast as possible. Britain cooperates in raids and air tactics. So on and so on.

THURSDAY, 14th.

"Stoneheap Luqa".

Will pack once more, for a change. Kit bags, blankets, all the blasted lot. The other mob came about 3:00. Had no dinner naturally. One waiting for us at Luqa. 5 sights on leave, altogether 50 men. Damned glad to see the back of Stoneheap and the Drome of planes. Got to Luqa ok. I paid off, got paid 57 shillings 6 pence. That included ration money, colonial pay (Egypt), and 2 weeks' pay, plus credit. This must last us 2 weeks. Bed at Kings Head Sliema. Me, Frank, Harry, and Jack went to the Regent. Some dance. Ambique (8 bottles) and lemonade. Bloody poison wow! Fell on my face once. Danced with the four lads. On fire hah, so help me it hurt.

FRIDAY, 15th.

"Luqa Camp" (leave)

Felt hellish, with guts in lousy condition, and a sore hip. Laugh! Went swimming, great. Went to Tini Barracks for dinner. Ok. Went to Pictures, Regent. Pissed again! Ah well, so what! Good dance. Sweat like hell.

SATURDAY, 16th

Great life! Cup of tea in bed. Good beds, good grub. Swimming again. Ok, went out about a mile. Lovely dinner at Tini. Ok, lots of drinks. Pretty hot. Went Regent again. Lots of Ambique, wow! Did Harry get pissed, what a laugh, yowzah! Sweat. Went to St Paul's Bay. Had a boat out. Lost Joan's watch, bloody shame. Got back to Regent, no beer! Got 25 shillings left. Good dance, dames ok. Up at 6:00 and got the bus home. Late though! An hour's punishment- 6 Dixies out and in. On fatigue.

MONDAY, 18th

As above, all in, on fatigue party, etc. 2 letters from Joan. Good kid. Snap and blade. Lovely snap. She looks lovely. I shall write a few letters to her. Russians hold Gerry. British still pounding away. Churchill meets Roosevelt. Blasted fatigues, had to carry water by the can. Short of water. Up till 8:00.

TUESDAY, 19th
"Luqa"

Up at 5:00 for route march and firing practice, at St Lucien. Breakfast 5:30. Cold tinned bacon and bread. Lousy. Light M Kit, webbing, water bottle, haversack, rifles, gas bag, and tin hat. Hell, what a load for a march of 10 miles. Started off at 6:00. Ok, cooler at that time. Uphill and down Dale. Got there, and hung about while the Maltese regiment fired. Had a swim, glorious, and warm. No firing. Start back. Hell, it was terrific, the bloody load and heat 120 degrees, uphill! We were saturated with sweat. Got some grapes ok? And so back. Had a shower, dallying, etc. Letter from Joan, June 4th, nice letter. Russians withdrew, and a few towns were lost. R.A.F pounding away.

WEDNESDAY, 20th.

Done some drills etc. I have no enthusiasm for it. I did have once, no more. I see it gets nowhere. Got a 20-hour pass. Went swimming etc. stayed at Joe's. went Regent dance. Pretty good. Had about 6 bottles of Blue, and some wine.

THURSDAY, 21st.

Blasted low-level raid on Luqa. No damage but we were delayed and got in late. Orderly Sgt. got us off ok. felt damned tired after a piss-up, swim, and dance. Hah! Had a good kip. Went "Birkirkara" ok. Saw film. Down to 12 shillings now. Must go easy. Went home. Having a good time all together. Grubs are lousy here. Had some lovely grapes and melons. Gerry advanced steadily, 12 miles from Leningrad. Looks serious. Things are speeding up. Doesn't look too bright for a quick finish though.

FRIDAY, 22nd.

See most of the old draft in, on 3 days' leave. Nice to see em again. On fatigues today. Easy. Lots of letters coming in. Got 3 from Joan. Written in May. Mentions Harry again doing well. Went to pictures. Nothing much to do today.

SATURDAY, 23rd.

Tried to get a 24-hour pass. "Fox" wouldn't give. Sod!! Said we already had it from last week. Had some P.T. Hambrough, some gas drill, and kit inspection, and passed off ok. Got away by 4:00 and caught Lorry and Car into Sliema. Went swimming, not so good, choppy. Still ok. cleaned up at Joe's. went Regent. On Ambique, Shandy, Lemonade. Felt good. Had some swell dances. Picking up, Tango and Fox Trot. Dames ok, had a great laugh. Lots of dames. Yeah, man. Scrammed about 9:00. So what! Got through, it was tough. Lads asleep. Started on foot for home. Wow! 5 miles. Finally made it. Italians over-dropped incendiaries. And so to Kip.

SUNDAY, 24th.

Down to 5 shillings. Most of the boys are away on M.G. Out at a new stretch in "Haba" Pretty isolated out there. 5 out of each detachment. Up at 6:00 for our lousy bloody grub. Detailed for ammo carrying. Feel lousy, Ambique gut. Went by Lorry hell of a way! Chucking 200-weight boxes of ammo. Moving all got messed up, and damned tired from last night. Eventually finished. Leave stopped. Leaving tomorrow. Got out anyway. What a bloody army. If they carry on like this in action, God help us. Messed about, and went to a bar. Malt there played guitar, lovely. Boy and how. Wish I could play like it. Sounded great.

MONDAY, 25th.

Up at 5:00 and worked like hell until 10:00. Moving, carrying, shifting, buggered about. Pick it up put it down. We finally finished. It's bloody maddening the things we do. They call it a rest by hell! Lorries came 4 of them. Piled stuff on anyhow. Crushed everything. Bloody daft. Off we went, travelled to the other side of the Island, near the water. Very open here. Isolated, near "St. Julian" Village. Plenty of dames. Lots of grapes etc. good mungy at Infantry Barracks ok. Got stuck with Lorries in the roads, and busted a tire. Hell, what a battery. The daft things they do. Nobody knew the way. Well, well! After bashing about the Lorries got through. Stopped all men at the new T.H.Q. out in the glaring sun. had a lousy dinner of bully beef and spuds. Finally, by donkey and car, we got over to the sights. Bofor came about midnight, what a struggle. Knocked walls down. Field of camouflage tents. Got it in finally, one of the new types -semi mobile-4 firing.

TUESDAY, 26th.

"Krendi"

Had a good kip. Got a hell of a headache though (grapes). Ate too many, I guess. Cleaned up on the gun, stripped b.block and autoloader. Good grub at infantry. Can't get out at all. Fired up grub in the tent, yessir good mungy. "Fox" came during the night. No guard on. Playing hell with "Slats". The rest of the detachment came to wake us up. Hell, what a bloody mess up. Men moving and packing Kits in pitch darkness. Blinding and swearing. I was stuck in bed. Nuts to it all! I should worry. I stay put. "Fox" ordering and screaming etc. So what! Got no fags or rations. If we hadn't been near the Infantry. we would have starved.

WEDNESDAY, 27th.

Raid-2 Italian Savoia's dropped incendiaries. They were both shot down by Hurricanes. Good sight. The enemy rear gunner put up a good show. Got fags and rations. I think we move tomorrow; we shall see.

THURSDAY, 28th.

Got everything packed again. Cleaned gun down. Made camouflage nets. "Guest" came. Also, a runner from Battery. We're not going. Staying permanently. Well, I'm blasted! Unpack again. Got a hell of a headache over right eye. Either grapes or neuralgia. "Frank" is pretty bad. Guns are nice and clean. A lot of work to be done though. About 2, 000 sandbags to fill and build the gun pit. Pretty isolated here. Can see Valletta on a hill overlooking the sea. We're about a mile from the sea here. Village is ½ mile away. Good grub at infantry regiment. "Frank" in bed with Malta's guts.

FRIDAY, 29th.

"Krendi"

Filled sandbags. "Fox" around again, sod, sneaking around. Also "Happy". No leave until pits are built. Bloody battery is hopeless. No dough or leave now about. Donkey carts to transport kit with. Getting stuck in the roads, knocking walls and houses down. Guns breaking loose, lorries buggered up. What an army. If they do this sort of thing now, what about fighting a war? Had got down to Kip again. Got a fierce headache. I've eaten about 10 lbs of grapes. My head is burning. Took aspirin etc. stuck in bed. Between flies and heat it wasn't too comfortable. Kit inspection etc. I missed it, handy. Who said swing the lead? Pay tonight. Tons of blasted work. Had to lug 65 boxes of ammo about 200 yards. Killing work that. Each weighed about 250 lbs. Lost our rest hour. "Happy" and "Fox" are about all the time. Once they get H.Q. it will be hell here, I can see. We're putting in for transfer. Had a few drinks at the canteen. Decent bunch of boys here.

SATURDAY, 30th

Stand to 5:30. It's also reveille. So, we're up mighty early. Hell of a long day. The British take Iran completely with the Russians. Signs of the Finns wanting peace now that they have their territory back. It would relieve pressure on the Russians. Russian counterattack raids started on the central sector. R.A.F. batter away. Iran is under control now. Vichy hands over North African ports. What an attack of neuralgia I've got. Hell, my head coming off. Every morning regular, over right eye and down side of face and neck. Can't work, had it for 4 days now.

SUNDAY 31st

All quiet here. Very high wind blowing. Lots of dust, some rain. Very cold at the stand. New Lt. "Bid" came. So changed leave now. Go with the Yorkshire lads. Headache still is terrific. Filled about 1, 000 sandbags. A lot more wanted. Started pit. Started leave ok. not much news. 40, 000 French executed since the war. Laval pretty low. Lost 7 ships of a convoy.

SEPTEMBER

MONDAY, 1st.
Blasted neuralgia driving me mad. High wind still about. Much colder these days. Plenty of good mungy here. We cook at night. A big field of tomatoes nearby. No fresh news from home yet. Hell, when's this war going to end? On and on. The blinding army gets me down. Same thing over and over again. Oh, for England. More sandbagging every day now. We're on from 5:30 to 8:00. Rest hour in the afternoon. Kit laid out, fully dressed, brass cleaned. We do an hour's guard at night. Can't get a pair of laces now. Have to keep on changing over from the work boots to the good ones. Frank almost walked on his socks. Can't get my boots mended. What an army! Headache etc., eased up. Me, Frank and Harry on leave, went "Siggiewi" for the bus, 7:00. So got to Sliema late. Went to Regent. Did some Ambique and lemon at 1/6D a bottle. Ok to get a list on with. Had a good dance or two. Lousy though, tight squeeze. Hah, nuts! I got mad as hell, bleak, yeah no more.

TUESDAY, 2ⁿᵈ.
Had a good kip. Got in about 12:00. Harry already in. Damned nice bed for a change. Frank had a night out. 8 smackers Hah! Got 2/6 left from 10/ shillings. Not much left to go on leave with, what! Ah well, one learns to spin it out. Had a good feed of macaroni. Messed about till pictures. Had a talk with Tony, invited to stay with him one night. He's worth money, got 2 shoe shops and a swell bar. Worth sticking to. Harry thinks may have a chance at his role sometime. Germans dead 2, 500, 000 claims Russians. Gerry claims 5, 000, 000 Russians are dead. Russians using 50-ton tanks. Big raids started on the Russian front. London was without an alert for a whole month. War is 2 years old today. I remember distinctly "Chamberlain" broadcasting the declaration of war. What a shock. At Mrs. Whites. Then the 1ˢᵗ sirens. 3 in succession. People rushing about didn't know, what it was. It proved to be one plane crossing the Channel. Friendly. I knew I

was doomed for the army. I felt pretty bitter about it. There was Joan of course. And now I look back over 2 years wow! I didn't give a dam if I'd only known. Ah well, I'll look back even on this one day.

WEDNESDAY, 3rd.

Pit going up steadily. Plenty to do yet. "Fox" played hell again. We were sandbagging and he called for an inspection. Ticked me off for having dirty brass and buttons undone. I ask you, where's the spirit? Still sandbagging. Only 2 on leave now, so every 6 days. I'm flatbroken anyway. No news from home. Usually get em early too. I wonder! Good grub at infantry still. Getting a bit of a paunch but I get no fatter. Boys suffering from the stomach. Water, I think. Plenty of grapes and melons about. Gee, am I browned off? This blasted Island! I'd like a move. Although I am completely safe here. War with Russia is much the same.

It looks workmanlike, but that's a pose! The guy sitting down is more like it.

This is how we get rid of the unwanted or malingerers. A few bursts, then hack the head off. Bamboo Jungle in the background

What the hell is this? I don't know. Work it out

THURSDAY, 4th

4 raids last night. Incendiaries and H.E bombs. About 10 planes in all. Got over before the sirens. High moon, so lights weren't good. Had lousy sleep. Pretty cold at night now. Very warm during the day, though. Sgt. won't speak to "Fox, " so it looks as though we are here permanently. Blasted sight this is. We've about stripped one field of tomatoes here. We fry up at least 10 lbs, of tomatoes every night besides onions, chips, etc. I'm getting quite a paunch.

FRIDAY, 5th.

Krendi"

Woke up about 4:00. Machine gun fire above. All got out. 3 Hurricanes. We filled an Italian bomber full of lead. He came down in flames. What a crack-up. Sandbagging all day. 2 on leave a night. Me and Harry will go tomorrow. Pretty cold at night. On 1 hour guard. Feel pretty good these days. Think I'll use my last roll of film. Might as well, or they might lose strength. Not a film on the Island. Major P. paid us off. The blasted struggle to keep going on 10 shillings. Letter from Joan, all's well. Jean may have a baby after 12 years. Wonder what Bert thinks? Am I browned off? I'd like to move again. A hellish battle going on in Russia around Leningrad, Odessa, etc. 3 divisions were destroyed at Leningrad. 24 hours of rain. Heaps of dead (Rumanians) before Odessa. 200 Gerry planes down in 2 days. British flying fortresses bomb from the stratosphere, no sound, no planes, just bombs. 2, 000 planes were delivered to Britain in April. Japs quiet. Vichy hands over more African Ports, Biserta, and others.

SATURDAY, 6th

Quiet last night. Brilliant moon now. Planes operating from here all night. Fleet air arm over Sicily and Italy. Bombing machines, drones, and harbours etc. While heavy bombers, Wimpies and Blenheim's take on convoys, Libya and the Straights. A terrific number of enemy boats sunk trying to get supplies to Libya. 2 reccos came over. Hurry birds met em, shot em down. 9 Machis and 2 hurry birds lost. Good going. One was an Italian ace. Our fighters are too good for them. Me and Harry on leave. Left at about 5:00 and got the bus to Sliema. On beer got well oiled. Harry shouting and roaring. Went and saw Vincent, and will stay at his place. Went to Regent, and could hardly stand up. Tried to dance, but my legs refused. Staggered back to Vincents, had grub. So, to his flat. Some laugh, Harry thought I was in danger. Not me, they don't know the experiences I've had. Hah! Sweet memories. Who said "Wolf" gave us a snort of cognac. Ok a bit stiff though. I was well out again. Had fairly good kip.

SUNDAY, 7th.

"Krendi"

Left Vincent's after wash and shave at his place. Had grub. Went swimming, ok too but the cold coming out. Winter drawing on. Had a good mungy at Vincent's. Pictures etc. Tea. Vincents again, cost us nothing. And so home. Not too bad but I was broke yeah as usual. Reckon I'll flog some kit or paraffin. Got back too late for grub. Too bad, starving. Mungy tonight.

MONDAY, 8th

Forging ahead with sandbagging. Nothing much today. Charlie Mitchell came over with Sponder. Had chat. Good to see em again. All is well. Grapes going off. Lovely and sweet though. Short of fags. Mail from Joan. Not so frequent now. Took 4 snaps of us lads. Not much doing.

An interval while sandbagging for what we called a grape gorge.
Some grapes, big white & blue ones. Pretty hot then too.

A spot of bayonet drill. How to rip & rend. By an Infantry Sgt. In the background is our tents and camouflage. On the right is a massive fig tree, then yielding tons of figs.

Bit of a farce here. Too bad

Supposed to be "action" as it often was, but the boys wouldn't conform to my directions

TUESDAY, 9th

Hell of a night. 4 raids, about 20 bombers in all. Ju 88, Italian Savoia's, and Breda's 120. Moon up. Lights couldn't get em. Light was very bad. Fighters engaged once or twice. Some damaged I guess, but nothing definite. H.E's on Ta Qali, Luqa, and Harbour. Also M. Baskets over Halfar same night. No action for us. Reports of Canadians and Norwegians landing in Norway. We shall await developments. Otherwise, fighting is just as fierce in Russia. "King" came, dogged about till he left. All ok. Finished off camouflage nets. Mungy ok. Steak, beans, tomatoes, chips, bread, tea, lots of milk and sugar. Everything is pinched or scrounged. Ha, belly first. Have hellish dreams in consequence.

WEDNESDAY, 10th.

"Krendi, Kenilworth sight."

Quiet last night. Up stand to 5:30-7:00. Shave. Set kit out in army regulation rules. Clean up on cook house. Fatigues today. Ok this. Plenty mungy, tea, etc. Not much to do. Very windy today. Dust was everywhere, like in Egypt. A new squadron of fighters was brought in by Blenheim. 15 in all. The latest Canon carriers. Fairly good news today: British, Canadians, and Norwegians land and take "Spitzbergen" Norway. Important coal fields there, they are still in possession. Russians break through Gerry's lines, taking town after town. Wiped out 6 divisions-2, 000, 000 casualties. Terrific battle going on. 200 planes down in two days (Gerry). Very little activity over Britain. Heaviest raid yet on Berlin. 400 British bombers raided that city for 6 hours. H.E.s, Incendiaries, while Russia raids Belgrade, Bucharest, and others. 20 British bombers were lost. Slight activity at Tobruk. Quiet out east. British bomb and sink Italian convoy. Usual strafing, etc., over Italy and Sicily. And so it goes on. People are very optimistic now but it is unwise to hope too much yet. The Gerry is still very strong. Although it certainly looks favorable. I believe the Russians can hold out now. Messed about in cook house, etc. Borrowed dollar from "Don". Leave full, awkward this week.

THURSDAY, 11th.
"Krendi, Kenilworth Sight"

Quiet last night. Stag-3:00. Went to sleep, woke up dead at 3:00, not bad. Still warm enough. Usual day. We are starting a football sweep. 4d a man per week. I find I have no credits now, blasted luck! I guess that railway warrant in Glasgow knocked me back 3 pounds 12 shillings. Ah, well, I guess I'll make the 10/- spin out some more yet. Letter from Joan. She received the snaps ok. That's fine. All is well at home. No parcels, though. I don't suppose I will receive them. Harry and I got away ok. Saw Vincent, ok. Went to dance. Had a bottle of Ambique between us. Getting used to it, though. It took no effect. We had only 10/- between us. Alarm, so dance finished. Had good grub at Vincent's. Stayed at his joint.

FRIDAY, 12th.
Harry is up at 6:30. Cry wolf! What a laugh. Well, well, this guy (Vincent) is worth 3-4, 000 quid. He has laundry, a couple of shoe shops, and a café not bad. Not a bad day. Had a good swim and so on. Got back for grub ok though and paid.

SATURDAY, 13th.
Same again. Stand to at 5:30. Got gunfire. Ok. The raid last night. Barrage. First time in months. Not much doing. 50 Hurry Birds and 5 Blenheim's, all new, came in today. What a sight. Did they roar, yessir! There must be nearly 200 here now. Going east I expect via Iran to Russia. Russians counterattack heavily, retaking towns. British bomb Italy, Turin, Genoa, Naples etc. Speech by Roosevelt. Yank escorted British convoys to fire on any enemy craft. They're simply promoting trouble.

SUNDAY, 14th.
Quiet last night. Slept 2 hours on stage in the pit. Ok, bar the rats, snakes, and beetles of large dimensions and a dog or two. Took it easy all day, no work. Had a decent book. Still warm but cloudy, much nicer and cooler. Pomegranates are ripe now, huge too. Tomatoes are still strong. Huge fig tree alongside of us. Yields tons of figs. A nest of 4-foot snakes live in its roots, lovely black,

slimy things. Haven't seen the paper for 3 days. Don't know how things stand. Putting on weight 11 stone 7 now, not bad, never felt better. The two new squadrons went out. I guess they're for Russia via Iran, etc.

Our ration cart & horse are all decked out on Sunday. Maltese boy & ration orderly.

MONDAY, 15th.

As per usual, slept on stag. Ok. Good mungy. Bully beef, beans, sardines, chips, and tomatoes, altogether in the pan. I made cocoa out of crock. Pretty good, too. It's the plain stuff. Tons of rain, bloody great spots, big as eggs.

TUESDAY, 16th

Again, the same. "Fox, " says we're here permanently. Wanted to know the sweeps and numbers. Either invasion or evacuation. Personally, I'd prefer the latter. Might be of no consequence. Number 3 won the sweeps. Record crowds at the matches at home, and we are carrying on here. Hell, it could be a lot worse, but it could be better. This jumped up the Island, fields, walls, goats, and the heat. Gee, I'll go nuts, and be short of cash always. I've 3/ for leave tomorrow night. I'll have to borrow from somebody or another. I've just paid back 5/. No raids. All quiet. The rains are settling and getting chilly. Also, for stag, the pit is progressing. Telephone and predictor are in a pit now.

WEDNESDAY, 17th

"Krendi"

Same all day. Chipping solid rock with a pick. The British style all over. Grub remains good. Leningrad is in danger. Terrific battles still. British aircraft in action there. Convoys blasted; Dromes strafed. Towns and places were bombed wholesale. And so it continues. Got into Valletta ok by a Maltese work truck. Some ride, wow! Went to Sliema. Vincent's, dance, etc. No dames. Went west, funniest experience yet. Well, well, I wouldn't be credited, no sir. All buckshee. Messed about Valletta, pictures, etc., started with 6/ returned with 3/. Not bad. Well, must work it out somehow. Bit of drill, etc. Harry slept through stag, so I had uninterrupted sleep. Oke poke!

THURSDAY, 18th

All quiet as routine. Pit coming on fine. Grapes have vanished now. Found a field of melons, water, sugar, and banana, huge sods. We raided it in the dark. Bloody dogs heard us. We sprinted across fields and walls, with dogs close behind. Made it, though, with about 4 each, ha-ha. Went to a concert by the boys at Heavy Battery. Not bad; I saw some of the old drafts.

FRIDAY, 19th

Routine again, no change. Got telephone and wiring in. Getting cold now. Windy and rain. Lots of lightening at night. Not much news these days. Gerry forcing the issue, and Russia fighting like hell. Leningrad is in danger. Kiev reported taken by Gerry. No confirmation. R.A.F. playing hell and so on. Reports of large concentrations of Gerry troops in Sardinia, Bulgaria, and Greece. Also, much movement in Libya. Large British army on the Nile. I guess there will be a big push there this winter, once the weather permits. Well, I don't mind if anything takes place from here. I would mind a try or change. It's blasted monotonous here. Same thing every dam day. Malts, walls, goats, and mungy. Hah! I'd like a move anywhere. Unlucky in the army but lucky in so far as danger, at least imminent danger, is concerned. Although we've had our share here in dive bomb attacks, machine-gunning, etc. Yeah!

SATURDAY, 20th

Raid last night at about 3:00. Stuff dropped all around. About 10 planes, a couple of 1, 000 lb. D. A's fell about 100 yards away. I was in bed. It didn't take long to get out. I heard the whine and thud. I threw myself on the floor and waited. Hell! I thought they'd blast everything out of existence. Finally, they blew up. Hell, I felt my ears come out. Terrifying. Mines and bread baskets were part of the equipment they dropped. On predictor course today, easy. Observation of tracer, etc., not bad. Thursday next on Sub calibre firing course. Bren gun mounted on Bofor and predictor. Should be ok. Got 4 letters today. 1 letter and 2 postcards from Joan. 1 letter from Vi, very nice. Everybody ok. Weather lousy, raid free. Harry living with Jack.

SUNDAY, 21st

Guess I'll have to miss a few days. Why? Well, I just neglected the old diary for a few days. Anyway, from today up till now there is nothing unusual occurred. A couple of raids, very negligible. On Leave. Saw Vincent, ok, got pissed. On Blues and Whiskey, buckshee also grub and fags buckshee. Worth knowing this guy. Wrote 4 letters. Received 4 letters from Joan, Vi. Ok, dated Sept 3rd, not bad. All's well, quiet. Boy, was I boozed. Slept at Joe's. 1 ship from England. Lots of papers and parcels. Joan's haven't come as yet, it's doubtful. Good to see English papers, Mirror, etc. Lucky sods back home. Nothing to do. Leave etc. Everything is as usual. "Blondie" in England and the rest of the ships gunners. Jammy swine's what! Well, I guess we're here for a few years yet.

THURSDAY, 25th

On Firing course. Sub caliber. Bren mounted on Bofor and planned by the predictor. Observation of tracer. Master layer number 2, that's me, hah. I smashed the target. Good shooting, they said. I'd like to try 40 mm now. Beau fighters, 12 came in. Kiev is full on. Reports of Leningrad fallen also. Terrific battles. 60-ton tanks used, 1000's of planes. British in action there. Substratosphere bombing by the British. Everything points to a move this winter from Italy or Libya. Sardinia full of Gerry troops.

Latest reports Leningrad still holding out. Terrible slaughter. U.S. tried to repeal the NC Lease and Land Act so as to arm M vessels and take more drastic steps. Ark Royal and part of fleet outside Island. The strip here gradually takes shape. Guess they'll use it this winter. That makes 5 Drome's here now. The fighters will use this one I believe. The Drome is filled with planes now. Dozens of Wimpies and Blenheim's. New mills bombs (Br. hand grenades) were sent here now, as well as Italian throwing grenades, Molotovs, Tommy guns, and ammo. Boy! Are we well equipped? Ok, for invasion. Couldn't sleep for boil. Hell's acre, the pain was terrific. M.O. said to apply a poultice and all duties. Ah, nuts! I got Frankie to squeeze it out, whee, terrific. Almost keeled over, but it came out. An enormous amount of stuff. Much better, wow! Raid, 20 planes off the Island. No attack. I guess this is a forerunner of what's to come. No action. The weather remains lovely, not cold or wet. On drains around the tent, for coming wet weather. Harry Rostrum gone to Malt battery. Still 11 on sight. Expect to have Sgt. Quinnell on here soon, they tell me. Nothing but salt water at St Andrew's barracks. Pretty rough tea.

FRIDAY, 26th.

"Krendi"

The raid last night. No action. Night fighters engaged. Don't know the results. About 7 planes over. Slept through night stag. Worth it. Have a good night's kip then. Read of E boat invasion of Malta in Mirror newspaper. July news. Pretty good. I had a good view of it all. On cook house fatigues. Ok, plenty of mungy. Got paid 12/- Nothing of further importance.

SATURDAY, 27th.

A couple of raids last night. Bombs dropped on St Paul Bay and Mosta. About a dozen planes. Heavy barrage, no fighters. Worked on pit all day, coming on fine. Tried to pinch some stakes from K.O.R.S. didn't work. Capt. spoke to Slats and got hell. Numbers 1, 2, and 3 guns gone to "Delimara."

Convoy expected in, large one.

Mosta Dome, Mosta. 3rd largest in the world. Marvelous place inside. It will hold 10, 000 seated people.

Roman Catholic. 8 months later (10/03/42), the Hun has smacked it. It's now a heap of rubble.

SUNDAY, 28th.

Took it easy. Make tea about 4 times a day in Dixie and Primus. Ok, got our own milk, tea, sugar, and mungy, also gramophone and records. Ok. Weather remains fine. In good health, the boil is almost gone, but stuff still coming out. Must eat fruit, it's lack of green stuff. 95 % of our grub is tinned. Macaroni, bully beef, carrots, beets, peas, cabbage, tinned fruit, bacon, fish. Terrible. No fresh stuff, although plenty of food. Plenty of tomatoes still, melons, and figs. Me and Frank got away for leaving 5:00. Air alarm, 25 plus. Slight dive bomb attack on a convoy coming in about 1.5 units of the fleet and 7 Merchant men. Fine sight, all well loaded. Dozens of planes flying about escorting them. All the big ships of the fleet from New York after repairs, came with them. Nelson, Ark Royal, Barham, Sheffield, Renown etc. I guess the U.S. Fleet has relieved them alright. 1 merchant vessel torpedoed, and the Nelson hit. The merchant vessel lost, but the Nelson ok. Lots of troops and R.A.F. The R.A.F. has played hell over Italy. Turin, Genoa, etc., bombed. Beau Fighters, Hurry birds strafing Dromes from here. A great shortage of food in Italy.

MONDAY, 29th.

All quiet. Good night. Went to Regent. Saw Harry picking up the Tango, ok. Dames, nil. Stayed at Joe's and went to pictures. Saw a good film about R.A.F. in action in Germany. Wimpies coming down low, Gerry A.A in action. Damned good. Got back ok.

TUESDAY, 30th.

Carrying on working on drains around tents. It's nice and easy. "King" inspected, pleased with pit, etc., best in the troop. Very windy, with tons of dust. Blasted boil still erupting. "Don" down with boils and blood poisoning. Lot of scabies on this Island. Saw a young girl while on leave, legs covered with running sores. Terrible sight. Fag issue. Letter from Vi, from July off the last convoy. Russians hold Gerry. No raids over Britain. Terrific battering to Italy and Germany by R.A.F. and so on.

OCTOBER

WEDNESDAY, 1st.

Good night. Windy. Cookhouse fatigues. 2 alarms, nothing occurred. Grub is still good. Order for me to report to T.H.Q West. Had preliminary drill, etc., for a week's guard at the governor's palace. Every 6 months, a different battery does it. So, ours fall next week, a man from each sight. I was picked from ours, maybe because I am tall. Anyway, for a week. The usual all day, just mess about in general. There's the pit yet. Ammo pit and others as yet. Plenty of work. Pretty lowering today. Plenty of rain, I guess.

THURSDAY, 2nd

Report for drill again. Fix and unfix the bayonet drill. Sentry go drill. It's the Castille Valletta we guard. Hordes of officers floating about. On prolonged salute. Still, it's a change. Saw the boys, etc. Rain today is pretty heavy. Nothing much to do. Played crib for 1/ and 6pence and bottles of beer. Did ok. Last night, with a tin of jam and ingredients, George made a huge Duff. We all sat around and scoffed at it. Dammed good. I just managed to get to my bed and collapse. I had about 4 chunks as big as a loaf each. Tonight, we shall make some pancakes. Mungy, can't beat it.

FRIDAY, 3rd.

Wow! Some feed last night. Made about 20 pancakes, each a foot in diameter and 6-8 inches across. A tin of jam and ingredients for sauce sure was good. Had 2 myself. Argument arose that "Slatts" accused "Frank" of having 2 men's rations. Some laugh! "Joe" knocked Dixie of tea over. Went on leave and danced. Hell of a scrap, Sailors and R.A.F. Blood, snot, and sweat. M.P.'s mixed up. Chairs, bottles, etc., they carried 2 out and carried on. Gee! It was great. Worth a bob. Sailors won. So endeth that great battle.

SATURDAY, 4th.

Slept till 10:00. Lovely Kip. Golly. Walked about a bit. Went to the pictures and already saw it. Cost 1/- too. Bloody things are dear. 1/ 6 for a writing pad, 9 pence a quart of sweets, 10 pence a lb of apples, and so on. On my 10/- a week, some laugh. Tons of stuff coming off the convoy, trucks, grub, etc. 7, 000 troops. Russians holding out. Quiet in England. Few raids here. Expecting a blitz this winter here. Dishing us out with extra blankets, bombs, sub guns, flame throwers, tommies, Lewis, Molotovs, and mines. Oh yeah! All in the telephone dugout. We play cards in there with a lamp, smoke, and chuck dog ends about matches. Ammo all around us. Make a nice bang, you know.

SUNDAY, 5th.

2 raids last night. Nothing much; about 12 bombs were dropped. Woke up but turned over again. Weather's fine, grub is good. The K.O.R's are gone on a shoot. Our C.O. said the best gun pit in the battery. Rumor has it we are fully mobile now, ready for a move. No mail as yet. The war is much the same. Chinese drive Japs back and slaughter 50, 000. Not bad, eh?

MONDAY, 6th.

"Krendi"

All quiet. Drill this morning. Sentry go. Bayonet drill is easy. One thing I can do, and that's the above. After 12 months of it, I should. Got back by 12:00 and had a game of Solo in the afternoon. Also, picking up Cribbage. Guess I'll give Pop a game one day.

TUESDAY, 7th.

No drill this morning. On sandbagging ammo pit. Almost finished it. Filled and laid 250 bags, which is not bad. Lovely weather. Boys of K.O.R's gone on firing course so were eating on our own. Grub ok. One satisfaction is we can always make our own at night. Never go hungry. When my guts are full, I'm happy.

WEDNESDAY, 8th.

Sent a letter to Joe to register air mail. Letter to Joan 1/8. It ensures its passage. Good service, also as much as you wish to write. Also wrote to Pop. Still, mail coming off convoys and parcels and tons of papers. Had no recent stuff as yet. At 2:00, we had orders to make gun mobile, and 8 men got packed up to move. Nothing was said as to where or why. Well! Hells bloody delight after the sweat and care that we put into that pit, it's got to be torn down. Could have wept, all of us. Made gun mobile. Knocked the wall of the pit down and pushed her out. Packed up, light kit, rations, cooking stuff, etc. the usual mad rush to time. The truck came, all piled on any old how. Bloody usual crush, scramble, and mess. Dashed along to strip covered in dust, me and 3 other guns and teams, all by 4:00. Off again to Kalafrana Bay. Squadron of seaplanes coming in. We are the defence. Messed about waiting, starting, losing the way. They had maps, King and Fox, but of course, they lost their way. The people cheered as we went roaring through. The fighting 59th hah! Finally, at about 8:00 we got to our position, high above the Bay. Lovely view, Kalafrana, Bugibba, and Delimara on the fronts. We can see our old gun positions, searchlight, and Wolseley. Got into action and so endeth the day. George made us a good tea.

THURSDAY, 9th
"Kalafrana Bay, Sight Manchester"

4 Sunderland's in, a couple of Swordfish and a Yank. Big things. There are 12 guns all around the Bay, so they're looking after the place. We have a good little storehouse and plenty of rations. The sights ok; a bit far off, though. Predictor came. We put that in. doubt if we shall use it much. The weather is lovely. Thousands of blasted sand flies about. God, I couldn't sleep with them. Vic got 2 parcels. Mine haven't arrived yet. I guess they are lost. Tyler has come to make us up. Joe didn't get my snaps. I guess I'll have to go in for them. War in Russia same as usual, although Gerry is supposed to be putting in the last reserves. Don breaking out in boils. Terrible all this bloody tinned stuff. I've been raiding the fields like hell for tomatoes, melons, pomegranates, etc. Played Solo for fags hah I got about 4 packets. Passes the time. Gee, what a life, every day on and on. I'm mighty sick of it all.

FRIDAY, 10th
All 4 seaplanes left today together. Well, I hope the mail is aboard. A fine sight to see them take off. Massive things, the Sunderland's. Still, it was a lot of fuss for 4 planes, uprooting us like that. It relieves the treble guard now. 1 only. Fox says do no work,

sandbagging, or anything. So, we lay about. Grubs ok but not a lot of it. When my guts are continually full, I'm happy. So, let's get back to Krendi. Plenty of mungy there. The trouble is there are no tomato fields or melons etc. around here. Don's arm was very bad, moaning and groaning at night. He can't sleep and can't get proper treatment. It's this blasted diet. 6 out of 8 of us have boils and skin trouble. No fresh fruit or greens in the rations. Fox came ok and returned 2 of my letters, bloody luck, incorrectly addressed, so I missed that airmail. Too bad. Fox says we are going back tomorrow. Fine.

SATURDAY, 11th

Altered again, not going back. Why the hell don't they get some system into it? Good god, the modern British army is all to hell, no method. Bloody good thing the Russians are fighting this war. Wow! Went to Sliema and saw Bill Cross, Leiser, and Curtis. Got films. Good set and adds to my collection. No reels have yet been released. Got back in time for tea. Hell, it gets me down going into town. Can't help it. One sees a bit of life, etc. My dreams are a bit messy, yowzah! This blockhouse we're sleeping in is crawling with all sorts of bloody great spiders about half a foot across. Big bugs, black and shiny, soft, slimy ones. Find them in our blankets. I got up at about 3:00 and shook a few out. Missed stag, hah, to hell with it. I didn't feel like getting out. Sunday, tomorrow, oh boy, to be home for Sunday dinner.

SUNDAY, 12th

2 raids. Reccos and escort passed over, also 2 more at night. Heavies opened up, and no bombs dropped. Sunderland came in about 4:00 from home. There should be some mail on her. Pretty windy and stormy. Generator won't work so sent for ordinance people. Nothing much to do. Few raids, but nothing materialized. Played crib almost all day. Blasted days seem long. Stand to at 5:00-6:00, same at night. George cooks grub alright, but there's not enough of it. From dinner at 12:00 to 7:00 the next morning, we have 2 pieces of bread and jam to keep us going. Blasted rations are so small. Bloody starving now. Let's get back to

Krendi, where the mungy is plentiful. So damned isolated up here. Also, the 3 men guard.

MONDAY, 13th
"Kalafrana Bay"

Didn't bother with stag last night. It rained like hell. Flooded the pit and shelters out. Had to cut holes in sandbags to let it out. Messed about with guns, etc. A couple of alerts, the plane was still in. Me and Frank went scrounging. Had ideas about knocking a few chickens off. What a hope! Too many Malts about. Finally bought 10 eggs at 4pence each, 4/ a dozen, for breakfast tomorrow (eggs, this is) Raining like hell again. First stage, boys went to die league for some grub. Came back with a few cakes.

TUESDAY, 14th
Little action this morning. At 5:30 alarm came through. 20 enemy planes headed for the Island at 11, 000 feet. Very fast, in 10 minutes they were over and came down machine gunning Luqa Drome, then Hal Far, Hal Safi. Boy, did the light A.A. put up a barrage. Wow! They came down in lines of 4 and 6's, spitting lead all over, then over Hal Far by the Drome and out over this bay. I got them in my sights just as they came up and over. We let them have about 60 rounds. The sky was filled with green tracer. Boy, have they got some Bofors about now? It was hard to see, bad visibility. Don't know the results of the attack. I should think some were hit. They were Macchi's Italian fighters.

WEDNESDAY, 15th
Pretty stormy, with lots of rain. Another Empire flying boat in, also a Yank Catalina. That makes 3 in now blast it, we shall never get away from here. It's so damned open. Can't get leave or time off. Grubs are so short. Ah well! Could be worse I suppose. 1 Macchi was shot down yesterday by a Hurricane. No damage was done.

THURSDAY, 16th

At last, the Sunderland went out at 4:00. Big raid on, too, 12 plus bombs dropped, etc. no engagements by fighters. Today, the Catalina and E boat went out. So that leaves the bay empty. Relieves the 3-man guard now. 3 alerts today. Predictor and gun ok now, and running fine. Terrific battle for Moscow. Gerry is within 60 miles. 13, 000 dead at Orel. 15, 000 tanks used. Civil Guard and soldiers side by side. Russians say 125 planes of Gerry were brought down. Russians have new dive bombers well armoured called "Sturmovic". Also, the new fighter "Stalin." Terrible carnage and slaughter before Moscow. Hitler's throwing everything he's got. Reports 75 divisions trying to circle Moscow. Gerry shelling its Moscow defences with long-range guns. Hundreds of dive bombers were used. Russians fired on Infantry and tanks at point-blank range. Thousands of paratroops were wiped out. It's one hell of a shindy. God knows how it will end, and only he can bring this end about. Ah, it's terrible. God, in all your mercy, bring peace to this weary, shattered world.

FRIDAY, 17th

Slept through Stag last night for about 3 hours. So what! H.Q. doesn't seem to mind. Anyway, I woke up with the watch in my hand at 3:00, had a fag. There was a raid. Then woke Don. Hell, smithy was terrific last night. Thunderous is the word. It woke us all up. All had a chuckle. Must have been the M.V.'s. Bay is all clear still, easy today. Had practice on Predictor. Ok. British R.A.F. is playing hell over Germany. 300 bombers used, including Halifax's etc. These are capable of carrying as many as 3 Wimpies or 8 Blenheims. Hell of a load, about 7 or 8 tons or more. U.S.A. is trying to repeal the Arms Act. I think it will succeed. Japan seems to be trying again. Dismissed the cabinet. All legations and embassies were evacuated out of Moscow, as well as the population. Looks pretty serious. They're fighting like hell. Rumanian's claim to have entered Odessa. The battle still rages. An increasing amount of Yank planes coming over. The U.S. Minister says Russia is getting the supplies demanded of her by way of Iran and Vladivostok. Japan would like to stop that. Gerry is urging this move.

SATURDAY, 18th

As usual. Went into town after dinner. No films about it. Went to pictures. A film called "Angel" not bad. Big dance at Vernon's. Plenty of dames. Holy ole doodle, enough to drive a guy nuts. Am I starved, or am I? And how! It's a blasted crime. Got back ok.

MONDAY, 20th

Nothing to write about yesterday. Quiet, we didn't do much. Hung about. King came around, quite charming. We were playing crib. All in a state of undress. Beds all over the place. Ok, he said, stay put. Promised stuff would come tomorrow. It did today, minus my bedboards and boots. So, I'm still on the floor with the bugs and beetles. Hell! Last night, I found them in my blankets and dozens all over the floor, scuttling about all over the place. Ah well! They can't eat you.

TUESDAY, 21st,

Out of fags, all of us. Can't get any anywhere. "Leiser" saved our lives. He brought 200 from Naffi. Hell of a lad, Tommy. No mail. Gee, there are about a dozen boats(flying) in a week and no mail. Odd. They brought us a table finally and some more cooking things. We've been making tea, boiling, and cooking in one dixie. Each night now it's been 2 slices of bread and jam. As a change, bad cheese and onion. That is all between 12:00 dinner time and breakfast the next morning. Hell, I'm half-starved. The spuds are bad, the cheeses are bad, the margarine and bully beef, and M.V's are 10 months over their time. They literally stink. Don has huge boils all over, and he's mighty run down. Most of the lads have screaming shits through this and water drawn from a stagnant well close by. There are dead things of all kinds in it. So far, I have escaped with a boil on my neck. But on a civilized Island such as this! The British have been established here for donkey's years. It's a bloody crime and organization. Good God! The Island is attacked by the enemy and all the R.A.F. can manage to do is send out 6 Wimpies and 6 Swordfish by night and Blenheim's and Hurricanes by day. There are dozens of air crews doing absolutely nothing and haven't reported at their stations for weeks. Those in charge don't know and don't care. I've got this from the crews themselves. Now is the time they should take advantage of the lull. They raid, yes, but not often enough and not enough planes (6). Gerry uses 50, 100, and 300 Yeah, and does it right. Hell's delight, what an army, what a lousy British system.

WEDNESDAY, 22nd

Sunderland in again. That's 2 now. Usual routine today. We're not doing much, playing crib most of the time. Just messing about, etc. Grub's still poor. I haven't been down to any of the villages yet. Too far. Anyway, between buying beer and fags I've bugger all cash left. On leave. Alarm, 6 plus, came down and machine gunned Luqa and Ta Qali Dromes. Also, Blenheim coming in. The Bofors drove them off. Hurry, birds mixed it. No results, out of range for us. They're getting mighty bold these days. Got away by 6:00 into Sliema. The dance was not bad, had heavy boots on though. They sent all our Kits from Krendi, but my boots weren't among them.

THURSDAY, 23rd

Slept till 10:00 at Joe's, ok. Damned nice the soft bed and clean sheets. Makes a hell of a nice change. Had a good breakfast. Went to pictures at the Coliseum. Saw the latest news, pretty good, convoys, etc. Got back ok. Met Sargent at the dance, just over from the western desert. Plenty of dough, throwing whiskey about wholesale. I felt pretty good after about 6. Met some of the boys. Can't get much stuff also, very dear. Wow, a hell of a lot of troops about, sailors. Most of the convoy is gone now. All empty and away. Big one coming from "Alex, " it is said. When I got back, everything was packed and ready. Gun out of action and mobile, of course. We don't move till 8:30. When it's nice and dark. Just like the army. Anyway, trucks came, 2 of them to take our stuff, which was enough for 4 trucks. We had all our kit crammed on when an officer told us to take it off again to get the Predictor and Generator on. Did this after much sweating and swearing. Finally got it all on, hell's delight for the sake of another truck, all this work and time. Captain King drove, what a ride, about 10 miles of dust. Truck conked out twice. Eventually made it. More grinding, sweating, and swearing to get it all off and gun in action. Finished at about 1:00 then we had to do sentry. Well, well, what a system, what an army. Thank God the Russians are fighting it for us. To top it all, there were no rations.

FRIDAY, 24th

"Kenilworth"

Well, it's good to be back again. Plenty of grub again, a better sight altogether, also more life about. Good to see infantry boys again. The buildings are going up pretty fast, nearly finished. While we were away, 2 of the boys of the infantry tried to commit suicide. One lay down with his rifle. He's pretty serious. Another turned the Bren gun on himself. This is because they are driving them so hard. Manowars, tests, guards, drills. Poor sods, they're going through hell. Had 2 raids, and they came pretty close, too. Got paid, etc. Plenty of grub. Feel much happier.

SATURDAY, 25th

Had a good kip. Weathers ok. Still, plenty of tomatoes about. Had an early raid, but nothing happened. Cleaning up the pit, etc., plenty to do now. Pit to rebuild and ammo dump. Had a raid about dinnertime. 17 plus. 4 bombers in formation came over with the rest escort. They bombed the docks from about 20, 000 feet. Hit an oil dump. No sirens sounded. I guess there were some casualties. The dump burned like hell. Huge pall of smoke. I can't understand the policy of the fighters. Didn't seem to be many up and those kept away. At one time, they would have gone in and played hell with them, but not now. Well, I guess this is the beginning of the winter blitz they're expecting. Ah, well, I think they want waking up. We shall see. I guess we'll get a good bashing this winter. We counted 26 Wimpies take off last night from Luqa. Also, a Swordfish. The Blenheim are out all day. Naples was pounded for 4 hours Tuesday night and Berlin for 5 hours. Getting a bit hot.

SUNDAY, 26th

On cookhouse fatigues today, easy going. The fire from the burning dump is still going. It's been on all yesterday and night and today. Thousand of tons of petrol and kerosene went up. Serves them right. All stuff like that should have been underground. They have the finest rock to work with for underground storage. Nothing much to do today. Greasy work in the cookhouse though. Grub is good. We've fixed up the pit ok again.

MONDAY, 27th

The weather is pretty bad, rain and cold. No further raids as yet. Me and Frank went on a dark expedition. Cauliflower, tomatoes, spuds, etc. Made a fine feed. Got some dates and raisins from the cookhouse and made a duff. Hell, and what a duff. Still, it filled the gap. We made some pancakes without sugar. They also went down. As I write, Frank is making some macaroni. It looks promising. At the moment, it is raining like hell. I've seen it rain in many a country, but for heavy rains, this beats them all. The battle still rages in Russia, just outside Moscow and on the central fronts, etc. Russia created reserves and a couple of armies. All quiet in Britain. R.A.F. bash Naples and all others besides Germany.

TUESDAY, 28th

Not of much consequence, the usual. This afternoon, 4 Fortresses came in, Boeing Yank, 4 engined bombers. Sure, are tough-looking articles, fast and heavy. Hope they've brought some mail.

WEDNESDAY, 29th

Didn't bother with leave. "Slats" wanted to go. Finished off the registered letter to Joan for tomorrow. Guard has been cancelled until Friday. Wish it were cancelled altogether. Don't fancy it at all. Parading the guard in front of a crowd, band, etc.

THURSDAY, 30ᵗʰ

Blenheim, new, crashed while coming in yesterday. 4 bags of mail lost. The crew got away ok. There were 4 came in. The Fortresses left. On leave. Got the 9:00 bus ok. Went Valletta. Sent in registered letter ok 1/7 hope it makes it. Sent 3 snaps, also enclosed. Rained like hell. Met Vincent on the bus, a decent bloke. Got a coffee, etc., and cheesecakes. Had dinner with him also. Lots of spaghetti done Maltese way, garlic, peas, tomatoes. Ok. Went to pictures. Met Frank, he came in for me to report for guard tomorrow at 8:00. Like hell! Not this chicken. They don't oblige me. I stayed, as did Frank. Took in dance ok too. Had a good time.

FRIDAY, 31ˢᵗ

Got the first bus ok. got to Kenilworth in time. Then to T.H.Q. for guard inspection by "Broach". Passed off ok. Got some mail from B.H.Q from Joan, Harry, and Vi. All is well. Harry will be called up for R.A.F. soon. I guess he'll go into the electrical branch of ground staff, etc. Vi at Herriers doing ok, with good hours and cash. She's in digs by herself. Harry with Jack. Pop ok. Joan, bless her still ok. Dam and blast it. It must be hard for her at times. What a filthy war it is. She sold my suits to Norrie, good girl. That's better than nothing. I guess she's right after all. Thank God she's well, etc. Russians are retreating slowly. Gerry is 40 miles away now. Hellish slaughter going on. A veritable holocaust.

NOVEMBER

SATURDAY, 1st
That fire caused by the raid burnt out a paraffin and clothing dump. 300 tons of paraffin went up, and tons of army clothing. The clocks have reverted to summertime as a consequence. A new squadron of Blenheims came in. One crashed, some mail lost. It came down vertically with a smack. The crew escaped. Also, new Wimpies. Was told by an R.A.F. bloke that there were 80 Wimpies, 4 squadrons, Blenheims besides Glenns, etc., on Luqa now. 27 Wimpies went out last night, bombed Naples, Sicily, Libya, and Tripoli for 9 hours. The Blenheims (2 squads) went out 3 times today. Last night, 12 Italian bombers came over here and dropped Anti-Personnel Bombs. They are small and delayed action, a slight touch and up they go. There were thousands dropped. So far, 4 signalers and 10 civilians have been killed by kicking or striking them or picking them up. They have a blast like a grenade.

SUNDAY, 2nd
Wrote 4 letters home. Usual today. Fixing up winter quarters (an old stable). Bloody filthy and crawling with bugs. Had 2 alerts. A couple of fighters near, not much doing. One tried to be funny, it didn't work. Next time there will be blood. So endeth the day.

MONDAY, 3rd
Frank and I on leave. Got away alright. Caught the 9:00 bus into Valletta. Messed about somewhat. Went to the fair, what a do. Some laugh. Saw Vincent, ok for free grub. Cheesecakes and curried rice at a Malt café. Pretty good. Rissoles at Vincent's, plenty of garlic, and then spaghetti. Hell's delight! Went to the pictures, news pretty good, fall of "Asmara" and "Massawa." Went to a dance, not bad. Pretty warm though in a pullover. Dames plentiful. Blasted rain. And so on.

TUESDAY, 4th

Damned good kip at Joe's. Sure is nice to have clean sheets, etc., once a week. Caught the 6:00 bus back. They're exploding those small bombs that the Italians dropped over the island. The CEPS gathered them up as though they were vagrants. Bloody fools. Already, 10 have died through picking them up. 4 R.A.G.L. blokes were blown to hell and back by 1, 000 pounders. Had to sew them up in a blanket to bury them. Poor sods! I knew them well. Also, 7 signalers. Well, that's the price some have to pay. Went on guard drill, ok. Some more letters from Joan and Vi. Joan writes hers half-drunk, celebrating Wally's 7-day leave. I had to laugh. I'll bet she felt good, or rather sentimental. Drink does that as a rule. Good luck to them. Wish I was there. Also, half a page was cut out. The censor had done his foul work, ha! Something about air raids she wrote, I think. Vi is ok. I am writing to all, also Christmas cards. Lots of mail about. Whitley Bombers, Bombays, and also Blenheims have been coming in. They are not getting our mail too well though. It's been 3 weeks since she last heard, and I write dozens of letters. They're building our hut now. Good! I must learn to control myself, damn it. Squabbling and scrapping. Ah, nuts!

WEDNESDAY, 5th

To hell with this island. I'm right browned off, there's bugger all to do. Gee whiz! One dance hall in the whole of the island and lousy at that. Bloody ancient pictures. No organized entertainment for the boys whatsoever.

SATURDAY, 8th

Frank and I on leave. By the time we had breakfast it was 9:00, so we missed the last bus. We walked halfway to Valletta. Decent day. Went to a carnival and dance at Vernon's. Partly lousy, all partnered. Didn't dance much. Cripes. A few pips and stripes, etc., what a difference. It makes one sick, this difference in the British Army. What an outfit! And to fight for it at that.

SUNDAY, 9th

Met Harry and Ox. Damned nice to see them. Went to Regent together, ok. Short of dames. Swished a few about. Harry up to his usual tricks, what a laugh. Raid about 8:00, that finished it. The dance finished. What a lousy outfit. Well, well! Slept at Joe's, ok. Those sheets again, what a change. Missed the bus this morning. Walked back to the site. What a life! Buses start at 6:30 and finish at 8:30 to save petrol. Heartily sick of it bloody all. Received letters from Joan. She got snaps, ok. They're getting letters alright now, so glad.

MONDAY, 10th

Not much of interest. Still working on the site, almost finished. On predictor drill for a shoot on Wednesday another sub caliber do. We fire Tommy guns, Lewis's, and try hand grenades. Should be interesting.

TUESDAY, 11th

Armistice Day. What a farce. 23 years ago this was promised. Peace. Lest we forget, and did we? Yea, and how. A much bigger and better war altogether. The folly of it all. I'm writing on my knee; this will account for the scribble. "Slats" is ill, bad diet is to account for it.

WEDNESDAY, 12th.

Up at 5:00 to go on a shoot. Light marching order, rifles, etc. Got a lorry from T.H.Q. to St. Andrews. Longish ride, about 10 miles. Pretty cold. The usual: Predictor on truck and Bren fixed to Bofor. Hung about for an hour or more. Finally started. The first lot was pretty bad. I could see the trouble, bad wheel movement. Tracer was wide and low. Advised "Don." We had a good shoot. Congratulations by "Fox." Threw bombs, grenades, and Italian grenades. Fired Tommy and Lewis guns. I managed pretty well, hit the target. Had our dinner of 1 sandwich and corn dog. Got back at 2:00.

THURSDAY, 13th.

Had a damned good kip. Rained like hell during the night. Terrific lightning and thunder. Had to get up and tie the tent flaps down. The site is complete now, nothing much to do. The Malt's are coming on with the billet. Nice spacious building. Should be ok. Had letters from home. All are well. Joan received my snap. Grub is excellent. Feeling damned fit.

FRIDAY, 14th.

Raining like hell. Mud and slime everywhere, pouring into tents, pit, and ammo dump. Some storm. Had to dig trenches and drains to let the water away. Hung about, late for pay. Guard was ok bar the foot drill at "Floriana, " which was lousy. Their step is different from ours, so half were doing the short halts, etc., and the other half the long. It looked and was funny. "Fox" came at 6:00. Frank and I just managed to get the last bus.

SATURDAY, 15th.

Went to a dance last night. Same old faces and dames. Ah, nuts! 9d for a half pint of beer, lemonade 5d a bottle, and fags 9d a pack of 10. What's the good? We walked out disgusted. Visited a few bars, dives, etc. Bloody hopeless. The sailors are in the majority on the front here. Plenty of dames about. Finally had a lousy meal and went to bed. It's blasted torture these days on leave. To see it all around you and yet can't touch it. It's getting worse. Such time wasted too! Holy suffering smoke. Messed about, pictures, etc. "Ice Follies" not bad. Rained like hell. Ark Royal sunk. And so home. A miserable leave. The shortage of cash is pretty acute.

SUNDAY, 16th.

Not much to shout about. Rain like hell, simply roaring down. Everything washing away. The telephone pit leaking like hell. Pretty uncomfortable. Grub is excellent. We're being helped by infantry cooks. Old George makes fine pastry. We flog the biscuits, bully beef, and M.V.'s for all sorts. Me and Frank went foraging. Brought back cauliflowers, cabbage, and tomatoes. Cauliflowers are lovely. Our hut is going up rapidly. In battle dress now. Like old times. Last time I used this battle dress, I was on leave with Joan. Happy days. Russians take the initiative, driving Gerry back here and there. Bad weather prevalent. Looks brighter, very much so. The neutrality act has been revised in the States, releasing ships. They are to be armed and can go into all ports, so that's a big lift.

MONDAY, 17th.

All's wet, still raining. "Slats" gone to hospital with yellow jaundice. Too bad, he has been suffering a lot. Bdr. "Monger" has taken his place. Sgt. "Bradley" coming shortly. Too bad, we were quite happy without a sergeant. Ah well, I guess we'll manage. I shall, it's no odds to me. Let's get it over with. The Malts are collecting snails around here. They eat them raw. Received a letter from Joan, a year old, dated November 14th, 1940, to Woolwich. Ain't it wonderful?

TUESDAY, 18th.

"Kenilworth"

Not of great consequence, the usual: on guard drill. Went by lorry to Floriana. Drilled on the square. Pretty ragged. R.S.M. gave us a lecture on C.O.'s inspection. Said he would inspect from every angle for an hour. Our persons from our boots to our nails. Hell, what bullshit. Wartime, bah! Got fitted for brand new battle dress and everything else. We were engaged on this all day.

WEDNESDAY, 19th.

Lovely weather, nice and cool, and plenty of sunshine. No flies or mosquitoes now. A lot better than that terrific heat. A bit warm in battle dress though. I'd prefer the tropical outfit. Received a letter from Harry, says he's accepted as a wireless mechanic in the R.A.F. A1 physically. Damned glad his ear is ok now. I guess he'll get on ok. Hope he remains on the ground. No recent letters from Joan.

THURSDAY, 20th.

Stand to at 6:30-8:00. Have good kips these days. I cut open my paillasse and made a sleeping bag of it. Damned successful too. Yowsah. Wrote about 6 letters. Unlimited sea mail going home on those few boats, I guess. I wrote to everybody, including Glasgow. Sliema ah! Should be on leave with Frank, but the guard tomorrow alters that. I'm glad. I can go on my own. I prefer that. Can work better. Yeah! As of yore. Stand to 5:30-7:00. Hour and a quarter stag, not bad. Dugout is warm. We have lamps, so we can read, etc.

FRIDAY, 21st.

4 alarms during the night. Heavy barrage and fighters. No result. Plenty of bombs and sea mines dropped. Machine gun attack this morning. 30 planes over, 5 waves of 6 came down and razed "Hal Far, " hit a few planes, damage done to the drome. The light A.A. put up about the heaviest barrage for months. 6 flew in our range, we got off 150 rounds and 2 were hit, into the sea. They were "Macchi's 100" fighters. Boy, what a sight. Thousands of shells and tracers going up. About 2, 000 shells were used. About 40 Bofors fired, apart from Lewis, Bren, 3", and so on. By Hell! Is there a defence here and how. Gerry wouldn't stand a chance of invasion. Went on guard drill, ok as usual. Came home late. Didn't wait for "Fox" with pay. Borrowed 12/6 off Joe and beat it. Went to Vernon's, knocked back 5 pints, went to Sliema, saw Vincent. Went to a dance, not bad. Pretty near all buckshee. Should have a few bob left. Felt mighty damned good. Yowsah! Not often I have any beer.

SATURDAY, 22nd.

Got away ok, didn't cost a lot. Went to pictures, not bad. Met Harry from "Birkirkara." Raid, big dogfight overhead. When I got back, I heard 4 were shot down out of 15. The result from Friday's do was 8 - 5 by light A.A., the rest by fighters. Some of my mates were killed on the site, and another site wiped out by a 1, 000 lb bomb. Bloody shame. "Brown, " a bloke I knew well. The British have started an offensive in Libya. They penetrated 65 miles, relieved Tobruk after their stand of 8 months. Longest in history.

Churchill, in a speech, said we have started and shall not stop. We are equal to Germany in forces there. Our R.A.F. outnumber them also.

SUNDAY, 23rd.

Huge tank battle in Libya. "Cunningham" says this will decide the war there. Reports say we are using huge 10–50-ton tanks and are superior to Gerry's. The S.A.A.F. under "Cunningham" are using squadrons of Glen Martins and bomb-carrying Hurricanes, machine-gunning with cannons, etc., and dropping anti-personnel bombs. Also, units of the fleet are bombarding from the sea. In Russia, Gerry is gradually getting in. Pretty serious around there. Terrible slaughter, huge tank battles, bad weather, Gerry freezing.

MONDAY, 24th.

Rained like hell all day. Some storm at night, wow! Thunder was terrific and lightning, rain poured in through the tents. Got wet— everything: blankets, kit. Hell of a night, just as bad all day today. Went to a lecture by "Fox" on air defence. Terrible, he didn't know what to talk about. Agony listening to it.

TUESDAY, 25th.

Decent night. Had to report with full kit for B.H.Q. Packed up ready, then suddenly Disha news came through, this is a general invasion warning. Reports came through that bombers, gliders and troop carriers were massed in Sicily. We had to get fully armed. Extra ammo out and every weapon. Besides bombs, mines, etc., extra positions had to be dug. We slogged our guts out in the rain and mud to put them up. I'll never forget it. All men to sleep with guns. This lasted until the next day. The guard was forgotten. The show gun had to be brought back.

WEDNESDAY, 26th.

It finished about 12:00. Still raining. Hardly one alarm so far. It proved the concentration of stuff at Sicily was reinforcements for Libya. Ordered to pack and move again. I went, plus kit, by donkey cart. Waited for 3 hours for the lorry. Finally got to B.H.Q., had a cup of cocoa. Nearly bloody starving. By cripes, what a life!

THURSDAY, 27th.
"B.H.Q. Tal Handaq"

Grand parade, drill, etc. easy. I don't care a damn for it, it's easy anyway; I can do it blindfolded, more bullshit. All webbing to be scrubbed white, all brass to be polished, boots, etc. I spent all afternoon doing nothing but this. New battle dressthey all had to be one colour. Good God, it's intolerable. Grub is lousy, a plate of the inevitable macaroni for dinner. Had to kick up a stink to the orderly officer about it. Well! I got a bit more after an argument with the cook. Issued with soap, etc. Must buy all other stuff. 1/- bottle polish, 10d for boot polish, by hell it leaves a guy nothing for leave. Not out of 10/- anyway. Fort Capuzzo, Bardia, and Tobruk captured by Allied forces in Libya. Terrific tank battles, about 100 tanks engaged. Yanks and British - 6, 000 prisoners so far taken. The R.A.F. doing well. Blenheims from here are doing good work. Russians still hold out.

Tal Handack Valley with huge underground tunnels & stores for Aviation Petrol & Ammo. Note entrance of tunnels 98 Foot below solid rock. It's used as shelter also.

FRIDAY, 28th

"B.H.Q. Luqa"

Same again. Guard, drill, changing, forming. Dead easy. Arms or rifle drill is easy. I got on ok with it, tons of b.s. though. Scrub equipment again, polish boots like glass, clean all Kit. Scrape and scrub brushes white. Everything new, spick and span. Oh, its hellish doing all this for blasted guard. Wartime. When there's guys being slaughtered in Russia and Libya. Gee! The people at home think we're risking our lives out here they have no idea how the public money is being spent. It's costing the Battery over 100 quid. I got paid 12/6.

SATURDAY, 29th.

The same again. Grub is lousy, a bit of cold tinned bacon for breakfast. Same through the day. Hell, I'm starving. Got to buy biscuits etc. and it's all so bloody dear. Hell, what a life. And rifles Wow! This officer came around with a match poking in holes and cracks for dirt. He found plenty. Went to "Krendi" to sight for boats. Had hell of a walk back - 5 miles wow! Went on leave, went to dance, met 2 Harry's, not bad. Had good kip. Old Joe charged like hell! 4/-3 ruined me. Left me with 5 shillings, can't last the week out on that.

SUNDAY, 30th

B.H.Q.

It was hell all day Sunday. Nowhere to go just walk about seeing Malts and soldiers. A few clubs with bugger all in them. Just streets and other servicemen same as yourself, walking about aimlessly. Charging 2/ at pictures and old shows at that. I didn't go, they won't rob me of 2 shillings the swine. If it wasn't for the services those bars and cinemas would go broke. I saw a lot of the boys, Bill Cross made Sgt. Couple of Air raids, this was the 1, 000th over Malta. Some record. Went to Vernon's club dance with Harry and crowd. Not bad, plenty of dames, had a few dances, but too much opposition these days. Ah well, nuts, who cares! I beat it to Harrisons. Wow ok there. And so home. Found all kit etc. had been moved to another room. Hell's delight, 16 of us in a room 12 feet by 6 feet. It's terrific, stinking, sweaty and otherwise. No room to move. Well, well and we are to keep stuff clean.

DECEMBER

MONDAY, 1st

Rained all day and we cleaned our stuff all day. Holy ol' doodle all day! Polishing, shining, scrubbing, cleaning kit. Terrific, enough to drive us mad. Still, "Jono" livened things up a bit. Some guy, "Jono." Boy! he'll make a cat laugh. And so it goes on. Saw the changing of the guard. Pretty damned good. Frightened some of our boys when they saw it all. Ah, hell, nothing to it. I'll do it easy, doesn't frighten me. And so back again.

TUESDAY, 2nd

"B.H.Q"

The same, up at 6:00. Breakfast of nice cold tinned greasy bacon by hell, with 2 slices of bread and tea. What a meal for a growing man. Well, to get on with it. General clean-up: rifle, equipment, etc. Bit of a drill by the Sgt. and B.S.M. Easy. Began to rain. Spent the afternoon, after a lovely dinner of maconochies (stew) with soggy spuds, doing up the stuff: brass, boots, and equipment. 4 solid hours. What a mess, they're worrying like hell over it all. Change this, and that, and the other. Everything brand new wow!

WEDNESDAY, 3rd

Much the same. Still raining. So on with the cleaning. Spent the best part of the day at it. Wrote 6 letters to family a page each under conditions that were pretty good, I reckon.

THURSDAY, 4th

Up at 5:00 for rehearsal at "Castille." Marched up Merchant Street to Castille Square. Paraded, changed guards, and so on. Made a hash of it, wheeling and left form. Still, it wasn't bad.

FRIDAY, 5th

Same thing. Bullshit and rehearsals. With massed bands this time. Much better. Everybody very pleased. B.S.M. bought a crate of beer for us all.

SATURDAY, 6th

Same again. Raining like hell, holding up things. Plenty of work though. Got pay, the usual 10 shillings, also leave at 12:00. Went to Valletta, had a smack at "Tombola" nowt, houses of 6-10 pounds, very handy. Went to "Gut, " messed about, slept in a dump near there.

SUNDAY, 7th

Up at 9:00. Left with 2/6d, so couldn't do much. Short on grub, what a bloody hole, hell's delight! Glad to get home again in time for dinner. Cleaned up a bit. 41 new planes came in. 4 letters from home, Vi and Joan. Snap from Joan what a laugh, good God it was awful. Some hat, oh boy.

MONDAY, 8th

Up and at it, cleaning, etc. Hell of a mess with new suits, etc. Anyway, got everything ok and away by 2:00. Got to Castille ok, way up the top. Nice barrack room, camp beds. Changed, all ready, paraded by R.S.M. Inspected by R.S.M., orderly officer, and adjutant. Hell's delight, what an inspection. Lasted an hour odd. We were at the port for 10 minutes, it was agonising. Still, we passed ok, 8 of us. All our officers were watching Broach, " "King, " B.S.M., and so on—giving advice. Said the Governor would be out front, also C.R.H. and the Brigs. Hell! Felt a bit sweaty. Waited for the signal. The band started and we marched to it. Easy to keep in step. Then we rounded the corner. Good gad! What a crowd! Thousands of them. Our guns were drawn up with teams, the old guard also. But the people—wow! Well, we wheeled and flanked lovely, went through ok, but what suspense. Could see everybody. Hard to stand still for a long time with a crowd like that. Well, it went off. We got in ok. The C.R.H. sent congrats, our officers also. We did well, but later we turned out for the Governor. The sentries came with us, "Hurley and Grant, " what a laugh. They should have remained there. Well! Then again, the sentries didn't present to the gun as it moved off, but it passed off.

The Governor holds an inspection. Pretty, very pretty

The R.A. H.Q Castille where we did all the brigade guards.
Pretty stiff and how. All the R.A.F & Signal Services are done
from here. Taken when all was quiet. It's now a heap of rubble

TUESDAY, 9th

"Castille Valletta"

Cleaned up after 6:30. Had tea and supper. Damned good grub, excellent. What a difference. Slept well. Up at 5:30, shaved in a mug of water. Lucky I got Joan's blade. By hell, what a shave. Me and "Jack Gustar" paired for guard together. We do 4 hours a day. Pretty good. Had the morning off. We went on in the afternoon. Ok, I gave orders and signals, so we worked fine. Had to distinguish ranks.

WEDNESDAY, 10th

Jack and I on early. Bloody cold, feet were frozen. Wow! Still, we did ok. Pretty high on the steps of Castille. Good grub. Plenty of time to read and write. Got a bar of chocolate each day so far. Turned off the guard twice. C.R.H., hell, what a guy, like a butcher.

THURSDAY, 11th

Up at 5:00 for the first trial with the new guard. Shaved in a mug of water. Had a good breakfast, etc. Marched out, then new guards, in Malt crowd. R.A. Pretty good too. Very slow drill. Members were very smart though. Went through ok, done it twice. We were ok. Inspection after by O.O. and R.S.M. Pretty tiring. Back to the guard room. Me and Jack on guard. Not bad. I gave orders for movements for present or butt. We had 2 turnouts. C.R.A. and Brig's ok. Bloody funny though. Different, little things such as Hurley coming out without a hat, and somebody doing the wrong drill. The R.S.M. broke 2 teeth off his plate biting a bit of cotton off a bottle. Hell, what a laugh.

FRIDAY, 12th

"Castille"

The battleships "Prince of Wales" and "Repulse" were sunk by Jap dive bombers. 2, 000 of the crews were saved. Bloody shame though. 2 Jap cruisers and 1 battleship sunk. The Japs started their invasion 2 days ago. The States, the Philippines, and others, also Panama, Cuba, and the Dutch East Indies, declared war on Japan. The Axis declared war on the U.S.A. In fact, every bugger is declaring war. It's bloody silly, even the Government of Poland in London. By cripes, it's crazy. The U.S.A. is bombing the Jap troops and transport. The Russians are driving Gerry back. Gerry is retreating everywhere. "Rostov" is nearly regained. 75, 000 Gerry lost. Terrible slaughter. Official sources reckon Gerry has lost nearly 2, 000, 000 dead while Russia claims 6 million. The British are slowly driving Gerry back in Libya. There have been air alarms at Los Angeles, Australia, Cuba, and Canada, by hell! The Japs are using 100-200 bombers every raid. Bloody clever sods. They've invaded Indo-China, the Philippines, numerous islands, Thailand, and so on. Got paid.

SATURDAY, 13th

Last trial with band and guns. Not bad. Ok. Bloody tiring though. Up at 5:00 and on the go until 9:00. The Malts are good. Received letters from Joan and Vi. 7 in all. Everything is ok. Harry is working out. Vi is earning 5 pounds odd a week at Harens. Joan cut her finger. She sent a horrible picture of herself. Wow, bad photography. Good thing it is just a snap.

SUNDAY, 14th

Jack and I on guard. Bloody good mungy. Lots of porridge, bacon, and beans. Good tea, with sugar. A bit warm today. Off at 12:00. Messed about. Nice walking, really hot, lovely sun. Everything very quiet and so on. On at 4:00, relief ok. Down to the Gut, few drinks, etc. Friday night ruined me though 5/-

MONDAY, 15th

As usual. Hell! It was warm standing there. The sun was right in my eyes. Still, we managed. Finally, the change over. Large crowd as usual. Got through it ok. Malts weren't so good. Band ok, and away. By hell, our officers abandoned us as soon as it was over. 25 men and equipment in one vehicle, stuffed in anyhow. Dumped at B.H.Q. Messed about. Finally got back. Good God, how awful. I'm thoroughly sick of it all. Don't fancy the sight again. Same old faces, etc.

TUESDAY, 16th

Well, the old round again. Stags, short grub, damp billets, no lights but candles. Bloody fine state of affairs, by cripes. The usual petty quarrels and bickering, dislikes, and cutting each other's throats. Had alarms last night. Got up 2 times. Bombs fell close by. Hell, the Junkers came over about 1, 000 feet up. Heavies engaged. No fighters, lights, or light A.A. Could have hit it easily, but were ordered not to fire. Bloody daft policy. The blast of a 1, 000-pounder knocked us flat. By hell, it put the wind up us. Yes, Ma'am! About 30 yards away in a field. Made a nice hole. Another stick fell across the infantry camp. Made a mess of billets and men alike. We opened up, as some of the others did. The Junkers came down and machined us. Bit unhealthy that! He was bloody accurate too! Anyhow, he got away.

WEDNESDAY, 17th.

On leave today. Had 4 alerts, none of importance. Coming in, 6 destroyers, 2 cruisers, a battleship, and 2 merchantmen. 8 Beau fighters brought them in. Should be more mail from Alexandria, they say. On their way in, they intercepted and sunk 2 Italian cruisers. H.M.S. Sydney and Dunedin sunk with an enemy raider. Bad losses now. Japs issue ultimatum of surrender to "Hong Kong, " but they will resist to the last man. Japs occupy "Guam." Set foot in the Philippines, Malaya, Sarawak, Borneo, and numerous islands. Fierce fighting. Resistance by Chinese, British, and Yanks. Outlook is not good for Malaya and Singapore. U.S.A. fleet and air force doing well, in full operation. Russians counter-attack "Kalinin." "Rostov" retaken. They've recaptured 100s of towns and villages, etc. The Gerry is in full retreat. Looks pretty good. Similar in Libya. The British are driving "Rommel's" forces west. Huge tanks used and heavy losses. Went on the local wine. Finished off the bottle. Felt pretty good. Went to the V Hotel. Not bad. Dames ok, cheap mungy.

THURSDAY, 18th.

Up at 8:00. Wash, shave, and breakfast by 10:00. Ah! Plenty of leisure. Hell of a lot of rain. Pretty sloppy all around. Bloody damp in billet. Blankets and kit wet. 4 alerts. Came over low last night—Ju 88's. Hit the Drome last night, got a Wimpy. Burned like hell. Had a decent night, though. Some letters from Joan and Harry—October and December 1st. Not bad. My letter was overweight—2/7d. Like hell! I'd be broke for a month.

FRIDAY, 19th.

Raids last night. Hit the Drome again, got a plane on fire. Some pretty close here too. Bit unhealthy. Don in hospital, had neck and bronchitis problems. Between the grub and conditions, I guess it's understandable.

SATURDAY, 20th.

On leave tonight. 3 alarms. Some Junkers came in, dropped bombs, and beat it. Went to a concert at H.Q. Damned good, enjoyed it thoroughly. Saw Tiny. Got a bus to Sliema. Pretty wet, raining like hell. Went to a bar, hung about like a devoted dog. Buckshee grub, not bad. Stayed at Joe's. Went to a dance and saw Harry boozed as usual. Spewed all over the place—some laugh. Boy, oh boy.

SUNDAY, 21st.

Up at 10:00. Shaved at Joe's. Had breakfast at Bergia's. Hell, 1/8. Bit heavy for me. Bloody half a beer doesn't last long. Went to Valletta. Raid on. 6 Ju 88's flew over and down on docks. Dropped bombs and gunned. Hell to pay. Some barrage. The fleet opened up with "Chicago Pianos." Holy smoke, what a lot of shit went up. 7 brought down. Went to pictures, saw "Babes in Arms" pretty good too. And so home. Another raid. 30 planes came over. Bombs on docks again. Always out of range for us.

MONDAY, 22nd.

Raining like hell, everything wet and muddy. Blasted damp in billet. Rain comes through onto us. Cold as a bugger also. Heavy raids last night. Ju 88's again. By hell, Gerry's back in the Mediterranean alright. Raid this morning. 15 planes. 4 Junkers dived on Luqa. Hell of a barrage, fired like hell. 2 Me's brought down, Hurry bird also down. Received 8 letters from Joan, dated April and March. Old stuff that's been held up.

TUESDAY, 23rd.

Heavy raids again last night. Barrages put up, also night fighters. Raid this morning 120 planes came over. Ju 88's on docks and Luqa. Cripes! Some fun. 25 brought down. Bombs and gunning all over the place. Holy smoke, what a racket. Whee! The smoke settled finally. Planes burning on the Drome. 25 shot down (Gerry) and 5 Hurry birds down. 3-gun crews wiped out. 2 destroyers sunk and a cruiser. Hundreds of houses and buildings hit. And so, we wait for the next crack. Boy, it's great, we pumped over 1, 000 rounds up. British troops near "Benghazi." Gerry retreating there and in Russia. Japan's still advancing.

WEDNESDAY, 24th.
CHRISTMAS EVE "Kennelworth"

2 alerts last night. Bombs dropped by Ju 88's on Krendi strip. It's a decoy, though. I guess they're not aware of that yet. The bombs were very near the Klondike site. Well! Paul, the Maltese boy, brought 2 chickens for dinner tomorrow. Not bad ones. We exchanged 10 tins of Maconochie's for them. Good deal that. 12 crates of beer, a 6 lb. joint of pork, 90 fags each, oranges, nuts, and writing material from the Overseas League came for tomorrow. Frank and Joe stripped the chicken. Started on the beer, cleared up about 4 crates. Went to the canteen, won a Tombola line—7/6. Bought the boys a round. Lost 10 bob playing Brag.

THURSDAY, 25th.
CHRISTMAS DAY

Cold and grey day. Started on the beer about 9:00. Tyler and Slatts came back pissed from the village. Don's in hospital with boils and ailments. Too bad! Blood poison, I guess. 4 Christmas puddings from the Battery out of Battery funds. 1 pudding and 3 mince tarts from Fergy, the infantry cook. Also, 20 fags, nuts, and a crate of beer. All well pissed by dinner, wow! I knocked off about 10 pints, at 11d a pint, on the book. Played Brag. "Fergy" well out. Made up my losses. Bloody fine dinner at 2:00. Baked spuds, cauliflower (from fields), peas, chicken, pork, stuffing, etc. Bloody fine. Well cooked too! Mince pies, pudding, 6 bottles of fine beer (by Hammond and King), nuts, and oranges. We sang and smoked till our throats were sore. Rotten drunk. Played Brag like hell. A couple of raids, not much. Disconnected the phone and put it in the billet. Had a smack at Tombola, no good. We drank and ate until we couldn't move. By hell, what grub. Not often we have it, so we made the best of it. Old "Joe" drank 2 or 3 crates himself, and he wasn't oiled. Boy, can he take it and how. "Tyler" had to go to bed, he was pretty bad. It was a bloody fine Christmas. King came with a crate of beer buckshee. We brought some of King's own back, Q.M.S. etc. We had to put them to bed, they were so far gone, what a laugh. We ended up playing Brag until about 3:00. And so to bed.

FRIDAY, 26th

Woke up about 9:00, felt lousy, thick head. I was still pissed. All the boys felt lousy, so we all had a drink and felt better. Had breakfast. "George" couldn't cook, so "Joe" took over. Raid. 40 planes, 10 bombers, the rest fighters. The fighters knocked 2 of our Hurry birds down. They were ME 109s, about 30 of 'em. It was bloody disgusting. Our Hurricanes (2 of 'em) flew around in a circle at 6-8, 000 feet in formation and did bugger all, while the Ju 88s in relays flew in at 10, 000 feet and dropped about 10 bombs each on "Luqa" Drome, right smack on the loaded Wimpies. They hit 4 Wimpies, blew up, and burned out. The Hurricanes didn't take any notice, just kept on circling. We fired 12 rounds at 2 Ju 88s as they came over this way. We were damned close too. We were getting better with each shot. I was number 2, pulling around to them, then we had a stoppage. "Sid Manger" said it was mighty close. Well, "Luqa" was smoking like hell. Gerry sure fooled them. They expected it to be the docks again, but he smacked "Luqa" instead.

SATURDAY, 27th

We boozed last night, played Brag, etc. Up at 9:00. Alarm right away. 6 MEs came in low for a gunning attack. They came in near us. The sights didn't recognise them, but we did. We let them have it. Bloody close. They came back over the top. Me and "Frank" were laying there, and we let them have it again. Hell, my ears were bursting. They came in twice. The bloody hurricanes flew about aimlessly, doing nothing. They could have got those MEs easy, or at least got stuck in, but no, they flew around about 20 of them getting in our sights and hindering us. Hell, those fighters flew about as they pleased. Well, we opened on em the 4th time and hit one. He staggered and hit the dock somewhere. I knew we hit him. I saw him pull up, then his nose tipped over. We got off 84 rounds anyway and one hit besides. We defeated their objective- strafing. Bloody fine shoot though. They all said we were close. 2 more alerts, but they didn't come in. Some laugh though. Somebody stepped on the dog. Hell, he made more noise than the gun. "Bill" fell off the platform, hah!

SUNDAY, 28th

3 alerts last night. About 6 Ju 88s came in at 5, 000 feet, one after the other. They've got lights all around the strip, using it as a decoy. By hell, they fell for it and how! They came in at 5, 000 feet and dived right over "Khartour" down the strip, dropping 10 bombs each. The first one we saw plainly. We gave him 17 rounds and hit him 6 times. He burst into flames and crashed into the sea. The crew bailed out. The second one, we gave 20 rounds. He returned our fire; his bullets were hitting the billet 40 yards away. The bombs all hit the strip. Good bombing alright. Had there been anything there, he would've smashed it all. A total of 60 bombs fell altogether. Well, we crippled a third one. He flew out over "Kalafrana." The Bofors there finished him off. What a crack-up. Wow! Lit the country up. The others didn't come low enough. They smacked "Hal Far" instead. We were up until 3:00. Boy, what a kick though, and what a target. A swish first, then his engines roared on. I felt my hairs rise. Cripes! He was as big as a house, 50 yards away. We smacked him right in the guts as he banked. Boy, did he come down.

MONDAY, 29th

Up at 9:00. Still on the beer. Been drinking for a week now. Feel great though, although I can feel the strain of late nights, beer, and bombs. They smacked the strip again last night. 4 Ju 88s. We belted off 30 rounds and claimed 2 hits. 1 came down over "Ta Qali." I won't bother to go on leave. I'm sick of it. Bugger all to do when one goes to town. Rather stay and be in the fun. A plot of 60 came over this morning. 30 Ju 88s bombed Luqa Drome. We caught one coming out of a dive. We gave him 40 rounds, and he was hit. He came down somewhere. The crew bailed out. The Hurry birds mixed it and shot a few down. That's about 4 we've shot down and a total of about 15 bombers in a week. About 3 Hurricanes lost, a searchlight and gun crew were wiped out. About 15 men (R.A.F) on Luqa were killed and 8 Wimpies destroyed. Hell, did they go up in smoke. Yeah! The Navy in the Harbour put up some fine barrages. My head was singing and ears were bulging from concussion. As master layer, I get most of the blast and was almost blind last night, couldn't see anything. I couldn't move through the nervous strain.

TUESDAY, 30th

We were up until 3:00 last night. They had the lights on the strip. 2 Ju 88 planes were about. I could hear one to the south a good way off, then suddenly a swishing noise. The crafty sod. The other was to attract our attention while number 2 shut his engines off and dove in. But I heard him and saw him. We were in our seats and on him. We got him with the 6th shot. He crashed at sea. His bombs fell about 100 yards off. The blast made my nose bleed. He returned our fire but was out of range. 4 raids today. We got off 40 rounds at 6 Ju 88s. They flew over "Luqa" and out at "Filfla" (small Isle to the south). We got 2 hits. The second raid was at about 4:00. We were just having tea in the pit. 6 Ju 88s came in from the north. Could see them in formation, gradually coming around to Luqa. Well, all hell broke loose, good God, it was terrific. There were 20 ME 109s above them like bees, 25 Hurry birds waiting for them. Every gun on the island let go. Wow! I had earplugs in, bloody good job too. We had a dirty big Ju in our sights. I saw his eggs come out, heard the whistle, whee! Here it is, I thought. I was paralyzed; what was the good? I'd be too late to duck anyway. We had a stoppage, too, to make things worse. Well, the bombs hit all of Luqa, some 50 yards away, some on the strip. One of our gun billets was smashed. A Malt was killed near here. A bomb hit a Wimpy with a 4, 000 lb bomb on it. Cripes, what a blast! It blew 10 other Wimpies up with it, so 11 in all were destroyed. Half the town blew up too. We fired 85 rounds, changed barrels. The barrel was smoking, it was so hot. Hell, what a do!

Then, I tripped over an empty case and busted my ankle. I'm laid up now. Of all the lousy luck. The pain was terrific. Went to bed.

WEDNESDAY, 31st

Well, had a good night. 2 alerts. Junkers flying about all night at about 5, 000 feet. I think they've got wise to the strip. They're not bombing it. Had orders to fire single shots because of shortage of ammo. We've fired 500 rounds in a week. I guess it soon mounts up. The predictor is out of action. Our Sergeant is no bloody good at it; he made a hash of a shoot. I went sick. Saw M.O. Went down by donkey cart. I haven't shaved in 3 days hell, I looked good. Anyway, he excused me from all duties. I'll get about though. Buggered if I can stay on my back. Grub's ok. Bloody cold these days it's surprising. Cold as Glasgow. Plenty of rain and clouds. Ideal weather for Gerry. Wrote several letters home. Haven't received any yet from home.

1942

JANUARY

THURSDAY, 1st

Will it end this year? I say it will. Ok, we shall see. About August or sooner. I shall be home for Christmas, ok, it's a bet. Some heavy raids last night. A plot of 56 came in, sailed right overhead. Stukas, Ju 88's. By cripes, we fired 45 rounds and the heavies put up a terrific barrage. The bombs hit "Luqa," "Hal Far," "Ta Qali," and all the dromes. Set about 4 planes alight.

FRIDAY, 2nd

A 1, 000 lb. bomb hit the "Breconshire" last night. Killed 20 men on board. They are a rocket bomb, a queer roaring noise when they explode. All the dromes were hit again. Some Wimpies destroyed. The 3.7 guns on the hill nearby are very active. The blast has busted all the windows and cracks have appeared in our billet. 4 alarms today, about 40 planes in all. They were in range, but the blasted Sgt. is yellow. Wouldn't let us fire. He made sure he got well down while the bombers passed overhead to their objective. There were about 10 bombers. Junkers 88 dive; some of our own fighters up. Naturally, it's suicide to send em up. They are no match for these Messerschmitts. About 30-40 Me's cover the bombers as they come over.

SATURDAY, 3rd

Well, they pounded hell out of us last night. About 16 bombers came over. They dropped about 10 bombs each, D.A. 500 lb. and 250 lb. A stick fell about 200 yards from here, in fact, all around us. By hell, and us in this stone billet, freshly made with a tin roof. The shrapnel smacks down on it and bounces off with a hell of a smack, and during the day, wow! The barrages are terrific. Shrapnel comes singing down. Lumps as big as your fist. As I had the first bomber in my sights today, I could see the shrapnel out of the corner of my eye. Well, in that raid today, 4 bombers coming out of their dive were in range. We gave the leading plane 40 rounds. He burst into flames. That was 2 to us, anyway. It's still bloody cold. We dress in all we've got, plus overcoats, balaclavas, and gloves. By hell, it's cold at night. I go to bed fully clothed, plus 5 blankets, and am waking up every hour shivering. Apart from that, the damp comes out of the walls and drips from the tin roof. The blankets are wet as a result.

SUNDAY, 4th

My foot is still a bit stiff. Can't go on leave, so I handle number 2 in action. I can manage that ok. Weather's still cold. "Fox" gone to field R.A. We now have "Hammond," a bloody nancy boy, and "Logan," just as bad. Talk of leaders, hell's delight, they are a couple of spineless chimps, Oxford drooling snobs. Well, "Slatts" handles this sight. We all like him. The Sgt. is hopeless as #1. He can't take it. There are only a few of us that can stand up to it. Well! Maybe I'll crack up soon if this continues. It's bloody nerve-wracking, especially at night. About 50 planes came over today. The fighters went in, and boy, what a sight. Right through the barrage, then the guns stopped firing, though they got 3 bombers. Me 109's came down and smacked 5 Hurry birds down. The sky was full of planes and parachutists. About 10 planes came down. One fell near us, a Ju 88. It blew up and burned. When we got there, it was a heap of ruins. We picked up the pilot, a Gerry about 28, single, Iron Cross. Quite nonchalant, didn't give a damn. Anyway, the drome was hit. Couldn't see it for smoke and dust. About 6 planes went west.

MONDAY, 5th

Hell, what a night! I went to bed about 10:00, then a raid started. It lasted until about 2:00. About 26 Ju 88's came over. It was terrific. They dropped sticks of 12 everywhere. It was a duet between bombs and the A.A. 4 sticks fell around here. I could hear them coming closer, closer, until the last one. By cripes, it put the wind up me. D.H. also and 1, 000 lb. This morning we found 3 pillars in our billet, cracked and leaning out. Big cracks and chunks out of the walls. This billet won't last long. I guess we'll have to evacuate soon. There are 30 D.H. bombs around here besides 100's of anti-personnel bombs. We've had it day and night for 3 weeks now. About 25 bombers and 10 fighters have been shot down. We've lost about 20 on dromes and about 12 fighters. In Libya, the British have captured "Bardia" and as far as "Tripolitania." Everything is going fine there. The Russians are still advancing. The Japs are gaining everywhere. "Manila" has fallen. The Chinese are preparing an army. "Churchill" confers with "Roosevelt" in the U.S.A. Results- 26 nations agree to fight side by side until the Nazis fall. "Wavell" appointed commander-in-chief of Eastern operations with U.S.A. chief as assistant.

TUESDAY, 6th

Pretty lousy weather. Low cloud base, driving rain. Still, we had 8 alarms. A single plot each time. The heavy A.A. brought 2 Ju 88's down yesterday. At 4:00, we got orders to move. Unknown destination. Everything to be taken. So, here we go again. It's raining like hell. I can see what's coming off. Now for organization. Well, we packed our kits by candlelight. There's mud and slime everywhere. We all went over to the canteen. Most of us were pissed. "Joe" bought 4 crates. He gets the money from somewhere. The whole of "Krendi" guns are moving, 5 of them. Our C.O. was about. Well, 30 boxes of ammo had to be lugged and carried. God, what a job, in rain and muck. At 11:00 the first truck arrived. All kit was squashed on. A tower came, got stuck. Another to pull it out while pulling the gun out that got stuck. So, 2 trucks and a gun were stuck. After digging, sweating, swearing, and wet through, we finally got them out. Refused an order, so I and the gun team were put under arrest. The officer wanted us to carry ammo hand in hand. Bloody swine! Well, we got going. We're for "Hal Far, " the fighter and bomber drome. Good God, of all places. That's where the Luftwaffe aims for. For 3 weeks without stop, he's bombed this place, so they're putting 20 Bofors around it. They've spotted a concentration of 87's and 88's on Sicily. They've got the wind up, so have the gun crews. All the boys are on the beer and wine. They are all grumbling. After all they've been through. A year now of hell from Gerry and yet they stick us on the hottest spots. It's bloody suicide on this place. Well, we got to our position, on the edge of the drome. Planes all over the place. Bloody huge craters everywhere. D.A's buildings in ruins. Some of the boys are dead scared. This battery is going to pieces. Some are looking mighty bad, after the beer etc. Well, I've never been so drunk so often in all my life. Well, in rain and mud, we got the gun into action, ammo off, kit off, all out in the open, no cover. Beds, blankets, clothes all got soaked. We revolted again. A sergeant major put us under arrest. No billets or cover, just an open field. Not even a tent was sent. So, we stood under some trees, miserable, wet, and tired. Hell, I'll never forget it. So came the dawn. George managed some tea and a sandwich. We got a tent later. 10 men in a tent supposed to hold 6. Kit was wet and everywhere. What a life, by hell! Do I appreciate home now! I slept in all my wet clothes. 6 Ju 88's made a dawn attack on the drome. We fired 80 rounds. He machine-gunned and bombed. 2 were brought down. We could hear the bullets hitting the stones and whining off. One came down to about 500 feet, we could see the bombs easily, even to the fins. The blast stunned us for a while.

WEDNESDAY, 7th
"Hal Far" Fighter/Bomber Drome

Bloody cold and windy with squalls etc. The tent won't stay down. Had to get up at night and tack her down. There's about a foot of mud in the tent. We have one candle and one primus stove. We do our cooking also in the tent. By hell what conditions!

THURSDAY, 8th
Much quieter now. A few raids of 1 only at a time. They aim for the Dromes. Our R.A.F. with 12 Blenheim's went out at daylight and bombed the Sicilian Dromes. Then Wimpies, about 10 at night, dropped incendiaries, H.E's, and 4, 000 lb bombs. Played hell! Destroyed 26 Ju 52's, a troop carrier, about 10 Ju 88's, and 10 Ju 87's. Played hell with the ground. Anyway, it's made a difference as they've stopped the Blitz. According to R.A.F. observers, Gerry has evacuated Sicily. Hope so. Russians are 50 miles from "Smolensk." The war is going well. All signs of collapse this year. Haven't heard from Joan for 2 months. I guess

the Blitz has stopped the "Sunderland's" coming in. "Tripoli" bombed every night without stop. Wimpies with 2-ton bombs, by cripes! I've seen these things on "Luqa" hell what a size and blast! Whee!

FRIDAY, 9th

We got the telephone in tent. Up at 8:00. Shaved in mug. Serves a lot of purposes, these mugs. Still raining and cold. Bloody cold in bed. Haven't taken a bath for weeks or even a change. Still fairly quiet, only a few alerts. Very quiet. Our people are operating like hell. A stalemate in Libya. No pay as yet.

SATURDAY, 10th

Same again. By cripes, what a life! Bloody awful conditions we're under. "Slatts" absent without leave. He chucked his stripes in. He's a gunner in the stores. "Brad" is gone to Luqa. A new bombardier and lance bombardier coming here. "Lewsly" gone home okay. "Don" still in hospital. The team is breaking up slowly. Been with "Slatts" over a year now. What a pack of stupid bloody officers we have. "Hammond" is like a milk sop. The old school tie is strangling him and "Logan." Holy smoke, they're hopeless. Leaders of men, they'd have been purged long ago in the German army. Got paid 12/6.

SUNDAY, 11th

Well, the days are passing fairly quickly. I'll be damned glad to get back to "Krendi." This Battery is going to pieces. Some of the blokes in hospital, others going to pieces, others the beer and wine, others absent without leave. They're not much good for anything. They've had their whack of action. About time some fresh blood took over.

MONDAY, 12th

Had a lousy night. About 24 plots on the board. We weren't manning. Went to bed, but the Ju 88's dropped sticks of 10 all around the Drome. By cripes, there was havoc. The noise was terrific between the guns and bombs. Some fell amongst the Hurricanes, about 100 yards away, destroyed about 5. The new

Sgt. and L.B. came. Not bad guys. Brad has had a stripe taken from him (inefficient). I've been given a stripe. Me, of all people. Why, I can't see it! Oh well, they'll have it back shortly. Also "Johns" and "Carver." I guess I shall move to another site. 6 raids today. Bombs on "Luqa" all day. No opposition. No Hurricanes up at all. Good gad! They come in as they like. About 6 Ju 88's and 10–15 Me 109s. The Hurricanes are no match for 'em.

TUESDAY, 13th
"Hal Far"

About 4 alarms last night. Usual thing, bombs all around us. Some of the boys are losing their nerve. They're sleeping in a huge cave near the sea. It's about 40 feet down. All the Maltese living near sleep and live there. Well, I'll try not to start that! Once one does that, one can't stay away. Well, about 12 Ju 88's and Breda 20 dive-bombed us today. Machine-gunned us as they came down. About 40 H.E's fell amongst the dispersed Hurricanes. Bad bombing though, only 2 were hit and burnt out. We fired 5 rounds. Had stoppage. Hell of a moment to see these huge bombers diving down overhead and unable to fire at them. Well, they got away. Later, 3 M.E.'s came over. We gave em 74 rounds. They tackled a "Glen" Recco coming in. We shot one down. The "Glen" shot another down. 2 more came in. The Glen crashed in "Sliema, " and not a bloody Hurricane took off to help the "Glen." Bloody shame, she was outnumbered. Talk of air cooperation, wow! The A.A. are doing all the work. That was the 80th enemy plane shot down by A.A. The Gerry comes in and does just what he likes. No wonder we're making a hash of everything. Hell! They haven't learnt anything yet.

WEDNESDAY, 14th
Heavy raids last night. About 10 planes crossed the coast. "Hal Far" and "Luqa" got hit. A lot of planes burnt out. The Wimpies and Swordfish are operating alright through every night. The Swordfish from here smashed up a large convoy last night. Wimpies are battering "Tripoli" and "Naples." Also, Dromes on "Sicily" by Blenheim's. 7 alarms today. Heavy rain and clouds.

Base at 6, 000 feet, sometimes 2, 000 feet. The bombs come, can see them easy but can't see the planes. We've beaten them, and we're stuck in the pit hoping for the best. On leave. I have about 25/-. No chance to buy anything. Haven't been on leave for 5 weeks. Rain and raids, also moving about prevented that.

THURSDAY, 15th

Plenty of raids again. A stick of 5 50 lb bombs fell about 50 yards away. Luckily, most were duds. Bloody huge caps, noses, and the bomb casings fell all around us. By Christ, they were whizzing over from all directions. Old "Bill" got under the gun, "Hammond" fell flat in a welter of mud; I didn't move in time, it was too late! A piece weighing 300 lbs. fell 10 yards away. Splattered us all with mud, stones, everything. Good gosh! It was nerve-wracking. Well, they hit 4 planes on the Drome. They burnt out. They were out of range for us. And so passed the day. By hell, the boys are going to pieces. Some are on 5 days' leave. I guess we shall soon. Rumors of the Battery moving again. It's about the 50th time. Last night, flares and parachute mines were dropped on "Fort Ricasoli, " as of old. They do the damage, the mines. Hell, Valletta is good proof of that. Russia is still driving Gerry back. Russians are about 60 miles from "Smolensk." British capture "Sollum, " 20, 000 prisoners taken. Seem to be doing okay there.

FRIDAY, 16th.

Monday the 12.1.1942 I was made up. This is for reference in case of accidents. Fairly good night last night. 1 alarm. We were duty gun, so 4 of us slept in the pit. Good kip. Fairly warm and dry today, hardly any rain. This Sgt. is a sod for work. Good head though. Built telephone pit today, lots of sandbagging. Had 1 alarm this morning. Hurricanes at long last intercepted and drove the plot off. Another in the afternoon, 15 plus. 22 Hurry birds up, but as usual they were miles away when the 3 Ju 88's dive bombed "Luqa". Then the fighters went in, but the Ju 88's were too fast for 'em. I think they engaged. Got paid. On orders as regards my promotion. Believe to be going to Sgt. Collins' sight. Should be ok there.

SATURDAY, 17th.

Raining like hell again. Mud and slime everywhere. Hellish conditions. 4 alarms, bombs dropped. "Taylor" working like mad, build this, build that. Whee, I'll be happy to get away. Ration cart came for me at tea time. Go to "Collins'" sight. Damn nice chap, big fella, weighs about 16 stone. I knew most of the boys: "Gorbould," "Curtis," "Hudson," and "Bachelor" well. Sleep in a tent with them.

SUNDAY, 18th.

Going well so far. Rota lists and colors so far, only job. Nice lot of chaps on here. Heavy raids. 47 hostile planes came over. Hurry birds went in. Still rain and mud. Bloody awful conditions. Can't do anything.

MONDAY, 19th.

Very cloudy. 70 hostile aircraft came over and dive-bombed a convoy coming in. They missed them. Boy, what a racket. Pom Poms, A.A, bombs, roar of about 50 dive bombers. Hell, it was terrific. 4-1, 500 lb. bombs in a stick dropped near us. 1 died and a few gunners were injured. Hell of a blast. A Malt jumped on me! Well, we've been at it all blasted day. The boys' nerves are all to hell; in fact, the whole Battery. They've stood too much of it. They always get the hottest sights. Rumors of the 59th leaving the Island again. Yeah, and how. What a hope. Well, 3 Merchantmen and 6 of the fleet came in ok. They say there are a lot of troops aboard.

TUESDAY, 20th.

Every bloody meal time there's an alarm! No peace at night or day and never a meal without an alarm. On guard last night with "Smudge." Hell, they were over every hour. 3 or 4 sticks fell close to here. Could hear them whine. We were duty gun too. Fairly bright today. 15 Ju 88's came over Docks and left.

WEDNESDAY, 21st.

Well, I'm making out pretty good as regards job etc. Starting pit at present. We have only a foot-high wall of stone as protection; of late, bomb splinters have been falling near or in the pit. Must have some protection against this and blast. 5 alarms today. 15 Ju 88's and 20 fighters came over. Dived over the pit and onto the Drome. Hit the runways. About 5 Hurricanes, 1 Albacore, and a Swordfish were hit and destroyed. They were about 150 yards off. We have Hurricanes and Swordfish all around us, so naturally the Gerry goes for this part. We couldn't fire. He came out of the sun; couldn't see him. Heard him and the bombs though. On leave. Set out in the middle of leave. A Ju 88 came over. I saw his eggs come. Hell, I thought they were right for me, but they fell about 200 yards off. A few Hurricanes went up in smoke.

THURSDAY, 22nd.

3 alarms last night. About 10 bombers came over in plots of 1 each, laid mines etc. But I slept at "Vernon's." Fairly good kip. 4 alarms today, on "Hal Far" again. By hell, it is continuous, without a break. It's bloody nerve-wracking. The boys are all to hell. The way they crouch in fear at the sight of the bombers diving. Well, they have my sympathy. Can't help it; they are not made of iron. By hell, it's shook me up more than I'd like to say. Much more of this and we'll all go nuts. Strong rumors of going home again. Ship supposed to be being fixed up for troop carrying. Ah! I guess it's bull like the rest of the rumors. I doubt if we'll leave until this war is over. Japs are progressing out east. Using a lot of bombers of all types. Looks precarious for "Singapore." Russians retaken "Majaisk." Still advancing. Operations held up in "Libya." Very bad storms etc. And so it goes on. Mud, wet, poor grub, bombs, and horrible conditions. Isn't life sweet!

FRIDAY, 23rd

"Hal Far"

Hell of a night. About 13 alarms. Our tent is about 50 yards from the edge of the Drome. A big stone wall between us. Alarm at breakfast again, and then right throughout the day. 6 Junkers came over. God, what a sight! See em about 5 miles off, all abreast, slowly droning on. No fighters to intercept them and no A.A. About 15, 000 feet. We could only crouch down, watching them come on dead for us. Then they tipped their noses into a dive. I was fascinated; couldn't keep my eyes off them. Saw a string of 10 bombs each leave them. Could see the bombs grow larger, larger. The noise was appalling. 3 Swordfish, an Albacore, and a Hurricane went west. They fell about 200 yards away.

SATURDAY, 24th.

Again, the same. Heavy raids last night. Sticks dropped on the Drome. Hell! Can't get a decent sleep. The same all day, 15 bombers altogether. Again, the watching and waiting. We're getting so good now we can judge where the bombs will fall. I've watched them through the glasses (binoculars), watched the traps open and the bombs come out and down. About 50 aircraft came in today. All smacked this Drome. They don't touch Luqa these days. It's the Swordfish based here that's doing it. These Swordfish have been smashing up the convoys going to "Rommel."

SUNDAY, 25th.

Heavy again last night and all day. 5 Ju 88's and about 18 Me's 109 came in and great surprise, the Hurricanes actually went up and intercepted them. What a scrap, wow! 5 Hurricanes were shot down, 4 Me's and a Junker. Boy! The air was filled with planes coming down and parachutists and bombs. The bombs hit the Drome; an Albacore went up in flames.

MONDAY, 26th.

Fairly quiet last night, but had a lousy sleep. Keep on dreaming of raids, Ju 88s and bombs. I got a chest cold, the old phlegm brand. It remains cold and raining. Lousy conditions. The Predictor is useless, so they are taking it away. We are now an open sight gun. Two men were taken away: "Tom" and "Fitz." The Sgt. here is a damned fine chap. About 6'4" and 15 stone. Played for Bristol Rugger. Damned fine disposition. The Russians are doing well, nearly at the Latvian border. Japs set foot at several other places. A danger to Australia.

TUESDAY, 27th.

Pretty rough again last night. About 15 bombers crossed the coast. The moon is nearly full. Bombs dropped nearby on the Drome. Hell of a racket.

WEDNESDAY, 28th.

Can't get much sleep these nights. Blasted heavy A.A. and bombs, the JU's coming over low. Expecting bombs every moment. Doze off, then crash—bombs. Doze again, crash! A.A that's off duty gun. When on duty gun, it's worse. In pit all night. Freezing bloody cold these nights too. North wind. Wow! Had about 7 JU 88s come over. Dive-bombed us. Bombs fell all around, also hundreds of incendiaries. They scattered them everywhere. They fell within 10 yards of the pit. They burned fiercely, then exploded. First time he's dropped them during the day. We heard the whistle and thump; didn't know what to make of it. Got off 3 rounds. One of our Bofors in good range brought a JU down. That's a total of one a day now. No Hurry birds up as usual. It's no use; they only get shot down by Me's. These new Me's do 450 mph, also new Italian Macchis. The Me's have 1, 500 hp engines. Also, sleek and small. They knock hell out of the Hurry birds. 6 Hurricanes were brought down yesterday, and no enemy aircraft down. Bit expensive that!

THURSDAY, 29th.

Went on leave, not bad. Went to the pictures twice. Messed about. Met some of the boys. "Hal Far" bombed again. The Swordfish and Wimpies have been operating every night so far. Swordfish from here (Hal Far) and Wimpies from Luqa. The Swordfish have smashed a convoy each night so far. Doing bloody fine work, these boys. Hurricanes are operating at night also. They go over Sicilian Drome's and smack the bombers as they take off and land. 12 a night so far.

FRIDAY, 30th.

Bloody awful weather. Blinding sleet and rain, and cold as hell. Low cloud. Had about 10 alerts; they came over low and dropped stuff on Docks and Drome's. They can't leave this joint alone. "Joe" on 5 days leave. I'll go next leave. I'll be damned glad to go too. I'll get some sleep. A change from this hell hole. New Blenheims and Maryland's came in. Russians still driving on, killing the Gerry off quite fast. "Rommel" recaptured "Benghazi." He's getting reinforcements now. Three convoys have arrived here this week. They're getting through okay. The Japs are pushing on too. Can't seem to stop 'em. Votes of confidence for "Churchill" in the House of Parliament. Somebody's getting tired of him. Too much of a dictator, I guess, so he's called his gang together for a back me up vote.

SATURDAY, 31st.

Much the same. Rain, wind, and mud. Plenty of it. Lots of raids last night. Full moon, but clouds very low. The Ju's came down to 2, 000 feet, buzzing overhead. Dropped stuff on "Hal Far" Docks and "Luqa." Pretty rough all day today. About 10 alerts. Cloud base about 1, 000 feet, Ju's just above it. Hellish! Can't see 'em.

FEBRUARY

SUNDAY, 1st.
Same last night. Stuff fell very near. Still cold and wet. Grubs pretty poor. Not enough of it. Invariably, I leave hungry. About 14 men eating here now at T.H.Q. Blasted mail is slack. Over 2 months now since I last heard from home.

MONDAY, 2nd.
Clear today. 20 Ju came over. Dead over the pit. Dived, dropped stuff all around us. Bombs, incendiaries, anti-personnel, and machine gun. Hell of a sight. Some of the boys look terrible. I rallied on. It was hell on earth, like a battlefield. Bofors, Lewis, Bren, Heavy A.A., and bombs, besides the bombers machine-gunning. Not a bloody Hurricane went up. Cripes, it was awful! We fired 150 rounds. A few were brought down.

TUESDAY, 3rd.
Pretty rough again last night. A stick fell near us. Right across the Monastery. Blew us off our beds in the tent. Hell, some sensation. About 30 yards away. Bad visibility today. Bombers came over in ones. One came low; we got off 15 rounds. So did the rest. Orders are to fire about 5 rounds, single shot, to reserve ammo. What a policy. No bloody use, single shot; these Ju's are too fast, 350 mph, we'll never get them that way. Single shot, bah! Auto, yes, a chance there. Most of the crew are paralyzed. Only 3 of us man the gun. Poor sods, their nerve is gone. Some T.H.Q. staff run like hell to shelter on an alarm.

WEDNESDAY, 4th.
About the same again. Pretty heavy last night. A stick fell near the tent. Smacked the Monastery. Blew us off our beds. By hell, it had us paralyzed. Bits of shit flying in every direction. Getting used to dirty big Junkers diving over the gun onto the Drome. It's an awful sight, though; can see the bombs like strings of sausages leaving the planes and not a Hurricane anywhere. The Me's patrol

overhead along the coast at about 50 feet above the water. They dare not send Hurricanes up. The Me is fast, wow! They shot down 2 Blenheims returning from operations, in full view of the Island, also a seaplane in the bay.

THURSDAY, 5th.

As above. The Me's patrol regularly now. It's bloody bad. Not a fighter up. About 60 odd planes came over today and bashed the Docks, Luqa, and us. I'm sick of it all, day after day. No encouragement, just A.A. We got a Ju 88 today.

FRIDAY, 6th.

Heavy raids last night. Can't get much sleep. The guns and bombs play hell. A lot of D.A.'s dropped last night. They've been exploding all day, fairly close too. We get the blast. We're moving tomorrow, Luqa again. Ah well, we're all glad. It's bloody terrific here on Hal Far, about the hottest spot of all. The 225 Battery is taking over. We're taking H.P.'s at Luqa.

SATURDAY, 7th

"Luqa"

Packed up, etc. 3 lorries, and away. All 4 guns. And so to "Lynmouth" on the west side of the Drome. Not far from the Wimpies, Blenheims, etc. Still, it's a good pit, etc., also predictor. Sweat and struggle to get the stuff down. We've taken over from the Malts. They were all cursing and blinding, etc. Checked up on everything; all ok. About 3 alarms lasted 7 hours. 1 of them, the Me patrol, were over. It has stopped operations definitely; the planes dare not go out while they're about. We fired 7 rounds at a Ju 88. About 10 came over. On 5 days leave tomorrow. The Battery messed up everything. No pay for me. What a bloody army. Got 2 letters from Joan, dated January 27th. All is well. She has received my proficiency pay: 8.19.0, not bad. Pretty bad weather over there. Snow and rain, etc.

SUNDAY, 8th.

Well! Started on 5 days leave. Naturally, they buggered my pay at Battery; it didn't even come. So, I borrowed 2 quid from "Will." Filled up my gas mask with small kit. Got away at 12:00 into Sliema. Put my kit in Joe's. Poor old Joe, ill with rheumatism. Well, mooched about, so on, pictures, etc. Bombs dropped on a street near my digs at night. Hell of a racket. Six people killed; cinema wiped out, also the dance floor at Regent.

MONDAY, 9th.

Slept until 10:00. Messed about. Met a lot of the boys. Gorged and drank down at the "Gut." Snooped about. Got tired of it. Went to TOC and read considerably. Went to dance; dames ok. Bed and grub ok there.

TUESDAY, 10th.

The raids continue day and night. Bombs dropped on "Qormi" killed 28 people. About 6 Ju 88's, none of our fighters about as usual. Went to the pictures again and so on.

WEDNESDAY, 11th.

Heavy raids last night. Hundreds of bombs dropped in the Harbour. A cruiser hit and sank. Bloody heavy batteries all around us at Sliema. What a racket. Could hear windows falling out. About 30 odd bombers came over. Bombs dropped on every important point on the Island.

THURSDAY, 12th.

Heavy raids last night. Can't get a hell of a lot of sleep between the A.A. and the drone of planes and bombs. So, I slept until about 1:00. Bombs on "Marsa." About 120 people killed. No opposition. About 50 Ju 88's came over, escorted by fighters, but none of our Hurricanes were up. It would be useless anyway. The Me's would mow them down. The Me's are carrying bombs also, one each. By cripes, there's been thousands of bombs dropped lately, whee! The Maltese are definitely hostile towards the English. They can't understand why there's no fight or opposition now. The Gerry

251

does just what he likes. The Me's patrol and stop operations by our bombers by day from the Dromes. They dare not go out. The Me's would soon pounce on them. So the Malts blame the English for it, understandably. There's a hell of a lot of Malts killed lately.

FRIDAY, 13th.
Got back ok. Got straightened up ok. We're moving to a new site again shortly. We are moving towards the strip where all the Wimpies are. They can't leave us at a peaceful site, oh no! Must stick us on top of this place, like Hal Far again.

SATURDAY, 14th.
Well, the Luftwaffe are still smacking us, day and night. Today he used about 15 Ju 88's and about 40 fighter escorts. The usual, start patrol on the coast. The Hurricanes fly one way, the Me's the other way. They caught a Glen coming in and shot her down. Damned rotten. They got a Blenheim yesterday, right on the base. Bombs on Luqa and docks, also various towns.

SUNDAY, 15th.
Getting into shape on the site. It's a good pit, lousy sandbagging though on the part of the Malts. There's no telephone pit. Bit awkward. Means doing an hour stay at night. The boys on this site are a decent crowd. Pretty heavy bombing today. About 20 Ju's came over. We fired 6–8 rounds. I was firing. We hit a Ju smack in the guts. He came down in flames. The heavy A.A. fired right into a formation of 8. 4 came down. The Hurry birds got 1 and 2 Me's, pretty good! A formation of Ju 87's dive bombers came over, spiral dived on the docks; 2 shot down. Boy oh boy, what terrific dives, straight down vertically to about 10, 000 feet, then spiral to about 5, 000 feet. They hit Valletta and the docks. A terrible sight, and what a noise. The roar and whine of the dives and the A.A. about 100 Bofors besides the 15 or 20 batteries of heavy A.A. A cruiser was sunk in the harbour. About 50 bombs hit the city. The A.A. put them off their target. A cinema was hit with about 200 servicemen in it, and another cinema completely ruined.

MONDAY, 16th.

Heavy raids last night. About 20 bombers crossed the coast. A couple of lumps of shrapnel came through our tent, just missed one of the boys. Some more towns hit. Heavy casualties. About 20 people in one town killed. 2 Wellingtons on the Drome hit and destroyed. 2 were brought down. We fired 30 rounds. The Japs have occupied all of "Malaya" and "Singapore." The Russians advanced as far as the Polish border. They're killing off the Gerry by the thousands, capturing a lot of booty also. Stalemate in "Libya." The British are fighting before "Gazala." All quiet over England. The "Kittyhawks" are doing well over "Libya." The force of 15 "Kitties" destroyed 30 bombers and fighters. The German battleships "Gneisenau," "Eugen," and "Scharnhorst" got away up the English Channel and the north. 600 bombers and fighters failed to stop them.

TUESDAY, 17th.

Very heavy rains and bloody cold. Can't keep warm at night. I have 5 blankets, my overcoat, and I sleep in my pants, all to no avail. The bloody tent is no protection. My gut ache has come back. Oh hell's delight, that bloody agony again. It's no use going sick; nothing will be done for me. I'd have to walk about 3 miles, then I'd be given some dope or other. Besides this, I've picked up crabs from somewhere. I'm trying iodine. Hell, talk of agony, wow! And so it goes on, day after day. Rain, damp, discomfort, no decent rest, raids, raids, and more raids. Bloody tinned food every meal, not a bit of fresh stuff. No wonder my guts are bad, gee! I think I'll go nuts if this goes on. I'm getting mail alright now, thank God! Everybody's well at home. Dear old Joan, she's a damned good girl. May God grant that we both come through this safely. Very severe winter at home. Tons of snow, etc., still she's looking after herself.

WEDNESDAY, 18th.

Went on 24 hours leave. Pretty good. Plenty of mungy. Messed about in general. Went to the pictures. Didn't feel too good whilst the raid was on though. There were about 20 people in there. After that, another cinema was hit; I guess they don't fancy it. There were over 100 killed, mostly servicemen.

THURSDAY, 19th.
Continuous raids night and day. Pretty bad visibility. They dropped their bombs everywhere and anywhere. Most of the towns caught it.

FRIDAY, 20th.
On a system of 24 hours off, complete detachment every 24 hours. Pretty good. We fired every day so far at Ju 88's. A total of 90 aircraft came over today. They hit a few planes on the Drome. 5 Ju 88's shot down, also 2 Me's.

SATURDAY, 21st.
Weather is better. Bloody tent is torn to shreds. We are moving soon to another position. We brought a Ju 88 down today. Shot his tail off. Looked good to see him come down and the tail floating down after it. 3 bailed out and one chute didn't open. That's 3 today; also, an Me not 500 yards away fell to pieces in mid-air. Hurricanes' cannons got him. Hell, what a mess. The pilot couldn't be found.

SUNDAY, 22nd.
About 80 aircraft came over today, mostly Ju 88's in sixes and threes, diving overhead or out of the sun. They come from every direction. The Hurricanes go in and have a go, but the Ju is fast and armoured. They usually get away. The heavy A.A. are good, but if they get caught in a light A.A. barrage, they'll never come out. That's happened a good many times.

MONDAY, 23rd.
The raids have lasted all day for the last 3 days. Me's come over and patrol the coast, etc., watching for our bombers, etc. Our aircraft are grounded while they are about. They dare not take off. The Wimpies are operating at night.

TUESDAY, 24th.
Had orders to move ammo from the dump to the position. Of course, the efficient staff at B.H.Q. bungled the job. No carts. "Ken" and I walked to B.H.Q.; the cart had left. We walked back

to the dump, no cart. At 3:00 in the afternoon, it came. We moved 15 boxes out of the 90 that are there. Meanwhile, we had 6 alarms. In each, a force of 6 and 3 Ju 88's with about 10-15 Me's. escorting them came over and bombed "Luqa" and the docks.

WEDNESDAY, 25th.

On the fob again. But it rained like hell. I was in charge. The donkey boys wouldn't work, so I had to send them home. We moved 12 boxes. And so it goes on. These bloody boys do what they like. Our people won't commandeer them. Vital supplies are left waiting. Same with the rations. Half the gun sights can't get the guns owing to these donkey boys. We got soaked coming back, right through our overcoats. Had to change.

THURSDAY, 26th.

Raining like hell, driving rain. The tent is flooded again. There are about a dozen holes in the roof and sides, owing to shrapnel. And so our kit gets wet. Ah! We are very happy! Raids last night and today. Pretty rough. Bombs dropped nearby again, also on Valletta. Some people killed. We should move soon. It's a good position, plenty of dry-stone billets, etc.

FRIDAY, 27th.

Ju 88's came over low today. Bofors and Hurry birds got stuck in. Marvelous view we had; saw it all. The Ju came down nearby; they scraped the crew off the ground. We helped. An awful mess. 2 or 3 Kites on the Drome got hit. A convoy headed for Malta got sunk completely. They were our relieving 4T Batteries aboard. So, I guess we don't go home now. Hah! What a laugh.

SATURDAY, 28th.

Got paid. Can't go on leave owing to ammo. It has to be moved yet. Until it's done, I can't go on leave. Bloody luck!

MARCH

SUNDAY, 1st.
And here we go again. Same as usual. Lots of stinking Junkers over last night. Not much to report. About 28 bombers and 50 fighters came over and smacked the Docks etc.

MONDAY, 2nd.
Much as above.

TUESDAY, 3rd.
Finished off the ammo. Ok. Darn good billet. 3 in all. It will be a good sight. 48 raids last night, bombs dropped everywhere. Today about 30 Ju's came over with an escort of fast 109's. Our Hurry birds were up and 3 were shot down. 2 Ju 88's shot down. Those M.E's are too good. Poor old Hurry birds don't stand a chance. I saw the tail of one JU shot off. He came down nicely. About 5 planes burnt out on the Drome.

WEDNESDAY, 4th.
Went on leave. Good leave all around. Didn't cost much money. Sent off a registered letter to Joan. Bless her. Thank God she is ok. I must send a telegram and photo next time. About 20 Ju's over today and bomb carrying M.E's. They carry a 500 lb. bomb each, sods! They come whipping in and out, but these blasted Ju's sail right through the barrage, then tip their nose straight at us and come out. We belt away. We've fired an average of 20 rounds daily. Got several hits, saw 6 up to date come down. The night Fighter got one last night. It's really a hopeless policy, the Hurricanes go up once a day. They are useless.

THURSDAY, 5th.
Heavy battering last night. Didn't get much sleep. Had 30 bombers over with ME's and bomb carrier ME's. Bombs fell all around us. Fred got hit in the leg. Compound fracture, pretty bad. Shit fell all around us. It was a narrow escape for all of us. We engaged the leading plane. The other sods came in behind, took us

by surprise. Japs attack Java and bomb hell out of Australia. Russians doing well, still advancing. Stalemate in Libya.

FRIDAY, 6th.

About 30 Bombers crossed the coast last night. Bombs dropped everywhere. Fires started on Drome. Night Fighters were up but no interceptions. About 30 Bombers came over today in waves of 6 & 3. Also bomb carrying Me's. Bombed the Docks, Harbor and Drome's.

SATURDAY, 7th.

It's bloody awful. Every damn day they come over. We spot them about 15 miles out, about 6 Ju's with 5 or 10 fighters. They creep in at about 15, 000 feet and speed of 200 mph. They're heavily loaded. An ineffectual barrage goes up. None of our fighters go up and if there are, they manage to avoid the plot. In each raid there's 2 or 3 Wimpies hit and burning on the drome (they cost about 30, 000 quid each). We've lost about 15 this week.

SUNDAY, 8th.

16 Spitfires and 4 Blenheims came in today. Encouraging sight. The Spits looked bloody good, small and fast. This will shake up the Me's. They are supposed to come off a carrier outside. Also a convoy coming in. Heavy raid last night. None of us could sleep. Blasted guns firing, shrapnel whining and sticks of 10 bombs screaming down. It was terrific. He's dropping 1, 000 pounders also. Some more shrapnel came through the tent. We dare not light a candle now because of the light showing through the holes. Ha! They won't give us a new tent because we're moving soon. About 10 raids tonight and today. Planes hit again. We won't have a bloody plane left soon on this Drome. They're bashing Hal Far too. About 80 bombs fell there today.

MONDAY, 9th.

Got paid. I've got 4 quid now. Can't spend much these days. Must send flowers to Joan. No mail from her yet. Over a month now.

This Islands almost at a standstill. No operations by day, no mail coming in, Only a few Wimpies by night. The weather is lovely now, warm. We spend most of out time in the gun pit. We had 1 alert today. Yeah, all day, from 7:00 till 8:00. We have our meals one at a time. They're dropping stuff so big now we can follow em from the plane to the ground. The towns and villages are being smashed up horribly. The Japs have taken "Java", are near "Rangoon" and gaining in the "Philippines". They've just about taken the lot. The Russians are advancing. Gerry is throwing in reserves and spring troops of all sorts, Poles, Rumanians, Hungarians and Finns. Quiet over England. 5 million men under arms there and so it goes on day after day. Grubs very short now. Rations cut down. A bit of bacon between a slice of bread and cup of tea for breakfast, tin of maconochies 3 times a week, corned beef twice and fresh meat twice, for tea a bit of cheese or a sardine. We're pretty hungry as a rule. We go out and buy it, but we can't get anything in the villages, no bread, milk or anything. Everything is controlled.

TUESDAY, 10th.
Had a close shave again today. 3 Ju's dived at us, dropped stuff all around us. Shook us up somewhat! Pretty rough all day. 16 Spits and 3 Blenheims came in. Damned nice to see them. Came in from the carrier. 8 Ju's came over and dived on Luqa. They got 8 Wimpies. Some fire wow! Also, a 6 and a 3, about 45 bombers in all. Not a fighter up. I guess the Spits will make a difference.

WEDNESDAY, 11th.
Got orders to move. Had to hire a horse and cart to shift the small stuff because the Battery didn't have that sort of thing available. We went without grub because they had no transport for water. No trucks running now. Well! The usual mess up at moving. Had to manhandle the gun, predictor, and generator. Hell, what a job. Sweat and curse. Got to our new site at 2:00.

THURSDAY, 12th.
24 hours off. Went to Sliema. Heavy bombing again. Valletta hit again. 3 or 4 streets in Sliema smashed up. Lots of people killed also. All the Drome's again. More planes hit on Drome's. Ju's and Me's brought down by H.H. We fired about 200 rounds; it was a bit sticky at times.

FRIDAY, 13th.
The Spitfires are operating. Bloody great to see em up. They brought down 2 Me's. Boy, can they shift. They are a match for the Me's. About 3 plots, about 60 in all came over.

SATURDAY, 14th.
Rangoon and Java have fallen. Japs set foot on New Guinea. Big naval battles. We lost about 8 units of the fleet. Terrific force of men and ships used by the Japs. The Russians are still advancing.

SUNDAY, 15th.
Raids on a much smaller scale. The Me's don't patrol the coast as of old. The Spits have shaken them a bit. Still have the old gut ache every blasted day, a couple of hours after each meal. I shall go nuts if it lasts like this.

MONDAY, 16th.
Just about the same as yesterday.

WEDNESDAY, 18th.
Weather is damned nice now, plenty of sunshine. Almost finished the new pit. Used 2, 000 sandbags. Bloody fine position this. About a mile from Luqa and Safi strip where all the heavy bombers are. Yesterday, 8 Ju 88's dive bombed it and got 5 Wimpies. We fired; 1 came down. The Spits and the Hurry birds brought down an Me and a Ju. Mail very bad; haven't heard from Joan for 2 months or the rest of the family since before Xmas, almost 4 months now.

THURSDAY, 19th.

Weather okay. Pit almost finished. Got predictor set up, although it's out of action. The fitters came around and made it worse. It jumps for elevation 5 degrees, which is 3 degrees too many. Heavy raids throughout the day. About 30 bombers in waves of 3 and 6. The Spits and Hurry's engaged. A Spit shot down. A good many planes lost on Drome. Really, it's bloody shameful. They have 4 Spits up. If they had 20 with Hurry's, they could stop all this. But no! After 3 years, they still meander along. Although they have built underground hangars in Ta Qali. Rations are being cut down weekly. ½ a loaf of bread per man per day, 2 ½ oz. of sugar, 2 oz. of milk, a bit of bacon (tinned), about an inch long. 1 tin of sardines per 12 men for tea. Maconochies and bully beef 5 days a week. The meat market was hit by a bomb, so we go without meat now. We are hungry after each meal, and one can't buy meals in the villages.

FRIDAY, 20th.

Terrific dusk raid. 50 Junkers with about 30 fighters dive-bombed Ta Qali. Fighters on Drome. It was terrible. Waves of 10-15, 6-16. What dives! It was awful; the barrage was terrific. Also, all the light A.A. had a go. 4 were shot down. They dropped 4 each. They hit "Musta Drome" (the 3rd largest in the world) in Musta village nearby. They also hit all other surrounding towns, besides Rabat (holy city). The death toll was high, and the result was 2 Hurricanes hit on the Drome because the rest and the Spits are underground.

SATURDAY, 21st.

Not so bad last night. This morning, 8 Me 110's came over and bombed Ta Qali. The Hurricanes got 4. Later, 43 Ju 88's bombed Ta Qali, and then later, 50 more. What a sight. In all, 175 bombers have been over today. 15 dived on us, straight down. We worked like hell, fired 200 rounds. Shot 3 down. The heavies got 4 more. We could hardly see the bombers owing to dust and smoke from planes burning. One crashed a few yards away. A Ju 88; the crew burned with it. The sky was filled with parachutes, H.H. bursts, smoke, dust, and bombers. It was the heaviest raid so far. There were none of our fighters up. What a lousy policy. We could see the bombs leave the bombers. There are about 600 craters all around us. The shrapnel fell like rain. A piece hit Roy in the hat, clang, knocked him down. A small piece hit me in the back, ripped my jacket and shirt, cut my back. Lt. Morgan was killed. Bloody fine officer too. Valletta and Sliema are a terrible sight. Whole streets are down. Casualties are high.

SUNDAY, 22nd.

Small-scale raids today. 6 Ju's bombed Luqa, got 2 planes on Drome. Hurry birds shot an M.E down. Fairly quiet though. Took things easy. All leave stopped owing to raids. Received a telegram from Joan. All is well with her, thank God. No letters yet. Operations have ceased now. No bombers left here. All been wiped out. 9 Spits and 3 Blenheim's came in. Reinforcements.

MONDAY, 23rd.

Food getting worse. It's mostly corned beef, Maconochies, and bread. No crops yet, too early. Sent cable and registered letter to Joan. Russians doing well, taken Kharkov. Japs advancing in Butera near Mandalay, also in New Guinea. The U.S. bombs Jap bases with Flying Fortresses. Heavy clouds. Convoy coming in. 40 Ju came over low, one at a time, and tried to bomb it. The navy barrage brought 6 down; the Spits, 3. The total of the invasion the other day was 18 bombers down: 12 by A.A. and 6 by fighters. We lost 2 Merchantmen outside; the rest got into harbour safely.

TUESDAY, 24th.

Clouds still low but broke up a bit. As the sun came out, 12 JU's dive-bombed docks and surroundings. 1 brought down. They came over later in sixes and fives. Later, 20 JU 87 bombers came over and dive-bombed Hal Far and Luqa. We fired 96 rounds, had 3 misfires (faulty mechanisms). Boy! What a sight. 20 Ju 87's and 15 109 fighters. They dived vertical from 15, 000 feet straight down on us. A terrific sight. They dropped 3-500 pounders each. Me's came down on us and machine-gunned our position. We heard the bullets whine and slap into the sandbags. We dug em out later; there wasn't much damage. The grub is awful, getting worse. We're hungry after each meal. Nothing but bully beef and tinned Maconochies. Got 3 cards from Joan.

WEDNESDAY, 25th.

Heaviest raid of the whole war today. 75 Ju 88 and 45 Ju 87 dive-bombed the docks and Hal Far, also the Breconshire anchored outside. It was terrific. They came in waves of 15. We fired at Stukas, M.E's. The docks were absolutely blotted out with smoke, planes, and barrage. An oil tanker was hit and set on fire. Black smoke pouring from that, also the power station; also, 4 other boats of the convoy were hit and sunk in the harbour. I believe 2 were left untouched. So, after battling their way from England, they wind up by being sunk in the harbour.

THURSDAY, 26th.

Very cloudy today. They came over in ones. The Spits and the Hurricanes went in, but a pretty hopeless show. They are always outnumbered by M.E's. I went on leave. Valletta and Sliema are in a hell of a mess. Buildings and whole streets smashed flat.

FRIDAY, 27th

Had good leave. Sent registered letter to Joan with snaps and so on. The Japs threaten Burma. The Russians still advance. Heavy losses at sea for us.

SATURDAY, 28th

Bad visibility. Not much doing. A few desultory raids. Finished off pit, etc. We haven't fired much lately. They're leaving Luqa alone. They've just about smashed everything worthwhile. No operations now. I'm to go on an A.A. course soon. It will be a break, I suppose.

SUNDAY, 29th

Still heavy weather. 7 Spits, 4 Blenheim's, and 8 Beaufort's came in. Received letters from Norman and Joan. All okay. My sister May is in Vancouver now. The Breconshire was hit and sunk. The fighter policy is lousy. 2 or 4 Spits and 6 Hurry birds up. Useless! They will never learn.

Here you are! The boy himself. Minus the mighty grin. Too bad.

MONDAY, 30th

About the same. About 60 odd Ju's came over in singles. Bashed docks and drome's. Not much of interest today. Fired about 40 rounds.

TUESDAY, 31st.

Weather cleared up. The fighters got 7, and the A.A. got 2 yesterday—14 altogether. Not bad! Saw 3 Ju's come down and M.E. Spits also.

APRIL

WEDNESDAY, 1st.

Not too bad at night. Much quieter. No raids last night. Today – good visibility. 16 Junkers bash Ta Qali, 12 Luqa, 23 Stukas on Hal Far, and then 18 on docks. About a hundred altogether today. A lot of planes hit and burned out on drome. No fighters up as usual. They come in in bloody great bunches at about 15, 000 feet, and then into screaming dives. Usually can't see anything over targets; there's so much smoke and dust. The Stukas come straight down on top of us. We fired 85 rounds, got 1. They drop 3 each. By hell, the barrage is terrific overhead. The stuff whines down all around.

THURSDAY, 2nd.

On leave. Not a bad night. Got caught in a raid on docks—25 Junkers. Hell, the bombs came down like rain. What an awful racket. The dust was choking. It was a near thing for me. A 1, 000-pounder fell behind the club. Plaster, glass, and all sorts came down.

FRIDAY, 3rd.

Hell, last night about 75 bombers came over in ones. Dropped stuff all over. D.H's also. About 50 yards from gun. Bright moonlight. Beaus up, but they seem to do nothing.

SATURDAY, 4th.

Heavy bash again. About 100 bombers over. 20 bashed Luqa. We had a hectic time. Still, we got about 150 rounds up. Ah well. They are doing just as they like now. The M.E's patrol the skies. No fighters up. A Mosquito was shot down coming in. Although Wimpies and Beaufort's, also Beaufighters, are coming in nightly and going out the same night. So, the new planes are getting through okay. The Spits can't seem to get here in sufficient numbers, though. Well, we can't wonder at it. We lost the last convoy. He's got the whip hand, alright. Japs landed near Calcutta. Russians still drive on.

SUNDAY, 5th.

About the same, all day raids. Got orders to be ready by 1:00 to move to the gunnery school. Got ready, etc., but they didn't turn up until 6:00 at night. Had 4 big raids. About 60 bombers in all.

MONDAY, 6th.

Got to "Bugibba" okay. About 10 of us in all on the course: 3 Sgt, 3 Bdrs, and the rest like myself—lance jacks. Decent crowd too. Sgt. and Capt. Paul are our instructors. Start off with reveille at 7:00, PT at 7:30, breakfast at 7:45, parade at 9:00. Work till 11:00, break at 11:30, and so on. Courses on 40 mm. in every aspect. Not bad.

TUESDAY, 7th.

A good day. Courses went over well. The grub is fine, and so are the sleeping quarters. Had heavy raids yesterday and today. 80 Ju 88's came over in 4 waves of 20 each. Bombed the harbour. None of our fighters up, naturally. Bloody awful. Later, 100 came over. 40 of them were Ju 87's. They bombed the bay near us. By cripes, I was about 200 yards with the rest of the boys away from the V.P. They came within 500 feet of the water and buildings. They smashed up the hangars with a lot of engines inside.

WEDNESDAY, 8th.

Another 100-odd bombers came over. 20 Ju 87's smacked the bay here. Our school overlooks this bay. We're about 500 yards from the V.P. We manned the drill gun. Got off about 9 rounds. They were coming straight down the barrel. A bit unnerving. I could see the eggs leave and see em coming out of the corner of my eye. By cripes, it was sticky. 3 of my mates were seriously injured on heavies. Bomb fell near. A lot of the heavy boys here on courses. Well, things are mighty bad here in Malta. The cities around the dock area are devastated. The wreckage is terrible. Street after street laid to the ground. People living in shelters day and night. The atmosphere of the shelters is horrible. The raids are continuous, so they dare not open the shops. The cinemas are all closed; also, the businesses. No people about. Nearly all the boats are sunk in the harbour. The installations are crippled; the dromes are smashed up. Nearly all our fighters wrecked. The A.A. are slowly cutting down on rounds to fire because of an ammo shortage. No shipping can get to the island. Consequently, the food is being cut down weekly. Also, cigarettes and chocolate, etc. Also, spare parts and equipment. The Army - yep! I wonder how long it will last? Unless the British government does something soon, this little island is going to be in a bad way.

THURSDAY, 9th.

Still pegging away at the course. Gunnery in all its phases. Good. I'm somewhat behind. I can see that my neglect of interest in the past is going to let me down. Still, we shall see. About 200 Ju 88's and 87's and 50-odd fighter escorts came over today. The docks and drome's got hit bad.

FRIDAY, 10th.

Big day for me. I'm 24 today. Yowsah! Time marches on. Wonder what my 25th will show. Some 80-odd bombers over today. Terrific damage done to docks, buildings, etc. Numerous big fires about. Me's coming down low and machine-gunning all around. The hurry birds shot a few down, also a Ju 88.

SATURDAY, 11th.

Course still going along okay. Managing okay. Trying to drum it into myself. About 100-odd bombers came over. Some stuff fell pretty near. 30 Ju 87's dive-bombed "Kalafrana" here, about 50 yards from this school. Wow, what a racket, bombs, roars, whines, bangs, cracks. Hell on earth. Weekend off, went to Valletta.

SUNDAY, 12th.

Holy smoke, what a mess "Valletta, ""Sliema, " and "Hamrun" are in. Well, after 100-200 bombs a day, one can expect it, but whole streets and whole blocks of buildings for miles around are down. People living in the fields homeless, without clothes, food, etc. Streets are blocked, impassable. Post office out of order; so is the cable office, light, and water. It's awful. Ships burning in the harbour, most of those underwater. Craters 100 feet across and about 20 feet deep made by aerial torpedoes. Walked back from Sliema 8 miles.

MONDAY, 13th.

4 letters from JoanBirthday cards, bless her heart. Everybody is well. Ginny and the baby are okay. Fairly quiet today. Courses okay. Good food.

TUESDAY, 14th.

Well, the Luftwaffe is still smacking us hard here. 180 bombers over today. Ju 87's and 88's come in waves from all directions. You're watching one lot, look behind you, and spot about 20 more coming towards you. It's not a pleasant sight. Some were pretty close. Saw the stuff coming straight at us, dropped 50 yards away. Aw hell, who cares? I'm so darned used to it now!

WEDNESDAY, 15th.

Everything going okay. Still batting away on the different subjects. Might manage it. Ballistics wow! Luftwaffe are easing up, it seems. Hardly anything about. I guess they're going home. Yeah! Another convoy is supposed to be coming in. Another letter and card from Joan, dated March 30th, pretty good. Her job is not so good. Too bad.

THURSDAY, 16th.

Had a go at the auto loader. Made a mess of it. Who cares! Anyway, got through the day on courses, etc. Lectures tomorrow. No bombs today. Luftwaffe is quiet. Something's up. Russians still battering away, killing off 3, 000 a day. Japs still advance into Burma. Yanks raiding Jap bases with Flying Fortresses. Still messing about in Libya. Ship and cruiser "Norfolk" and "Dorsetshire" sunk by Jap dive bombers in the Indian Ocean. Also, "Hermes" aircraft carrier. Italian cruiser sunk in the Mediterranean. Also, convoy of merchantmen. "Laval" in power in France again. Looks bad there. Almost complete collaboration there with Germany. Well, they've smashed up almost everything here in Malta. Convoys can't get in. Devices are being used, though. Getting mail okay—5 from Joan. All's well at home. Gladys married. Joan's lost her job or something. A bit vague. Malta's been awarded the "George Cross" for something. Hell of a lot of good that will do. Most of the troops aught to be relieved here, especially the A.A. they are whacked, worn out, nerves gone, tired. Yes, they've had enough. There are hundreds in Hospital, crippled, nervous wrecks, gone nuts and so on. Some will never be any good anymore. They've had continuous dive bombing to contend with for 2 years, mass raiding for 6 months. When not less than 200 bombers were used on V.P.'s sometime a 100 or 50, diving at once on them. And they can't take cover because they have none. Yeah! George Cross, huh!

FRIDAY, 17th.
Got through the lecture ok. Was cast and got the worst of the lot. Made it though. Also, redrill. It was first F.A.S and autoloader.

SATURDAY, 18th.
Written exam this morning. Bit stiff but managed ok, I think. Some pretty heavy dive bomb attacks today. 30 Stukas smacked "Kalafrana." Hell, it seemed as though they were right on us. One oil tank set on fire, and the hangars and workshops flattened again. Destroyed about 13 Spits in for repair. About 6 fires all about us. A fine target for night. Hell of a mess around here. People homeless, scraping among the wreckage for their little effects. Bloody pitiful, digging frantically for their relatives. Also, about 150 Ju's passed overhead on "Luqa, " "Hal Far, " and Docks. Boy, it's like a battleground. I saw 3 bombers blow up in mid-air. Direct hits by A.A. with their bombs on. They came down in bits. Half the Island was blotted out with smoke and dust.

SUNDAY, 19th.
Heavy bashing again, wow! About 200 88's and 50 87's came over in formation and then follow the leader in terrific dives. Great Scott! It's breathtaking. Can see the bombs quite plainly. Some carried 4, 14, 8, 6, and so on. Some only 1, and they were aerial torpedoes. They make holes about 100 ft. across by 30 ft. deep. Didn't get back to sight until late.

MONDAY, 20th.

And so back to the gun. Started off early; about 50 88's and 40 87's came in. Smacked the Docks and "Ta'Qali." 50 Spits came in, great sight. Later on, 100 enemy aircraft came in. 17 Spits and 4 Hurry birds went up. They shot down 5 Ju 88's and 3 ME's. Hell, 30 88's dived on our V.P. We had a stoppage. Cripes, dirty big Junkers all over the place. Hell! We were petrified; bombs fell all around us. Spits, ME's, Ju 88's all mixed up. Cannon fire, Bofors, Heavy's, bombs, machine, and Bren guns. Hell, it was awful; a regular Dante's Inferno. Ah! Well, we got 200 rounds off, and we live again by the grace of God.

TUESDAY, 21st.

The usual. 2 bloody great bashes. The usual went up, about 4 Spits and 4 Hurry birds. Can't understand it; 50 odd Spits came in, 17 went up, next day 10 went up, after that 4, and it has remained 4. The rest have been destroyed on Ta'Qali. Why! What bloody fool ordered them to be destroyed in that manner? The Ju 88's and ME's are coming very low, hardly any barrage. The guns of the docks have been ordered to cease fire (ammo shortage) the same with us. Only diving targets on our V.P. and within 1000 yards slant range. Why, that means they must be right on top of us. Well, we might as well pack up; we'll never fire. About 100 bombers came over in 3 raids. They smacked for the first time the hospital at "Mtarfa," the swine, and the Army Rest Camp at St. Paul's Bay, where we are going next week.

WEDNESDAY, 22nd.

As above.

THURSDAY, 23rd.

Bloody awful. About 150 Ju 88's & 87's came over. Whee! The noise, smoke, and dust were appalling. They hit Valletta and Floriana smack in the center again. All the Drome's, docks, and big towns. Shortage of fags now; we're issued 25 a week. Hell, it's awful; we are smoking tea leaves and Maltese fags (taste like nothing on earth). Shortage of grub also. Hell, we're starving half the time. What a life! The boys are going nuts! And there are raids every day! Good thing I can get to Sliema, etc. I was absolutely canned 4 nights in succession with the rest of the boys on the horrible wine they sell out here. I've been lousy ever since.

FRIDAY, 24th.

And so, it goes on. Russia still advances, Japs also. They still mess about in England, mouthing, yapping. And those toy soldiers at home! Wow! What a war. I'm getting to be quite a boozer. Ah! Who cares? Bombs by day and night and for every meal machine-gunned by fighters. Half starved, no fags, rot gut to drink, flies, and fleas.

SATURDAY, 25th.

About 200 bombers brought down over Malta since he started 5 months ago. We shot down 4 and 1 ME. An ME crashed 50 yards from the pit yesterday. The pilot was a fat swine of a Gerry. I felt like bayonetting him.

SUNDAY, 26th.

About the same. He comes over about 3 times a day now using 50 each time. He loses on average about 5 bombers and 2 ME's. Sometimes the R.A.F. are up but always outnumbered 10-1. It's sheer murder. The bastard that sends those pilots up like that ought to be stewed in oil. After the raid, they try to land; poor sods, there are swarms of ME's waiting to pounce on 'em as they land. But they are marvelous; they twist and wriggle out of it each time, by cripes. The bullets and cannons were zipping and whipping all around us. It was unnerving. Brums sight hit by bomb, smashed everything up. Knocked James out.

MONDAY, 27th.

On advance party for Rest Camp and 5 days leave. B Troop only, 4 of us N.C.O.'s from each sight. Decent place. Good billets at St. Paul's Bay. Came down on the advance party to St. Paul's Bay for the 5 days leave and weeks rest. Nothing much to do. Not a bad place, right on the Bay. Rather pretty here. Hung about drinking bloody rot gut wine and eggs and chips. No fags; it's bloody awful.

The boys came down ok. Got some fags (30); what's the good of that? Hell's delight! No fags, beer, or entertainment of any sort. Still on the Ambit, I helped drink 10 bottles last night. Good gosh: I feel horrible; my guts are absolutely torturing me. Sick, can't eat. I've been oiled now for 4 days. I went off it a day ago, and I'm still helpless. Whee! It's terrible. Got paid. Lost a quid at Brag. Went to town. Hell, it's even worse in town. It's a blasted rubble heap, flattened. Ah, nuts to it! Got back. Not so heavy raids now. Much better. 4-5 Ju 88's and about a dozen 87's. Yes, slackened off.

MAY

SUNDAY, 9th

Well, we finished our five-day leave on Monday. I spent most of it in Sliema at the "bash." Throughout the week, we had marching and rifle drills. I took the squad several times. Got in plenty of swimming. Received five letters from Joan, Vi, and Bert. Raids have been somewhat heavier—87's, 88's, and also Breda 20's. More RAF up these days. They shot down 10 yesterday. There's supposed to be a convoy coming in.

Big sea battle between the Allies and the Japs—Japs lost 18 ships. Heavy raids by Britain on Germany. Most places are flattened out—600 bombers used nightly. We lose an average of 10 planes a night. Russians are held up by the thaw. Gerry is losing an average of 100 planes a day. Small raids on Britain, with reprisal raids on cathedral towns. Saw two Ju 87's bite the dust near here.

The grub is bloody awful—bully beef and Maconochie every meal. Fags are very short—35 a week. The Malts get them from somewhere and charge us 1/3d per packet of 10. I spend an average of 5/- daily. Eggs and chips cost 1/8d. The bloody profit they're making out of us. Also, beer is available once a week at 10/d a half pint, and it's lousy stuff at that.

There's no entertainment around here whatsoever—just wine shops, and most of the boys are ill from drinking it. I am as well; my guts are playing hell with me—the old complaint. The blasted M.O.s do nothing for you.

Lovely weather now, with plenty of flies and heat to contend with. And so it goes on.

FRIDAY, 14th

Well, not too bad. Plenty of swimming. We had competitions among the detachments. I won the backstroke event—10 shillings. Came third in diving and second in the 2 lengths crawl (about 100 yards). There were seven competitors. Not bad at all. The water is lovely. I'm quite enjoying the rest—yep! Plenty of bullshit though, like brass polishing, etc. Food is very bad now, with short rations—bully beef and Maconochies every day. Slice of bread and jam for tea. Literally starving. I've lost about 6 lbs. in a couple of weeks. Everybody's complaining. I was an orderly Bombardier for two days. Pretty good, that.

I have a feed of eggs and chips every night—1/8d, a must, or we'd starve. Most of the boys are drunk on this blasted wine, Ambit. Terrific stuff, like a weak port but not bad to drink. The aftereffects are terrific though—wow! I was ill for a week, so I stayed off it— 1/8d a bottle. A lot of new Spits came in, about 75. "Gort, " the new Governor, seems to be waking things up a bit anyway. On each raid, about 20 to 50 Spits go up. There were 22 bombers brought down on Sunday and 15 the day after. Already this month, the total is about 60-odd Gerry aircraft brought down.

And so, back to the gun. Our reception was three Ju 88s coming down on us from the east. The Spits got in and shot two down right above us. Cripes, what a battle between the M.E.s and Spits. The two 88s fell near us and blew up. There were bits and pieces everywhere. An M.E. got a Spit, and it crashed in flames. Bullets and cannon shells were whipping past us too. The A.A. got two direct hits. The bombers had their loads on—they blew up, bombs and all. It was terrific. There were no parachutes!

The raids are much smaller now; Gerry is losing too much. The Spits met a formation of five Cants (Italian three-engine bombers) and 15 Macchis (Italian fighters). They shot down three of the Cants and five Macchis. There were parachutists everywhere—I saw 15 together. I also saw two Spits collide in mid-air—smack! The pilots were okay though.

Gerry started a push in the south, but the Russians were holding him. Russians are using massive tanks. Gerry is using 6" anti-tank guns to stop them. The Japs are near the Indian borders, and Britain is withdrawing constantly. Big battle between America and Japan—men-of-war. Eighteen Jap ships sunk, two aircraft carriers, nine destroyers, and also cruisers and auxiliaries. The Yanks are bombing all Jap bases with Fortresses. Britain is bombing Gerry industrial centers heavily. It's quiet in Britain. There's a gas scare on now—Gerry reported to be issuing new gas masks to troops.

Bloody rations are awful—we're literally starving. Fags are also scarce. What the Malts sell are at 1/6d per packet of Woodbines. No mail from Joan as of yet. One boat has come in so far and brought ammo for us. Rumors are that we're going home again on July 10th.

SATURDAY, 15th

It's getting very warm now, but we're still wearing battle blouses. It's bloody hot in them. Boy, I'll be glad to go on leave tonight to get a decent meal—we're starving. The whole day's meals wouldn't even make up one good meal. It's 1 ½ oz. of bacon for breakfast, two slices of bread, and a cup of tea—and what horrible tea it is, hardly any sugar. For dinner, it's five tins of Maconochies divided among 11 men. That works out to about a dozen tablespoons of this bloody stuff per man—just a small plate, and not even full. For tea, it's two slices of bread, a spoonful of jam, and more tea. What tea!

Our only variety, on alternate days, is 2 oz. of bully beef and about four small spuds for dinner. Well! We buy eggs when we can get them—they're very scarce at 6d each. There's no bread available. The bakeries on the island had such a severe bashing that they can't supply the demand, and of course, there's a scarcity of flour. If we're lucky, we can get an egg and a few spuds at some of the bars. For this, they charge us 1/6 - 2/-. Our issue of fags, at 50 a week, is not enough. The Malt shops get them from somewhere. They sell them at 1/3 a packet. Well, we buy them! We've got to have a smoke! The lousy profiteers. The blasted government won't control prices. We've been buying nuts just to keep going. We were lucky one day—we managed to get two tins of milk, Joe and I, for 1/- each, small tins. We drank it down—the thick stuff. It all helps. The boys, in fact everybody, are all grumbling. Bloody shame after all we've gone through.

And now they tell us this state of rations will last for two more weeks. If, by then, no convoy comes in, we'll be on bully beef and biscuits. Aren't we lucky! Well, I managed to get some grub in Sliema. There's no life in Valletta or Floriana now—they're just a shambles. The meals I got cost me from 3/6 to 5/-, and that was only for eggs, chips, and a steak with bread and tea.

Lucky, I have Joan—hell yes! I walked back from Sliema—about 7 miles. No buses, no patrols. The Spits are doing okay, averaging five a day since May 1st—100 brought down so far. Some marvelous dogfights between Spits and M.E.s. They come crashing down everywhere. The Spits tear them out of the skies: M.E.s, Ju 88s & 87s, Italian Breda 20s, Cants, Macchis, Savios, and Selcos. Yep, she sure is some fighter.

It's slackened off; we haven't had a bomber over for three days now. About 30 new Spits came in yesterday, and plenty of Wimpies too. I'm being paid for my stripe now. Bill Cross is to be B.S.M. of the Battery. I haven't heard from Joan for a few weeks but received letters from Pop and Vi. I must send greetings for their birthdays.

The Russians' offensive for Kharkov is going well—they've broken through the central lines. Although Gerry has taken Kerch in the south, the Japs are still advancing in Burma. The British are withdrawing. Americans are arriving in Ireland. They seem to be getting a huge force together in England for something.

All is quiet in Libya, although each army is building up and strengthening. And so, it goes on. I'm bloody well sick of it—short grub, this blasted island, and raids every day and night. Hell's delight—when will it end? The boys are going nuts, and they all believe they're going home soon. Hah! What a laugh!

SUNDAY, 24th

The weather is great now—very warm. We're all in shorts and shirts, enjoying plenty of freedom. It's also very dry and dusty. The raids have become quite desultory now, with only a few Italian Breda 20s and MEs. The Spits are in control and have shot down quite a few of them. I haven't received any mail for some weeks now; I guess it's on the way.

The grub situation is still bad—poor rations. We're hungry most of the time. What a reward after all the shit we've been through— semi-starvation now! They say a convoy is on the way. Yeah, right! The last one got here and is now sitting at the bottom of the harbor. There are about 70 serviceable Spits now, so I guess they should be able to take care of a convoy.

There are lots of mosquitoes, fleas, bugs, mice, and spiders about—oh yeah, all for our benefit! I found a snake under my bed yesterday. The Russians are driving forward at Kharkov, using thousands of 100-ton tanks. They've penetrated about 50 miles, but the Germans have pushed back the Russians at Kerch.

Malta 1942

WEDNESDAY, 27th

As usual, a few Italian Breda 20s come over daily and get shot down by the Spits. The Ju 88s have stopped coming by daylight— just M.E.s, Br 20s, C.R. 40s, Cants, and Capronis. A few Ju 88s come by night. The Italian fighters are Selco's, Macchi 200s, and Reggia 200s, along with Focke Wulf 170s. The Spits are the masters of them all; they shoot them down wholesale. A lot of Wimpies, Blenheims, Seaforts, and Bisleys come and go, and we believe they're feeding India. They don't stay here anyway. It's purely defensive now, but it may change to offensive once they get air superiority.

Meanwhile, the rations are bloody awful—we're more semi-starving now. Hell, it's torture to go hungry and think of those guys at home. By cripes! Here I am, stuck on this bloody rock with nothing but stone walls and goats around me, in stinking villages where the people throw their refuse out into the streets. There are pools of slop and streams of it running through the streets, countless flies, and dead animals lying around. The damned Malts charge exorbitant prices, but it's the government on this island, like it is in England, that's to blame for allowing it. Why not control it all? Yeah! I'm sick of it.

We've had six months of bombs—shit of all sorts, death everywhere, and our reward is starvation, no fags, and bugger all else. Heroes, eh? What a mug I was. I knew it, though. I'll bet that every campaign now going on, every defeat and reverse we've suffered, is caused by bad leaders, red tape, bullshit, and bungling. This island is a terrific example of it. The stupid things that are done—75 brand new Spits came in, and they left them on the Dromes. What happened? Fifty Ju 88s came over and flattened the bloody lot. A convoy of five ships lying idle couldn't be unloaded because of a dispute between the government and laborers. The result? 200 Ju 88s sunk the bloody lot—fully loaded. I saw it all! I witnessed the bombing, the ships burning, the gunners dying, and the food wasted. Yeah! After that convoy battled halfway around the world!

These are two instances of the great blunders made here—two of thousands! I'm paid for my stripe, but I've no interest whatever in anything. My guts are bad again. It's very warm here now. There's an average of five raids a day, with three or four at night—sometimes all night. Poor old Sunshine is dead, our second casualty in this Battery. Poor old sod, after about 20 years of service, buried under slabs of rock from a blast bomb. They'll bury him and forget him. Yeah, it's a lousy life. Get what you can; to hell with the rest.

JUNE

MONDAY, 1st
St. Andrews Hospital

Went up to the hospital and buried Old Sunshine. I was a pallbearer. Just a box with him inside, sewn up in a blanket. I had to sign for the body. The blanket cost the Battery 7/6d. What a farce it was! After 18 years of service, that's what he gets—a blanket and a last post. My guts are bad, wow! I reported sick and was sent to the hospital. So here I am, in bed in a ward with about 20 others, all with different complaints. Big hospital this— the only one Gerry didn't bomb. Lovely beds, all spotless. They've put me on a diet of milk and milk puddings, so I'm beginning to look like a skeleton. They've tested my bowels, and tomorrow they're going to shove a tube down my gullet and test the contents of my stomach. It's hell, though, this lying abed and inactivity. I'm reading books at 1 every 2 hours, so I've read all they have here. Well, I was to go on Sgt. Stone's site as Bradley and Whittle are gone. I guess I'd have been made up to full Bombardier then. Ah well, to hell with it all. I want this gut business cleared up once and for all after 2 years of suffering.

MONDAY, 8th
In Hospital

Entered the hospital on the 30th of May. This is my 9th day in, and I've been in bed and on a diet the whole time. Hell, it's driving me nuts! I get tinned milk at each meal, a slice of bread with jam or fish. I'm bloody starved! It's awful, whereas the guys around me are getting full meals, and I've got to sit and watch. Oh, for a good meal! I dream and conjure meals of every sort and variety. Still, all for a good cause. I must get through it.

They've tested my bowels by specimen and my gastric juices. They shoved a yard-length pipe down my gullet and drew off everything from my stomach. I was 3 hours like this. It's a very pleasant big hospital, about 600 beds. All cases are taken here: VD, war casualties, diseases, and so on. It's nearly full, too. No mail yet. The Japs are now pushing into China; they've taken Burma. The Yanks smashed a Jap invasion fleet, sinking about 15 vessels. The British are holding and pushing Rommel back in Libya, with about 600 Gerry tanks destroyed. The Russians are holding him alright. No major battles now; the Kharkov business has died down. He was beaten there, and they're trying to take Sevastopol now.

The British used 1, 000 bombers over Cologne, with 20, 000 dead and the city wiped out. It's been evacuated. The British are keeping it up, and the Yanks are also helping, or will help. Not much activity over here—just a few Italian bombers and fighters. The Wimpies are operating from here over Sicily and other places, so it's not so bad, but the rations are still short. A convoy is expected soon. Ah, to hell with it all! I'm absolutely browned off—half bloody starved, short of fags, beer, and any sort of fun.

SUNDAY, 14th
Luqa

Came out of hospital. All okay—fit as a fiddle! I'm bloody glad too; I was browned off. Still, my guts feel fine. I hope they don't trouble me anymore. I got back to sight okay. Not many raids— just a few Italians over the last two days. Beauforts and Baltimores have been coming in, along with a lot of Spits. A convoy is expected in.

TUESDAY, 16th
Well, the torpedo bombers and Spits have been operating all day from here. We've heard explosions and gunfire continuously. About 600 aircraft have operated from here. We learned that 1 Italian battleship, 3 cruisers, and some destroyers have been sunk. A convoy of 16 vessels came into the dock, and they were unloading like hell. Four Ju 88s came over; 2 were shot down. They put up a smoke screen. The Russians are holding all fronts, and the Germans are losing like hell. The battle in Libya is at its height, and the Japs are held as well. Thousands of Yanks, Canadians, etc., are arriving in England.

SATURDAY, 20th

Transferred to Sgt. Taylor's site on 16th June '42. He, through a tiff with King Company, left the site, leaving LB Gilkes in charge. So, I'm sent to help out. Well, it's my old team—Flint, Mitty, Smith, and so on. Not a bad crew, a bit tough, but we're pulling okay. Four out of six ships of the convoy bound for here were sunk by Ju 88's off "Pantelleria"—too bad. The remaining two got in okay and are now being unloaded. They're both 12, 000 tons, so they have a good load of tinned grub and flour.

Not enough long-range fighters here to go out and cover the convoy. Anyway, the Spits and Beaus shot down 10 Ju 88's and Italian craft. A convoy from Alex turned back on receipt of the results. They say it has started out again with a stronger escort. We hope so; things are bad on this island. Soldiers and civilians alike are hungry. Our rations are terrible: 3 tins of M.V. per 10 men, half a loaf of bread per man a day, and 1 tin of bacon to last 10 men for 3 mornings. Hardly any tea or sugar. No jam. By cripes, we're starving. Eggs are 6 pence each. Can't buy grub or meals at all from cafés—they're closing down. The civilians are blaming the Army, and the Army is blaming the civilians, saying they are hoarding it. What a bloody life.

The British pushed back to the Egyptian frontier but still held Tobruk. I guess we'll settle there now. Hah! The Russians are holding all fronts, but Gerry has nearly succeeded in taking Sevastopol. There's much noise about a second front in France by the British this year. They're massing and training for it now. I wonder. Britain raids Germany night and day. Churchill is in the United States. Molotov flew to Britain and the U.S.A. Big moves are being planned.

I'm getting letters regularly now from all the folks. Joan is in the hospital with a septic finger, and Betty also (bad heart). The Palmer tribe is all okay, I gather. Harry at P.N. is soon to be called up. Vi had teeth out and is okay. I've got about 5½ pounds of pay coming to me. Nice! Joan says there's 100 quid in the bank.

JULY

THURSDAY, 2nd

Left 61 okay. Back on the old site. The gut ache is back again, so I suffer once more. I knew damn well the hospital wouldn't make any difference after two years of this. They couldn't cure it in two weeks. I think I'm a confirmed dyspeptic now. Ah well.

Well, two ships out of six got in. Ju 88s sank the other four. One from Alex turned back—too much opposition. So, they've unloaded these. The rations are being cut daily. The army and civilians are suffering. Good God, our rations are terrible. We're getting worse every day. We go to bed hungry, can't work, and are losing weight. One can see the marked difference in weight and appearance of the men around. The prices are still outrageous. The black market is doing well. Fags cost ten at 1/6, and so on. The administration of this island is awful. The Maltese are complaining.

The raids are nothing now except at night; about six come in, dropping flares, anti-personnel incendiaries, and bombs, etc. There are hundreds of bombers and fighters on the Dromes here. Lots of Beauforts (torpedo bombers) are being used against the Italian convoys. Two hundred Spits and new Wimpies are operating at night, along with Bristol Bisleys (modified Blenheims) and new Baltimores (new Glens).

Well, Rommel has advanced beyond Mersa Matruh, within 100 miles of Alexandria, and is still going strong. They say we lack tanks or the right type of tank. They've gone to Russia. The 9th Army is moving over to reinforce the 8th Army, so it's touch and go now. I guess they've been telling the British a lot of soft soap regarding the strength of the 8th Army and Air Force, as usual.

The Germans are pounding Sevastopol day and night, using thousands of dive bombers, etc. They're gaining there, although losing heavily in men and material elsewhere. The Russians are holding them. The RAF carried out their sixth 1, 000-bomber raid, this time on Bremen. Churchill is back from the United States. Everything is set for the second front. One thousand bomber raids and strafing, etc., are preliminaries to the second front. But they must be careful. The Germans are gaining in Egypt. They're trying to close the pincers at Sevastopol and Egypt.

The Japs are quiet. The Yank Navy has crippled their supplies. The Chinese are pushing them back in China. There's a huge effort on the part of the Allies to finish the war in 1942. If it's anything like the organization and planning I've seen from the British Army, then I have no faith in them whatsoever. Tons of food have been lost on the docksides here because they lacked decent storage for it. Paraffin, food, clothing, medical supplies, ammo, and engines—tons of stuff—are gone, rotting now amongst the debris, while the people and army are going hungry. The bloody incompetent fools, like the rest of the empire. I hope Alex does fall; that will shake the complacent, self-centered, smug English out of their stupid, gross apathy. The Germans deserve success. They have great leaders and fine equipment—a fine army. I hope they do and dictate peace. Our foolish leaders would fight this war for years with human cannon fodder, relying on the blood and sweat of the workers.

TUESDAY, 7th
Luqa at Gun Position

Well, I was detailed for Brigade guard at Sliema as NCO. It was a snap. I did nothing but swim and drink tea beside the stray dames. All very gratifying. Yowsah! I made five days out of bread rations. It's hard to get grub, though—absolutely none to be had. All the cafes are closing, and the bars have no beer now. The breweries can produce just enough for the troops, so there's none for the civvies, and hardly any spirits.

Plenty of tomatoes, spuds, apples, pears, and plums are about, but the prices are terrific: 4/- per lb. for pears, plums, and apples, and 3/- for a meal that consists of a slice of pork, a few chips, a tomato, a lettuce, and a cup of tea—nothing else. My wages lasted me three days, and I've been broke the rest of the week. Fags? There's plenty of black-market stuff at 1/6 per packet; otherwise, it's nil, and you must be in the know to get them. Poor bloody troops are gasping for a smoke, while bloody Maltese kids aged 10 to 15 are smoking Players. I'm below 10 stone now, so I've lost one and a half stone, just like the rest of the boys.

We've been having some mighty hot night bombings—20 to 30 bombers dropping flares, anti-personnel bombs, and heavy stuff. They drop huge canisters that split open in mid-air, releasing hundreds of little bombs that explode on impact—enough to kill within a 30-foot radius. Some are DA, and if kicked, they explode. Several kids and gunners have been killed around here. One kid had both legs blown off nearby; he died as we got to him—a hell of a sight.

He's hit a good number of planes on the drome. By day, Italian Cants and Ju 88s with mixed escorts come over high and level Luqa here. The Spits shot down 16 bombers and fighters yesterday. The sky was filled with burning planes and parachutists, and there were terrific dogfights, too. The Spits play hell with them. A huge Cant fell near here with five crew members aboard. When we got there, they were ashes. The British are holding the Gerry 65 miles from Alexandria, but the Gerry knocked out 200 of our tanks. It looks as though we've got him, though. There's a big offensive all over Russia, and Sevastopol has been taken. The Russians are holding him elsewhere, and there's still much talk of a second front. The U.S.A. sank four destroyers of the Japs. This is the sixth year of war for Japan and China, and the Japs are forging ahead in China.

MONDAY, 13th

Luqa

Well, the raids have increased again from about 2 Ju 88s to about 15 to 20. By cripes, he's smacking away as bad as ever. It's a great surprise to us; we never thought he'd continue through the summer like this. I guess he's trying to neutralize us because of supplies to Rommel.

Every day since my last entry, an average of 20 to 40 Ju 88s have come over, always protected by about 20 fighters. They come in at 17, 000 feet, close together, with fighters above and all around—about 7 to 10 bombers at a time, but no diving. It amazed us; high level is most unusual for the Ju 88, and they're dropping anti-personnel bombs and heavy DAs. We've had numerous little bombs around here. The Spits have been taking a heavy toll on them—an average of 8 a day, both fighters and bombers. So, it's costing him something. The Beauforts and Beaufighters are having a go at him and the convoys.

Rommel forced the British from Knightsbridge to El Alamein, a distance of 60 miles from Alexandria, but the British turned and held him. We gave up Tobruk without much resistance, losing equipment and 25, 000 men. They are now recapturing some of the 25-pounder guns the Gerry is using from Tobruk. He smashed us back. Our tanks were inferior to his, although we had many more than he did and also air superiority. Still, we're holding him and have counterattacked; it looks okay so far.

The Gerry has started a huge push from Kharkov to Kursk and has crossed the Don River in several places. Things are serious—the Russians are withdrawing, and terrific battles are going on involving thousands of tanks and planes. Well, we're getting a bloody sight worse daily here in Malta. We get no more Maconochies (our main meal) and spuds only once a week. It's nothing but bully beef now for breakfast, dinner, and tea. The boys are groaning; they're all looking mighty thin.

For breakfast, we get 1 sausage, 2 slices (very thin) of bread, and a cup of tea without sugar. Dinner is a plate of watery Maconochies, which is now finished, and it's just bully beef and a few peas. Other days we get tomatoes or cabbage. For tea, we have a piece of cheese (the size of a half-crown coin), 2 slices of bread, and tea without sugar. If you're lucky, you might get a piece of bread, cheese, or a tomato. Some days, you get less than the above.

Now, the government has issued an order stopping the sale of all food in cafes, bars, and clubs, so now a soldier on leave cannot get food until they devise some scheme for feeding us troops. The people are hungry, the troops are hungry, and with bombs falling by day and night, we're getting little or no sleep. In Parliament, they're debating what should have been done and the mistakes they've made. To cap it all, the troops in Malta cannot be relieved because of the difficulty of shipping after all they've done here. By cripes, it's hard. We man guns day and night on literally bugger all to eat, and yet they say, Gallant Malta. They don't know at home; bloody good job they don't.

I had a good swim and heard from Harry, Vi, and Joan. Harry is now in the RAF.

SATURDAY, JULY 18th

Nothing unusual this week. The British are holding the Gerry in Egypt. We're using American tanks and Army Air Corps Liberators and Bostons. It has been revealed that we have more tanks and men than Rommel. General Ritchie has been recalled; he ought to be shot. The Germans are driving forward in their offensive. They have crossed the Don and are on the other side in force. It's a marvelous feat. They have taken several towns.

There have been big raids by Britain on Germany, and huge contingents of troops are reaching Britain. There's much talk about a second front. I heard from Joan; she's okay. The Ju 88s have stopped raiding here—too costly, I guess. The RAF and AA have shot down 105 planes in 2 weeks. The Manxman has come in again, and they opened a feeding center for troops. It's not so good—meals at cheaper prices, but there is not much to the meals. All bars and restaurants are closed, so this is the only way troops on leave can get food now.

We get our ration of bread, but it's bloody hopeless. Everybody is hungry. We get no spuds, no flour, no sugar, or milk. A tin of bacon once a week; we're living on bully beef, tomatoes, and 2 slices of bread per meal—none for dinner. We're eating nuts to sustain us.

TUESDAY, 28th
Luqa

Things are much the same, except perhaps that we are getting a bloody sight thinner. The rations have been cut to a minimum, and all restaurants have been closed. First, a Naafi opened for troops on leave, serving poor meals at huge prices. Our daily meals are starvation diets—same food every day with slight variations. No fresh meat, no spuds, no sugar, no vegetables—no bugger all. I've lost 2 stone now (28 pounds). We're all like rabbits. By cripes, it drives me mad to think back on our home meals and then the bullshit we read about what's taking place in England. The swell time they're having while we have to write home and say we're doing fine. The bloody bastards—such stinking irony! They could have saved all this with a little foresight, the stupid fools.

The bad administration, the stupid oversights, miscalculations— by cripes, we groan aloud! Now, after our sweat and toil, we still face dive bombings day and night, and on top of that, the weather is stifling. There are millions of flies to worry us, mosquitoes and flies at night, and bloody rats play about in our billets. I found one in my blankets the other night. The only consolation is swimming; I can do this once a week. There are no fields of vegetables around us; we are too near the Drome for that. The farmers have evacuated. Pears are 2/- per lb., as are apples. Peaches are 3/- per lb., and melons are at 1/9—bloody awful. Fags are still at 1/6, and the daily black-marketing bastards are thriving. The government just laughs.

I've heard from Joan; all's okay. I've sent home stockings at 3/- a pair. We're holding the Gerry in Egypt. The Gerry has taken Rostov, and they're pushing south into the Caucasus. The Russians are driving him back from Voronezh as they recross the Don River. Huge contingents of Americans are around in England.

AUGUST
MONDAY, 3rd
Luqa

Gerry's been knocked off a bit. We haven't had a Ju 88 over for three days. The Spits have stopped him. In the last raid, three days ago, four Ju 88s came over Hal Far, and the Spits caught them and shot down the bloody lot right above us. What a sight! They came down in pieces—chunks, bits, parachutes, bodies, engines. Wow! What a mess. There were blazing wrecks all around us. Also, ten ME 109 F's were brought down. So, they've given up except for fighter sweeps, and then the Spits take a toll on them. A total of 153 were shot down over here last month (July). The record is 157 for April. The A.A. got 101, a record for us. Had the Spits been here then, I guess it would have been 257. We get a few night raids every week, though. Some planes don't bother to come near the island, scared of the Beaufighters. They drop their bombs in the sea and go home. The Beau is deadly; he's got one nearly every day so far. One night, he got three. We saw one shot down. He trails the raiders for miles first, then gets close—closer—until suddenly we see the tracer from his cannons, and down goes another one.

The grub is still very bad: 12 oz. of bread per day and four tins of Maconochies per nine men. There's hardly any sugar or tea. By cripes, we groan aloud at times. We leave the table after every meal hungry as hell; it just tickles our appetite. The boys are all like rakes. The two dogs are like skeletons. On leave, we can only grab a bite at the Naafi place, which has high prices too. And you're still hungry afterward. We can't buy anything whatsoever at the shops—nothing, absolutely nothing. We get 50 fags a week—25 Army issue free and 25 Naafi at prices. One bar of chocolate per week. We can't get fruit or vegetables at all; the U kitchens are taking it all. Believe me, bud, we're in a bloody awful mess and have been for months. And us poor gunners, who went through the worst of it, are now suffering doubly—all for a lack of foresight on the part of the authorities. Apples cost 5d each, eggs 10d, grapes, and pears 4/- per lb. All cafes are closed except for one café in town that sells glasses of cocoa for 6d a glass. There's no beer; the breweries have stopped production. No spirits—the stocks are finished. Just rotgut Maltese wine.

Lately, Liberators have been landing here. Some plane! They brought torpedoes and bombs to drop. Also, Curtis Wrights, the largest twin-engine planes going, all passenger. A strong rumor is going around. It comes around every three months. Well, this is the newest: the R.A.s and R.A.F. are to be relieved by either Curtis or Liberator planes. Two thousand troops a week are to be taken via Egypt. Orders have been seen at a Drome in Egypt (Heliopolis) that troops from Malta are to pass through; every consideration is to be shown to this. For a fact, the R.A.F. have already gone— about 50 left the other night. The whole battery believes it. The whole island knows about it. But I suppose it's just another rumour. Woe is us.

The Germans have taken Rostov and are in the Caucasus. The Russians are retreating before them; terrific battles are underway. Gerry has crossed every river so far. He's using thousands of everything. It's a stalemate in Egypt; they're getting dug in now. Rommel is getting supplies by transport plane. The British will wait until he's strong, then he'll get in again. The British are bombing the hell out of Germany—600 to 800 bombers used nightly and hundreds of fighters (fighter-bombers). Bombers are used by day for strafing, bombing, machine gunning, and cannons against Dromes, railways, and so on. Terrific damage is being done. He's bombing our midland towns and cathedral towns.

MONDAY, 10th

The food situation is the same. By cripes, the boys are looking pretty pinched. I've known hunger before, but for a short time. This is day after day, weeks, months. The raids are mainly fighter sweeps, and the Spits take a steady toll on them. At night, a few Italians come near and drop their bombs in the sea. The Beau has got them scared; he's shot a few down too. They've closed all restaurants. The command Naafi is the only place to eat now.

When the troops are on leave, the bread ration is stopped for troops on 24-hour leave, and they have to take their unexpired portion: 1½ oz. of bacon, 6 oz. of bread, and 6 oz. of bully. What a bloody game! So, I forged a few five-day passes and got all the bread I wanted.

Things are bloody bad; prices are terrific. The farmers are watching their fields with guns for looters. There have been cases already of soldiers being shot or imprisoned for pinching grapes, tomatoes, etc. Poor sods are hungry; what else can they do? I had my five days of leave. It was lousy at St. Paul's Bay—lousy grub, 2/- for an egg and tomato—so I went to Sliema. I got my bread okay and ate at the fair. It cost me 2/10, but it was worth it. The Russians are withdrawing, and Gerry is well into the Caucasus. He's taken Rostov and several other cities and is now near Stalingrad. Terrific battles are underway. The British are going to Moscow. Things are getting sticky. The people at home are clamoring for the second front, but they say not yet—they're not ready, as usual.

Huge convoys from the States are arriving with all sorts, including troops. The British are bombing the hell out of the Ruhr, Düsseldorf, and all over France. Great damage is being done. There's trouble in India; Gandhi says the British should get out so they may declare their defense and policy. Britain says no! Gandhi's wife and 200 members of Congress have been arrested for rioting and shooting. Work has stopped as a result. Bloody fine at this time! The Japs will walk in shortly. The Yanks land at the Solomon Islands, lose several boats, but make a foothold. There's heavy fighting. The Chinese are doing okay, advancing somewhat. I received letters from Joan, Cled Parry, and Vi. All is well. Joan is in Bristol for her holidays. Pop is a firewatcher. Harry is in Scotland training as a gunner. Joe is on five days of leave. I'm in charge now.

THURSDAY, 20th

Well, there's no improvement in the food; it's still pretty bad. They weigh us each week to see how we fare on it. They've cut Maconochies right out now. It's all bully every blasted day. We get about 8 oz. per day and 1/2 oz. of flour per man daily. So, that's what we have to make pastry from, which makes one meal: a bully hash pie. The rest of the week, we have bully and tomatoes. By cripes, we have no strength left in us.

The convoy is in after a terrific struggle. They lost a Carrier Eagle, a Cruiser Manchester, a Destroyer, and an A.A. Ship, besides a few Merchantmen. They got 9 in here. The Gerry lost 68 aircraft in doing it. This convoy won't affect us because our stocks here are so low that they must be replenished; therefore, we shan't benefit immediately. There's quite a bit of activity around here. Wimpies and Liberators operate by night, with Beauforts escorted by Beaufighters and Spits (extra tanks) by day. The Spits go over Sicily on strafing and sweeps, along with the Beaufighters. The raids aren't much over here, just fighter sweeps. No bombers for weeks now, just a few bombers by night, but the night-fighting Beaufighters are deadly. We saw 2 Ju 88s get shot down in total darkness the other night.

They stick a huge smoke screen over the docks by day. It's still very warm here, with lots of flies—blasted things. Our routine is the same every day: up at about 7:00 for breakfast, clean ourselves and the billets by 9:00. I, as Limber Gunner, with the boys, clean the guns and all other arms, etc., then other jobs that may want doing. Sometimes men are detailed for a course or a job elsewhere. Dinner is at 12:00 (ye bully). We generally kip all afternoon; that's all we can do on the food allotted. Tea is at 4:00, then we wash our clothes, bathe, and play cards as a rule at this time (it's cooler then). We stand to at 7:00, and then supper is at 8:00. Some supper! One slice of bread and a cup of sugarless tea. We await the 9:00 news eagerly, received here at 10:00. So, we leave 2 guards on the gun for the night and then go to bed or play cards.

Now we do a bit of raiding; we've done it every night for the last week—for grapes, by cripes! We bring back about 20 pounds every night—beautiful, big, sweet grapes in bunches that weigh 1 to 5 pounds each. We estimate that we've eaten about 60 pounds of grapes each this week. The Malt farmers won't venture out after 9:00 because of air raids, etc. Our leave is stopped because of the convoy, and there's 100% manning all day and night—no breaks. There are plenty of prickly pears about now on the cactus trees, along with water, banana, and sugar melons.

I've heard from Joan, Pop, Vi, and Cled this week. Joan is enjoying herself in Bristol. Pop is okay. Harry is in the Army or the RAF; I don't know which. All's well, anyway. Everything went okay while Joe was away. There was a bit of trouble over the ammo; a wrong check was made of it, so I had to check it all over again. 90 boxes, 2, 680 rounds of it, in boxes of 24 rounds each, with each box weighing 150 pounds. Some job! The Russians are being pushed back in the Caucasus. Hellish battles are going on, with thousands dying daily. The Gerry is at the gates of Stalingrad. He's also gotten to Pozny, the oil area. The Russians have fired it all—everything destroyed. He's gotten south to Kletskaya and is headed for Baku and the Caspian Sea. If he succeeds, he'll cut the southern Russian armies off from the north.

Churchill flew to Cairo and to the Egyptian front. He spoke to the troops and all commanders, then flew from there to Moscow to confer with Stalin. So, big things are in the offering. Churchill got back okay. There are still large contingents of Yanks and Canadians arriving in England. It's all very quiet in Egypt. General Auchinleck is taking another post, and General Alexander is taking over command in Egypt. Many rumors are circulating regarding the second front. Yank Generals have a lot to say; they say they are ready. Huge forces of planes are all ready. The Yanks are to cooperate with Britain in bombing Germany.

In the last two weeks, a different city has been blitzed by hundreds of heavy bombers. Terrific damage has been done: Flensburg, Düsseldorf, Osnabrück, Königsberg, and so on. They promised even heavier raids yet. The British are using Sterlings, 4-engine jobs, with a range of 1, 500 miles and 8 tons of bombs. They use 4, 000, 2, 000, and 1, 000-pound bombs, which do terrible damage. A huge commando raid on Dieppe has taken place. The British affected a landing with Yank, Canadian, and Free French troops, along with tanks. They destroyed a six-gun battery, a location center, an ammunition dump, and so on. The R.A.F. took part, and 100 Gerry aircraft were destroyed. Throughout the day, we lost 85. So, it's obvious he has the aircraft ready. Big things are expected from this. It was a test and an experience.

WEDNESDAY, 26th

About the same. The rations are also the same—bloody bad. Day by day, we get thinner. They've started a fund for the dependents of the convoy crews: 6 shillings a week for 10 weeks. They went through hell for 2 days and were in England just before this. We haven't seen England for nearly 2 years and have endured 6 months of hell on top of semi-starvation. Bloody fine. Ah, this island is driving us all nuts. Joe and I spent a quid each on about 5 drinks. Can't get beer, so we had rum and brandy at 2 shillings a time. The Russians are withdrawing, and Gerry has crossed the Don again and is now storming Stalingrad. He has penetrated well into the south, reaching the mountains. Prince George, the Duke of Kent, was killed in a Sunderland plane crash. There are huge fighter sweeps from here now, with 30 to 50 Spits at a time.

SEPTEMBER

SUNDAY, 6th

Luqa

No difference. Rations are the same: bully beef every day, every dinner. Bully and tomatoes every day. Every day, we go to the table hungry and leave it hungry. Two slices of bread for tea and one slice for supper, two for breakfast with an inch of bacon or about four beans. Then, bully and bully, and best of all, not enough of that—6 oz. (half a tin). We're going nuts. I am going bald, thin, and my guts are still bad at night while on guard. My stomach is so empty. I retch and spew like hell, and then there's this horrible landscape of walls, Maltese goats, and heat, with flies everywhere. Gee, how much longer? Nothing of importance from here. Our leave isn't much good to us. We can't get food or see the pictures we've already seen. There's only swimming—thank God for that. And so, it goes on. I heard from Joan, Vi, and Pop; all's well. I made an allotment to Joan of 3 shillings and 6 pence weekly, as I'm getting a quid. Malt told me the other day that he sold his bike, a good racer, for 45 quid. He bought another for 35 quid. He also said he could buy flour at 20 quid a sack. Nice, eh? The black market. Our government can't cope with it. The priests and police are hand in glove with them. The Gerry are on the steps of Stalingrad. He's got 25 divisions and 1, 000 aircraft battering away. I guess it won't last long. All is quiet in Egypt. We lost 9 merchantmen, 2 cruisers, 1 destroyer, and 1 aircraft carrier in this last convoy. Five ships got through. We're still bombing Germany, and he's still turning out the stuff. Oh sure! The Yanks beat up the Japs at the Solomon Islands. The Yanks are in possession of 3 Solomon Islands.

WEDNESDAY, 16th

Well, things are pretty stereotyped now. Every day is the same. The raids are mostly fighter sweeps, of no consequence. The rations are the same—very little. I weigh 9 stone 12. Bloody poor. The majority of the boys are like it. We are like wolves; when our slices of bread are on the table, we size them up and aim for the thickest and largest piece. Whoever is last is mighty unlucky; he gets the smallest piece of all. That means a hell of a lot these days when you go 4 to 6 hours to the next meal, which even then only consists of 2 slices of bread and jam, cheese, or fish. I went to the 66 gun for 5 days. It was okay down there. Can't get grub at the command fair without a 5-day leave pass. The Gerry has reached Stalingrad, and he's bashing the hell out of it. Thousands of aircraft and tanks are being used. He's taken Novorossiysk, the Black Sea port, and is now headed east and south. He'll soon have the Caucasus in his hands. All is quiet in Egypt, with both sides massing. Only 5 convoy ships got in here, and there was a very small amount of food on them. So, it looks as though we are on short rations through the winter. Another 3 shillings and 6 pence per week for servicemen has been granted by the government. I shall send it all to Joan. I've heard from Joan frequently, as well as from Vi, Cled, and Pop. All is well.

OCTOBER

WEDNESDAY, 14th
Luqa

I've slackened off a lot. Actually, there is not much to write about—just 2 important events. Gerry is back, and I have been promoted to Bombardier. Why? I don't know. Well, it's been a month since I last wrote. Things have gone on the same. Rations are still bad. Joe came back off his course looking mighty thin, as we all are. Joan says I look thin in my snap. So what! It maddens me; I'll go nuts. Our best days are going to waste. What do we get? Nothing. Bloody mugs, that's what we are. But I've got myself to blame. I should have looked ahead a bit. We get 6 oz. of bully beef every day and 1 slice (2 oz.) of bread. That is our main food. I went on a gas course and got 91; it was okay. Brig's inspection. Gerry's back. About 200 bombers and fighters came in the first day. The Spits have shot down an average of 15 a day. He's already slackened off; losses are too great. Russia is still battling on, with snow falling. We're still bombing Germany, and so it goes on—no different. Just stalemate. Ah, we're all sick and weary of it all. What a poor, disillusioned sod I am. What will become of me? How will it end? Ah, nuts!

FRIDAY, 30th
An important event since I last wrote: General Montgomery has started an offensive in Egypt after months of preparation and terrific operations by the RAF against Rommel's supply lines and battle area. It started a month ago. Up to date, we have busted up a few of his minefields, pierced in places, and are holding our gains. The Navy is bombing, the RAF is playing hell, and, in general, things are going well for us. So, we watch it eagerly. It means our relief if the 8th Army gets through to Benghazi. We shall see.

Things are really acute on the Island. We've had a cut in rations all around; bread, fish, bacon, etc., are getting replaced with biscuits to make up for it. Our grub is not worth calling meals now. The boys are looking rough, and we have a lot of the Battery in the hospital. We can't resist colds, sores, or any small illness. I've had a small cut for nearly three weeks now, and it keeps festering. Not a man is fit. Grub is at a terrific price: a bag of flour costs 6.0.0 (black market), eggs are 1/8 each, oranges are 10d each, fags are 2/6 to 3/- a packet, spuds are 2/- a pound if you can get them (and that's impossible), and tomatoes are 2/- a pound. By hell, what a life!

The bombing has finished; the Spits stopped them. Now, there are only fighter sweeps, and very few of those. I think he's transferred them to Egypt. I'm a paid Bombardier now. My pay is 2 2/6 a week, but I shall allot 12/6 to Joan. I'm in good health myself; thank God, the old stomach pain is a thing of the past (so far). I sleep well, although I am always hungry. What a feeling it is to sit down at the table hungry and get up hungry! Boy, do I realize a few things now! Mail is poor; I heard from Joan, Vi, and Pop about three weeks ago. All is well. Our wedding anniversary is on the 21st of October. She sent me some nice cards and snaps, as did Vi. They also sent me cables. And Harry, he's come to life again! I haven't heard from him for ten months. Anyway, they are all well.

We've had the Brig around. All sorts of bull shitflying about. Good gosh, the ridiculous things we hear! Bloody foolish things that have no bearing on the war. We're just like a peacetime army: clean, shine, lay out, do this, that, and the other, with thousands of orders for the equipment. Bloody foolish things. The Russians are still holding Stalingrad. The Germans haven't had any spectacular success of late; the Russians are slowly bleeding them to death. The British are dropping tons upon tons of bombs—8, 000, 6, 000, 4, 000 lbs. by four-engine bombers on Germany, Italy, France, etc. The Yanks are helping; 94 Lancasters raided Lille, France, by day (one was lost). Hundreds were used by day and night recently on Genoa, Milan, Turin, etc. in Italy, causing havoc and enormous death tolls. It's all in conjunction with the drive in Egypt. Not much is said about the second front now; maybe this is it in Egypt. Anyway, they're very quiet about it.

They're still pouring troops, materials, etc., into Britain. The Yanks are advancing in the Pacific. Their fleet and bombers have sunk hundreds of Jap boats; they're doing extremely well. Britain is spending 15 ¾ million pounds a week. We've launched three new battleships: the Howe, Anson, etc. The Yanks are turning out four ships daily. The aircraft carrier Wasp was sunk. New Spits arrive here from Gibraltar (extra tanks). The Yanks have taken over in Liberia, West Africa, which is very handy for British possessions there. The British have now almost taken Madagascar. So, between these two events, they have ensured our reinforcements and supplies for Egypt.

NOVEMBER

MONDAY, 9th
Luqa

A few important events have taken place. The 8th Army has gotten through to and past Sidi Barrani. They've smashed and taken El Alamein and Mersa Matruh, and are still forging ahead. They've taken 60, 000 prisoners, 1, 000 guns, and 600 tanks. This is a very conservative estimate. The Nazis are fleeing as fast as they can. By hell, it looks good!

The next important event is that the Yanks and British landed in North-West Africa. From the Atlantic in Morocco and the Mediterranean in Algeria, about 150, 000 men and material have been landed so far. They've taken Oran, Algiers, and Casablanca, and are 60 miles from the borders of Tunisia. They are now using airfields and can provide air support to any of our convoys or fleet in the Mediterranean. General Eisenhower is in command. The battleship Jean Bart was sunk by Yank dive bombers, and a naval battle is in progress. Some Germans are surrendering. Vichy is resisting, but the Yanks are in control. So now it remains to be developed. This all took place on Sunday, the 7th of November.

We are standing by now, manning 24 hours as a convoy is coming in. Vic and Bob left us yesterday, going home on the Star. We all have great hopes of getting home now. The rations are still bad; we are all in a very weak state. We've had a further cut in rations. On leave, we managed to get a pork chop and some lettuce for 3/9. It cost us 39/- for grub. Beer is 1/- for half a pint, and the local wine is 1/- a glass (rot gut). There have been no air raids; he's buggered.

Thirty Beaufighters and thirty Beauforts came in, along with about twenty Wimpies. They are now operating. Italy is getting hell, as are Genoa, Turin, and Milan. The Russians are holding on and slaughtering Germans by the thousands. The Yanks are advancing in the Solomons and have taken a few points. The Australians are making progress in New Guinea. The Japs have had terrific losses at sea. Heavy bombers in large forces are pounding Germany and Italy every night, strafing and bombing continuously during the day.

Things are the same with us: hungry and browned off. The same old thing every day. We're having tons of gun drill and predictor work. The 419 is coming around tomorrow for a field check. I've got it all off pat (I hope). We still have the usual bull shit., such as C.O. inspections and stupid orders, etc. Ah well, we swallow it all. We're getting wise to it.

Mail is poor; I've received nothing from the family. I got a letter and card from Joan. She's doing okay at her job, getting the extra 3/6 alright, so as soon as I get my Bombardier's pay, I shall allot her some more. She's getting 35/6 now—not bad with her pay. I'll hang on to 15 bob myself. There's nothing to spend money on: no food, the pictures are old (we've seen them years ago), and there are no dances, theaters, etc.

DECEMBER
WEDNESDAY, 2nd

It's been a month since I last wrote. Well, things with us are about the same. We've suffered more cuts in the rations; we're down to a minimum. We can't get food on leave at all now, so leave is a washout unless one takes one's unexpired portion. That means splitting a tin of corned beef (1/4), half a tin of MV, two slices of bread, three biscuits, a spoonful of tea, sugar, and butter. That's the lot, and it's impossible to take, so we stay and are as miserable as hell. We get up hungry and go to bed hungry all day.

The Allies in Africa have taken all of North-West Africa and Morocco. They captured Darlan, who is now in control of all French possessions. The Allies are closing in on Bizerte and Tunis, now within gun range of both cities. The Germans are cut off in Libya, Tunis, and Bizerte. The 8th Army is now before El Agheila, preparing to go in and smash him up and out of Africa entirely. The R.A.F. and Yanks are pounding the hell out of him, with huge R.A.F. raids on Italian cities. The Italians are evacuating as fast as possible, with 8, 000 lb bombs dropped at a rate of one a minute and 15 incendiaries a second. Genoa is out of action. There is no air activity here; however, Wimpies, Beaus, Hurricanes, and Swordfish go out in force every night, pounding hell out of Sicily. Our fighters patrol the Straits by day, shooting down an average of five planes a day.

A convoy has arrived here: four merchantmen, four cruisers, and numerous destroyers. Plenty more are on the way. Our rations haven't altered so far; it's just routine here. Oh, we're bloody sick of it all—semi-starvation. The boys are praying for relief. I wonder how much longer? By hell, I hate this bloody island. All we can do and think of is food—food that we've had in the past, what we like. Hell, it's torture.

I am now war substantive, fully paid Bombardier. All are well at home. Pop has a friend again, and Harry is out of hospital after his appendix and is fit. Joan is okay at her job. Jack and Bert may be called up.

THURSDAY, 10th
"Luqa."

Things have changed somewhat. Convoys are coming in okay now; this is the third convoy, with about nine ships so far. We hold the coast up to Benghazi, so they get through easily. We're feeling the difference—not much, but there is an increase. Bread is up an ounce, sugar by ½ oz., and we have a small amount of butter and margarine. Later, rumor has it that the rations will be back to normal. Quite a nice scale for Christmas Day is planned: 14 oz. of S.K. meat with a good bit of bread and 9 oz. of spuds. We haven't had spuds for six months now. There are cabbages growing nearby, but the Malts won't sell them, so we knocked a few off. The issue of bread is now 10 ½ oz. per day, with 4 oz. of bully beef, about 3-4 carrots, or 1 small cabbage for every 10 men. We receive ¼ oz. of sugar and tea per man per day, an invisible issue of jam, a rasher of bacon about the size and width of a razor blade, and 1 sausage (this is for alternate mornings). Aw, this is hellish, but thank God things are improving. We pay 5/- for a fistful of grub on leave, all done on the quiet with black-market goods. There is absolutely nothing procurable. All we do is go to the pictures and come back.

We're getting tons of drill now. The C.O. has offered £10 to the best detachment in action. Our Bombers are doing well from here, especially the Swordfish, which have sunk a dozen boats so far. The Spits and Beaus go out strafing and bombing, and lots of Halifaxes are coming in as well. Hudsons are bringing ground supplies from Egypt, and the Douglas Troop Carrier brought in a few Yanks. I've saved £10; I guess I'll send it home. I'm hearing quite frequently from home now. Joan is well and working nights, earning good cash. Pop is courting, and so is Jack. They are all well.

There have been no raids on England, but the British are pounding hell out of Italy. Liberators bombed Naples by day, causing terrific damage and leaving a battleship and cruiser disabled. Turin, Genoa, Naples, and a few others are almost ruined. The Italians are evacuating amid tons of unrest in Italy; it may collapse yet. Gerry is fighting like hell in Tunisia, but the Allies are building up and closing in. It shouldn't be long now. The 8th Army is also doing the same, and the Yanks are advancing in Guinea. The Russians are doing extremely well, with a huge offensive underway and Stalingrad relieved. Armies are cut off and surrounded, and the Russians have advanced a good way as well.

1943

JANUARY

THURSDAY, 14th

Luqa

Well, Xmas has come and gone, and we are well into the new year. The events leading up to Xmas were nothing much, except for the 8th Army. They took all the coast up to El Agheila and are now past Sirte. There's difficult territory here, so they're slowed down, but they are still advancing towards Tripoli, which is 150 miles away. The 1st Army is meeting tough opposition and is stuck around Tunis" and ", Bizerte, and in the south. The Russians are doing well; they've practically driven Gerry out of the Caucasus and are advancing in Rostov and Voronezh. The Germans are retreating. Heavy raids in Italy and Germany continue by the Brits and Yanks. Genoa, Turin, and Naples are ruined. The convoys keep coming in here, with a total of 30 ships so far. Our rations have gone up a little—yeah, a very bloody little. We still go hungry. The Maltese bread ration is now 21 oz., while ours is 10 ½ oz.—a big difference. Yeah, the rations are lousy.

As for Xmas, well, we each had a tin of steak and kidney, some cabbage, and a few spuds. Not bad; I enjoyed myself. It was the first solid meal I've had in months. We had five bottles of beer each, a bottle or two of Vermouth, a bottle of Crème de Menthe, and some rotgut. Even then, we didn't get merry. We played cards until 3:00 a.m., and I lost 2 quid. And so passed Xmas—bloody lousy. Still, I don't suppose the 8th Army even got that. But when we think of those sods at home, we groan. We can't get any food on leave, except for black-market stuff (done on the quiet)—6/- a meal for a bit of bully beef, a few spuds, and watery soup. I tried to fill myself up once, and it cost me 18/-. Fags outside are still 2/6 to 3/- for 10. All this stuff is pinched off the convoy.

Well, the routine is the same, and by hell, I feel like going nuts at times. The bloody monotony is awful—day after day, always the same. Short on grub, nothing to do, and no hope of getting back home, it seems. Thousands of rumors, and all false. It's been two years this month. What a waste of time and youth. We're all sick of it. We see too much of each other. Some are pigs, ignorant fools. By cripes, what a life.

I hear from Joan and Vi regularly. I received one of Joan's parcels (Feb. '42). It's okay, though, and the contents are usable. Vi's engaged to Gordon. Pop is set to marry again. Great stuff. Jack is an outsider now—Harry's playing hell at home when on leave, can't hold his liquor, causing much fun.

FEBRUARY
FRIDAY, 5th

Well, I've had a move since I last wrote. There was trouble at the 67th. The Brig caught them all playing Tombola with the pit left unmanned without a sentry. The Sergeant was put under charge, and I was ordered to take command. I took over on the 1st of February, 1943. The position is pretty good—very old, though. The pit has been up for two years, and it's all in pieces, in a hell of a mess, with the site's store spread out all over the place. I've got a lot of work on my hands: a command post to be built, the pit to be reinforced, and so on.

Not a bad bunch of lads in the team. It's a strange start, but I'm getting things into shape. After a year at the 64th, one gets set. I had it all off pat and compact. The routine worked well there, but it'll take a little while to settle here. Not much has happened since I last wrote. The 8th Army has taken Tripoli, Zuwara, and are now in Tunisia, about 40 miles in—still chasing Rommel. The 1st and Allied armies are closing in now. It's only a matter of weeks, I should say, before the whole of Africa falls

The Russians have made tremendous progress. They have completely cleared Stalingrad, cutting off and annihilating 250, 000 Germans. They've almost cleared the Caucasus, are a few miles from Kharkov, surrounded Rostov, and relieved Leningrad. They're advancing rapidly every day. The Yanks are doing well in the East, gradually retaking numerous islands. Huge bomber raids from Britain—Berlin was raided twice by night with a huge force, and twice by day with Mosquitoes. Gerry retaliated by bombing London twice by night, with a fighter-bomber raid as well, but only a few got through. Fourteen were shot down out of fifty, and only six made it to London.

There have been huge raids by American Liberators on Italy and places in Tunis. On each occasion, an average of ten fighters attacking have been destroyed. Infantile paralysis broke out on the island three weeks ago, with about six soldiers dying from it and more in dock. Consequently, cinemas, bars, dances, and any place of entertainment have been closed. We have nowhere to go now on leave—absolutely bugger all to do. Hell, on top of all we've been through, and it's still on.

Lots of rumors are still going around about going home. Hah! By hell, I've given up hope of that. It's bloody sickening! The weather is great, though—a fine winter altogether. I'm okay and in damned good health, thank God. The rations are a bit better. The grub is good on this site. I've heard from Joan ten times this year (in six weeks)—all letters and cards. Also, I've heard from Vi, but nothing from Pop or Harry. Harry expects to go overseas. He's had a row with Joan again. According to reports, Harry has been drunk on each occasion of trouble. He can't hold it.

Pop is now married as of the 14th of January. Vi is engaged to Gordon. My bank balance is okay—168 quid, and I've got 15 pounds in National Savings Certificates. No news from Cled or Blonde, and so, we carry on. No raids whatsoever now, but plenty of bullshit to take its place. Proper guards by day and night, with NCOs responsible. By hell, after three years out here, by cripes, I'd like a change. So would the whole battery.

Let em come, I'll take em on

I was writing to you honey when my mate interrupted me.

That's only one of the positions in which I've written to you

SATURDAY, 20th

Tal Handaq Luqa

Since I last wrote, we have moved. We were warned about it, and there were many rumors. We were actually told at a conference that a complete regiment, the 65th, was taking over the Luqa area, with each VP having a complete regiment. We are supposed to take over Ta Qali, but that remains to be seen.

Anyway, we moved out entirely, with everything in tow, and arrived at our new position intact. We left the old position on Tuesday, 16 February 1943, and after a hell of a lot of hard work, we arrived at the new location around 4:00 in the afternoon of the same day. It overlooks Luqa at the end of the main runway. There's a good view of the harbor here, and it's very elevated. Everything went okay. I was in charge, with Mr. Yates supervising.

It seems we are here temporarily. Meanwhile, we've settled down and are staying in tents. We shall build a pit and are now waiting for developments. As far as I was concerned, things went okay, except for some trouble with the ammo. Ah, to hell with it. I stand to gain sod all, really.

Still, plenty of rumors are floating around. The Yanks have fallen back in Tunisia—they lost three airfields and three towns. Alexander has taken over supreme command in place of Eisenhower. We should see some progress now; that affair has gone on too long. The 8th Army is driving up from the south. The Russians have captured Rostov and Kharkov and are storming Orel and Taganrog. It's one hell of a drive, and it's succeeding.

All quiet here—no raids, no excitement. The rations are a bit better. The ban has been lifted. It's just routine now, with feeble hopes of going home. By cripes! How I'd like to get out of this. No women, no fun, just a waste of time. Not even a decent dance or picture. I'm getting plenty of mail from Joan. All is well back home. Pop seems to have settled down. I haven't heard from Pop or Harry for three months.

MARCH

SATURDAY, 6th
Rabat

We've moved twice since I last wrote. From Tal Handaq on the 24th of February to 68 (another site). I took over everything there, and the next day, the 25th, handed over to the NCO of the 194th Battery, 65 Regiment LAA, from Rabat. A bloody silly move in the first part, but I got over it. Took everything—Bren Gun, Predictor, and Gun. Ray went ahead to take over at Rabat. We got there okay and found a completely built position. Damn nice pit, ammo dump, and fine billets—the best we've ever been in, built by REs. So, we settled in okay.

I'm still in charge and getting along fine, although it's a little difficult. Some of the men are tough to handle, but so far, it's been manageable. We (B Troop—4 guns) are about 20 minutes from Rabat, overlooking a valley. Our job is defense against Troop Carriers and Parachutists. I've gone to Rabat quite a few times. There's a decent dance with some pretty good dames around. I think we'll do okay up here.

I've received plenty of mail from Joan, Vi, Harry, Pop, Wally, and Peggy. All are well. Joan is mixed up in Gladys's case. Harry is in the RAF Regiment and expects to go abroad. Next month will mark two years in Malta, and I'll be turning 25. By hell, how much longer on this miserable Island? Oh, to be home now that it's so easy.

Rations are a bit better; we're finally having fresh meat for the first time in nine months. They're giving us tablets to make up for the lack of vitamin B. What's next? My blood is in lousy shape—little cuts turn septic and won't heal up. The old gut trouble is back again. Well, it won't stop me. I'll get through this.

The Russians are advancing rapidly. They've taken Orel and Vyazma and are nearing Kiev. The Allies are closing in on Tunisia. The Yanks sank 23 ships in a Jap convoy. There were heavy raids on Berlin—100 tons of bombs dropped. All four-engine bombers were used, and 8, 000-pound bombs were dropped. There have been heavy raids over Germany and Italy. Retaliation raids on London have been very small with not much effect.

"B" Troop. St. Paul's Bay. I'm seated 1st on the right, 2nd row up.

SATURDAY, 20th
St. Paul's Bay

Well, we left Rabat on the 13th of March after just two weeks there. This marks my fifth move since the 1st of February. We got most of the stuff—ammo, gun, and predictor—onto a Scammell lorry, and it all went to Ordinance. We took the gun, our kit, and stores only. Got to Rabat okay and handed over all the stores. By hell, what a bloody mess—such disorganization! No proper check, items missing, etc. What an opportunity for some to take advantage of, and some did.

We are now staying in houses along the main street of St. Paul's. Not bad—electric lights and running water. I'm still in charge of the team. The whole battery is together but separated into troops. So far, all this week, we've done nothing but lounge about, go on leave, etc. Training starts next week—mobile work. Tons of rumors are circulating, the chief one being that there will be a mobile brigade held in reserve for emergencies. Well, the 59th is the Light A.A. unit. There are also rumors that we're going home. Hah! What a hope.

The food and accommodation are good, but hell, there's only one thing I want more than anything—home. It feels so close, yet the circumstances are awful. There's talk that men over 30 are being weeded out and that young NCOs are being promoted. I'm supposedly on that list too.

The Russians are doing okay, although they've lost Kharkov again. The Allies are gradually closing in on Tunisia. I received letters from Vi and Joan. Cled's father passed away; he's still in North Africa.

APRIL

MONDAY, 12th
St. Paul's Bay

This is our fifth week here now. The training period is set for six weeks—or so it's said. It hasn't been too bad: mobile work with guns and tractors for rapid defense work, and outdoor exercises. We've been all over the island and even had a night out, which was pretty good. It's a damned nice change, though it's a pity it's not in England.

We're continually on the move in this game. When we're not out training, it's the usual barrack square stuff—marching, rifle drills, lectures, Bofor, predictor, Bren, and Tommy Gun practice. Not too bad! A bit of commando stuff as well. The billets and food are very good, and the routine is neither strict nor hard. I'm enjoying it as much as possible.

They've placed a sergeant over me. In fact, there's been quite a shuffle around. Ah well, I don't care two hoots. The usual rumors are flying about, like going home soon and so on. Makes things worse.

The Allies have taken Sousse, and Gerry only has Bizerte and Tunis left now. It's just a matter of days. The Russians are also progressing steadily. I got through my birthday without mishap. I received letters from Vi, Joan, and Harry. Norman is doing well—he's working in a hospital as an orderly.

St. Paul's Island, where St. Paul was shipwrecked. Very pretty around here. All sorts of Bays, Coves etc. Lovely swimming, no beach tho.

A spot of boating again. We were just arguing over our direction. I stood up and hit him with an oar and somebody said smile. And so, the results.

*Few of the team. I took the snap as we were just ready to pull out
after the ceasefire on one of our streets.*

*The convoy at halt. All personnel dismounted and out of sight.
Routes etc. worked out*

I should remember this, my 25th birthday. Gun and tower on mobile work. With a cyclist. Another gun of the convoy is just behind. My boot in view.

MAY

FRIDAY, 7th
St. Paul's Bay

Well, just finished 5 days of leave—not bad. Lots of swimming and sun tanning. Went into Valletta a few times for dances and pictures. There's still no grub about; can't buy a damned thing. The prices are still outrageous.

The training isn't stiff at all, just a few mobile excursions for B Troop—getting in and out of action with the 4 guns at different viewpoints. Not bad, it's easy. We're all still together. It seems as though we're just filling in time here. Speculation is rife as to whether we'll be leaving for England or other theaters of war. By hell, the rumors are everywhere. Will we ever leave this damned island? Where the drains empty out onto the streets, creating horrible smells and millions of flies. Bully beef all our lives with no variation. Even on leave, it's the same cold chow.

No decent entertainment, lousy dances. They rob us left and right. It's 2/6 at the cinema for lousy seats, and it's a struggle to even see the screen. A drink (God knows what's in it) costs 1/10 for whiskey, and 2/6 for beer—only a bottle a week unless one is in with the black market. Then it's ½ for a half-pint. Beer like piss. Ah well! And so it goes on—the same thing over and over again. I'd prefer the 8th Army to this. Anything is better than this stale inactivity. It was better when the blitz was on; at least we had some excitement then.

Well, they're around Tunis and Bizerte now. Won't be long. Our people are literally blasting their way through. The Russians are still battling forward. These are the most important items these days. We hear nothing of England—no newspapers at all. Received letters from Joan, Bert, etc. All well. Nothing unusual happening back home. Got over my 25th birthday okay. I'm feeling well, thank God, and looking okay. Still retaining a little hair, too. Marvelous—it may last until I'm 30 yet. Some joke!

Lt. Hopkins-Welfare Officer, Lt. Hammond-Troop Officer, Capt. Blackford-Battery Captain. St. Pauls in the background.

Lt. Paul Yates- B Troop Officer. We love him. Village of St. Pauls.

Captain Broach-Gunnery Officer. Decent Stick

Survivors from an Italian Merchantman. In a pretty bad state. They were all that were left out of 60 crew. They're covered in oil etc. I helped round them up.

Our water carriers The Donk! On a lay down strike. It did this *every 100 yards or so. Note the bareness of this island.*

Nobby, Joe, and I were on the roof of our billet. We had some time here while training for the "do" in Sicily. The sea and St. Paul's Island were in the background.

JUNE

MONDAY, 7th
Fiddien Bridge Rabat

A lot has happened since I last wrote nearly a month ago. Our training continued as usual. We had a 3-day exercise on an oil tanker at Pinto, our V.P. We were about 100 yards from it (hourly for bombing). It wasn't bad there, though. We had one attack by 35 fighter bombers. We got a few shots off, but only one came in range. We were up at 12:00 the same night and moved off at 8:00. Hell, what organization again. Somebody had swiped a couple of wheels in the night from the 30th.

Back at St. Paul's, we took over positions there. We were up on Wardije Hill for 3 days, then back into barracks. I was glad of it, too. Gets on one's nerves, all the messing about. Getting in lots of swimming now. The water is marvelous, and I'm getting on fine with the Australian crawl. Entered the long-distance swim, 4 of us did. I came in second. It was about 600 yards—took some doing.

I saw a 20-ship convoy come in. Tons of ammo, oil, and petrol stacked everywhere. Tons of it. There are all sorts here now—Black Mauritians, Yanks, French, Palestinians, and Commandos from North Africa. Literally thousands everywhere. By heck, they're pouring stuff into the place. Five squads of Spits came in as well. Definitely something coming off soon. Four-engine bombers are in and out all the time; 12 came in together today.

We moved from St. Paul's on June 1st. A Troop was left behind, while B and C Troops went to the bridge. We have a decent site and are well settled now. Everything is built. There's tons of fruit around here and a few dames. We manage to trade fish, chocolate, etc., for spuds, onions, etc. There's a big water tank nearby, fed by a windmill. It's about 30x15 and 4½ feet deep. Lots of frogs and goldfish, but we get in amongst them anyway. It's alright, too!

Got mail from Joan and Vi. They've received my letters. All's well at home. Our address has changed to M.E.F. now instead of Malta (food for thought). It's causing much speculation. The R.A.F. is pounding

Germany terribly—2, 000 tons of bombs dropped in one raid. They smashed the huge power dams in the Ruhr. Estimated 60, 000 killed, hundreds of thousands homeless. The Russians are holding Gerry back. Both sides are building up for a big offensive now.

Two to three hundred Flying Fortresses bomb Pantelleria, Sicily, and Italy daily. These areas are taking terrific punishment—a prelude to an invasion on our part without a doubt. Churchill has just arrived home after a round trip to see Roosevelt. Staff talks were held for 2-3 days. The Mediterranean is now free to British convoys. They're coming in weekly, but even so, things haven't improved much here. True, we don't get as much bully beef now, but we mostly get dehydrated stuff, and it's bloody awful. No guts in it at all. Just shit, really. So, rations are still poor.

We still only get one bottle of beer weekly. Fags are okay—110 a week. Pipe tobacco cost me 5/- a tin (2 ozs.). There's nothing worth mentioning from the W.H.U.T—no decent books, games, etc. No entertainment in Valletta. It's not even worth going on leave. It's 2/6 to see ancient pictures in lousy seats, and there's no food available anywhere. A drink costs 3/-, and that's just for port. Prices are outrageous. I spent 25/- just going to the pictures, for my bed, and a few other things. The prices are unbelievable.

There are lots of rumors about us moving. We're a mobile battery, alright, but as far as I can see, only for this island. We've just about lost hope now of getting off before the end. No bombs, no publicity—we're forgotten in practically every respect. It maddens us to read and think of the extent they go to, to make things easy for the troops at home.

There are millions of flies here. We have no dining room, so we eat outside in the blazing sun with the blasted flies crawling everywhere—in our eyes, nose, and legs. We sweat and groan, and we get the silliest orders from Battery. They want to see this, that, and the other. By cripes, a Tommy is a patient soldier. We've had six more go home from this outfit due to various diseases, etc. The whole blasted show needs to go home. We're all thoroughly sick of it all. Boy, I regret the day I joined the army. Ah, so help me!

Verdala Palace near Rabat. I took this whilst the King was in residence. The flag is the Royal Standard. My unit formed the defense around the Palace and area whilst the King was there.

Chapter 8: Sicily June 10, 1943 - September 8, 1943

THURSDAY, 10th
Transit Camp. Day of entry into Sicily

A new regiment has come in and taken over from us. The 59th is now split up and has joined the 186th and 225th regiments, forming 6-gun Troops. We are equipped for invasion, and rumors suggest that we are due for a significant change is imminent. We left our previous site and moved to the assembly point. All of "C" Troop set off and arrived at Camp 2 Transit, where we were assigned to tents and will remain on standby until our guns and equipment are waterproofed.

Yesterday, Sicily was invaded by the Allies, with the Americans advancing in the west, the British in the east, and the Canadians in the south. So far, two Dromes have been captured, as well as the Port of Syracuse, and the troops are pushing forward. Montgomery (Monty) visited us, and we are now officially part of the 8th Army, ready to advance alongside it. One battery from our group is already on the ground in Sicily.

We are loaded with various arms and munitions; we're essentially small armies within ourselves. I wrote a final letter home and hope Joan can receive it. God bless her; she has supported me for the past two and a half years. There's no stopping us now; we're heading straight for Sicily, and it looks like we won't be seeing England for a while.

Our Spitfires are currently flying overhead and landing in the fields we have occupied, and we can hear the Navy engaging in action nearby. I feel great, and the whole unit is eager for this change from this damned Island. I don't care what we encounter; we're ready for it.

I received a cable from Joan informing me that Gordon was killed in New York. Poor old Vi; I wish I could be there to comfort her. I had a letter from her while on holiday. The orders for us now are frustrating—dirty boots, brass inspections, and dress codes.

Trying to look tough for the invasion of Sicily. The bunch of guerillas portrayed here had their hair shaved off for the sake of the dust, heat flies, etc., and we expected to meet them at the job. We were encamped at the time at "Mellieha" just before embarking. Mine was done under happy influence of beer and local rotgut. I didn't regret it either after what we encountered.

Aboard the LCI that took us from Malta to Syracuse Sicily. Our guns and vehicles chained to the deck. The gun is in action ready for a smack. In the background are some of the gun crew. A nice uneventful trip. Interesting from point of view the huge convoy and variation of boats. At sea between Malta & Sicily

FRIDAY, 23rd

Sicily

We entered Syracuse four days after its occupation on July 14th. We were up all Tuesday night and moved off in lorries. Arriving at the docks, we embarked on a barge that resembled a small cruiser, complete with two open decks for transport. About 100 vehicles of all types were chained down aboard. We cast off around 10:00, and thank God for that—the sight of Malta receding was incredible. After two years and four months of hell, we were finally leaving.

We positioned our guns on the deck and had to man them continually. The weather was fine, and the sea was calm. Our barge was one of about 20, accompanied by a substantial escort of smaller ships. The larger vessels were busy elsewhere. We met the Howe, accompanied by a mighty escort—what a sight!

After about six hours of steaming, we sighted Sicily and hugged the coastline. The Navy was everywhere, with hundreds of barges and transports in sight. As we grounded on Syracuse, the sky began to darken. Just as we entered the harbor, Ju 88s swooped down, and hell broke loose—we were right in the center of it. I've seen some barrages before, but cripes this one was unlike anything I had experienced. Millions of tracer rounds filled the air from Bofors, small arms, and heavy artillery (6" and 4"). The barrage lasted about four minutes, with bombs and incendiaries dropping perilously close to our ship.

This chaos continued throughout the night. We were dead on our feet, unable to sleep or rest, with the terrifying barrage erupting every few minutes until dawn. All the gunners were stretched out asleep. Our boat nosed into the docks, which were almost intact) Good bombing on our part. The city had been badly smashed. Thousands of Italian prisoners were unloading, looking in poor condition—lousy specimens, to be frank.

Once we disembarked, we lined up and circled around the bay, taking up positions all around the docks. There was a Bofor every

20 yards. Hell, it was bristling with them. Surrounding us were plenty of almonds, olives, oranges, lemons, melons and tomatoes. The sea right below us. Nob and I took a look around, armed with tommies, as snipers had been active. One gun crew had been killed by a thrown grenade. This area had only been in British hands for four days, and the local populace was still evacuating.

We found houses filled with abandoned belongings and stumbled upon an Italian army store loaded with rifles, ammunition, clothing—everything one could imagine. I kept a short bayonet as a souvenir. We even broke into a wine cellar—what incredible wine! We indulged in some and took a few bottles with us. As we wandered about, we encountered locals in caves who had taken refuge there to escape the chaos. They expressed their joy at our arrival, having waited eagerly for the British to come, as the Germans had treated them poorly.

I regretted indulging in the wine. Spewed and shit all night. Hellish gut pains. Wow! I'll never forget them or that night. At the chaos of 88s bombing the harbour, about 40 of em. Moved again to an airfield. The RAF took over the site 10 miles south of Syracuse, called Cassibile, near Avola. We were there for one day, taking over a field bustling with aircraft and transport vehicles. It was overwhelming, with convoys of vehicles stretching for miles.

Some of our infantry passed us, returning for a rest. They looked alright but tired. We left the field for another and traveled all day and night. I fought to stay awake in the back of the lorry. Signs of the advance were everywhere: our tanks, their tanks, all smashed and burned out, vehicles abandoned, and graves scattered about. Some tanks still held their crews.

It was a pretty horrible sight, and it sobered the lads a bit. Roads, blockhouses, villages, and railway stations were all smashed to hell by our 25-pounders. The Germans' 88mm guns were also wrecked and burnt out. When we reached Augusta, it was relatively intact, with plenty of our ships in the harbor and lots of aircraft, including seaplanes. We passed the port and carried on, noting that the countryside was in good shape, with great rolling orange groves, lemons, and melons, as well as healthy crops of grain.

It seemed that the battle had been fought along the road. We were to be in action by dawn, so we stopped for a while. From our position, we could see 25-pounders pounding Catania; there were about two to three miles of them. Flames shot up everywhere, creating a great rolling roar. The city was burning fiercely, with large blocks of fire and what appeared to be chemical factories ablaze. There was a significant glow high above us that puzzled me until I realized it was the active volcano, Mt. Etna, although we couldn't see the mountain in the dark.

As we moved on, leaving Catania to our north, we drove west and north. The city disappeared behind us, but Mt. Etna loomed closer. Finally, as dawn broke, we entered the Etna Valley, traveling on the road directly to Etna and Catania from the west. The boys were all asleep; the light was poor, and we were just creeping along. Suddenly, tracer rounds whipped across the ground in front of us, then stopped abruptly. It was odd.

As daylight broke, we got into positions in a field near a deserted airfield—no troops, no transport, no signs of life, just us. We could see where the Fortresses had bombed; plenty of planes were smashed up. As day came, we noticed long lines of black smoke rising about two miles away. Then we saw shell bursts and spotted our 25-pounders about half a mile away to our right, firing.

After awhile we identified German Tigers (tanks) and 88mm guns on the slopes, burning. We could see our shells bursting right among them. It was a surreal moment; we didn't know whether to laugh or cry. Here we were, stuck just two miles from a panzer corp. We watched the exchange of shells, wondering when they would find our range and send a few our way.

While scanning the fields with binoculars, I saw tanks breaking from the trees and our shells smashing into them. They blew up like 1, 000-pound bombs—what a sight! I went out on reconnaissance, getting within half a mile of the action, and saw some ghastly sights. Our boys were inching forward. Later that day, we received orders to evacuate—Gerry was massing forces, and a significant tank battle was imminent just where we were. We were given ten minutes to get out.

I had already spotted the forward elements. It turned out that when we arrived at the drome, our anti-tank boys had been firing at retreating patrols and light tanks. The airfield had been captured about two hours earlier, and the RAF hadn't arrived at all. We also heard that all our positions had been shelled to pieces. I worried that they would get our cargo.

We retired to another drome two miles from Lentini and eight miles from Catania, with Mt. Etna smoking and burning looming large alongside us. This new airfield wasn't much of a drome. A whole wing of Spitts here. We're in a blastedswamp, and we were being eaten alive by mosquitoes—there were millions of them. The regiment was all around us, and the grub was decent. There were tons of vegetables and fruit available, and army rations were good. We took what we wanted; we either took it or smashed it and took it. The farmers didn't hang around; many had fled to the hills, leaving their crops to rot and their houses burnt down in the wake of the advance.

THURSDAY, 29th
Lentini Field Sicily

We've been here for about five days, and there have been no attacks at all. There are about two wings of Spitfires here, totaling around 200 to 300 aircraft. This valley, located ten miles from Catania, hosts three airfields. Boy, we certainly have air superiority—the sky is always filled with British and American fighters, along with Marauder and Fortress bombers flying over every 15 minutes, usually in groups of twelve. It creates a continuous roar.

The front lines are about ten miles away, with constant firing and bombing. The Americans are busy bombing the roads and passes, while the 8th Army is holding off the Goering Division. General

Montgomery seems to be reserving his men, while the Canadians in the west are advancing slowly. The Americans in the northwest are advancing rapidly. To date, 83, 000 prisoners have been taken, and Palermo has fallen. Only 30 square miles remain in enemy hands.

This area is all marshland, teeming with millions of mosquitoes. We take four quinine pills a week to counteract malaria. Venereal disease is also prevalent here, and the heat is intense. We're surrounded by tomato and melon fields. The RAF is doing some smart work, tearing up landing strips by the mile each day. In one day alone, they shot down 63 German 52s. We could see the Germans blowing up Catania nearby, and there have been heavy raids on our ports.

There are hundreds of heavy anti-aircraft guns here, along with a lot of enemy equipment captured intact, including small 20mm Flak guns—nice finds. We pulled out on July 28th and moved 25 miles west near the Canadians, where we are now covering a Corps Headquarters in the town of Ramacca. What a poverty-stricken, dirty dump it is! The population is about 10, 000, and the houses, streets, buildings, and public utilities are all in a terrible state of disrepair.

God knows how the people live and eat. A few locals who speak some English told us that the Germans took 74% of their crops. They've had no bread and haven't seen tea for two to three years. The women are all in the family way, and the Germans have made a significant impact here. There's so much venereal disease that British troops are barred from these towns. We've seen some horrible sights on the way up and around here—wreckage is everywhere.

Fortunately, we have a good position right near the town, with available water and fruit. No mosquitoes or ants here, thank God. The night guards are stiff—two hours on duty with four men manning the position continually. It gets cold at night, requiring overcoats and blankets, but it's very hot by day. There's a grove of oranges and almonds nearby, but I haven't had time to explore yet.

Nob and I ventured into Lentini, but the MPs caught us; the town was off-limits to troops. This is our sixth position so far—three Dromes, two harbors (Augusta and Syracuse), and now the HQ. It's our fifteenth day here, and we still haven't received any mail. We've traveled about 120 miles by road, moving south, northeast, north, northwest, and west. The eastern coast roads and inland roads are all asphalted, which is a rarity around here. Some fine bridges have been blown up, and a big push is planned for tonight in this area.

AUGUST

MONDAY, 9th

Sicily

We're now in our sixth week since I last wrote. We have taken up four positions. The first was near the town of Ramacca, where we are defending Corps Headquarters. We are attached to the 30th Corps, which occupies the center of the line. The town is horrible—worse than any place we encountered in Malta. Every town so far has been like this; our cattle at home live better. There are no lavatories, no lights, and no running water. The people use the ground for waste, and the smell is appalling, with flies and filth everywhere. They are starving and don't wash.

Everyone tells us the Gerrys looted their homes and took their best women away to Catania. Wreckage is scattered everywhere, and the dead lie rotting in the streets. We moved onto a main road near where about twenty of our vehicles had been shot up and burned out. Our lads had been caught while asleep under the wagons; the bodies were still underneath, reduced to charred bones. The stench was terrible, and I'll never forget it. We felt as though we were eating and drinking it.

MEs strafed us, and we fired 30 rounds in response. We then moved on to Catenanuova, another wretched town just like the others. The population is beginning to return to their homes after seeking refuge in the hills during the fighting. We have a field nearby, and 5.5s, 4.5s, and 25-pounders are bashing away at Adrano, shelling it from seven and a half miles away. It kicks up quite a stink, and the people here are in a dire state. They have no shoes or clothes and are covered in dirt. It's indescribable—the women are offering themselves for bully beef, and their houses are filthy, swarming with lice and various insects.

We moved on to a valley near Regalbuto to cover the 7th Medium Regiment, an RA field. Some ride. The Gerrys had blasted the roads, bridges, and everything else. We had to make huge detours over bloody horrible roads. We climbed 800 feet, sticking to the track like grim death because there were mines on either side. And Regalbuto—good God! I've seen London and Malta at their worst, but this? It doesn't seem possible to cause such chaos. They hit it with everything. We shelled and bombed it, then occupied it. The Yanks mistakenly bombed it by mistake again. It was a city of about 25, 000 people, yet there wasn't a soul to be seen. Not a house, church, or shop was left standing. Water mains flooded, drains and sewers overflowed, and flooding the streets. Lines, wires and cables everywhere and the stench of the dead everywhere over it all. God, we were sickened; it was awful. Those who were left were weak and hungry, pointing to their mouths and saying "manja" (food). But our engines of destruction roared on, kicking up clouds of dust and noise. I threw some biscuits at a little group, and they dove on them, screaming and fighting like dogs. Eventually, we reached our V.P., four miles from the town, in a big valley with orange and almond groves. The riverbed is dry, and it's hot and dusty from the nearby road, long unused but now in continuous use.

The Canadians are nearby (the Patricia's) we got on well. Like old times to be among them again. They are on rest and heading south to regroup. Our VP, the 7th RA, will likely do the same, and we will probably go with them. It all points to the next push—South France? Italy? Greece? We shall see. Mount Etna is clearly visible from here, about 25 miles away, sending up clouds of steam and smoke all day.

A few of the natives got aggressive while we were negotiating for a couple of chickens; one flashed a knife, and I had to draw my .38 to stand them back. We got the chicken and almost managed to acquire the women too, amid much screaming and gesticulating. It's the only language they understand—the gun!

SUNDAY, 22nd
Sicily

Well, we pulled out of the muck and dust and got mobile again. We traveled up the coast road and through the center of Catania" A damn nice city that wasn't as smashed up as we expected. It has big, wide streets, large shops, and impressive buildings, with plenty of people about. And some damn nice girls too, although it was a bit dirty here and there, with open lavatories and such.

We passed through Acrieale and stopped at Ionia and Riposto, but there was a bit of a mess there with the road blocked. We took some roundabout roads to reach our V.P. and ended up sticking our gun right in a grape field, where millions of grapes lay trampled and crushed underfoot—big blue ones. Plenty of dustaboutand there were great groves of lemons, many of which were rotting. The fields are just below us, and the sea is about half a mile away. Nearby, a couple of big tanks have been shot up and burned out (105 mm guns).

We've moved together out of action and are now resting, waiting for the weather to improve. The next push is into South Italy. Sicily ceased fire on August 17th. The Yanks and Brits reached Messina together, with around 200, 000 Gerrys and Italians killed or wounded, and a nice quantity of booty captured as well. We are now shelling Italy from Sicily, and it's not too bad here. We're alongside the sea, under lemon trees, about a mile from Riposto.

I went into town; it's in relatively good condition. Initially out of bounds, but that restriction was lifted. There's a curfew at 8:30, and not much in the shops. I managed to get some cosmetics for Joan. These people have been starving for three years, and there are no goods whatsoever in the shops. By hell, some of the streets are horribly filthy. The people have no decent sanitary arrangements. They shit everywhere—even the women. The girls here seem to have no morals, and the blokes are doing well; there are quite a number of brothels. Food will bring it, and they'll do anything for a tin of bully beef or similar rations.

The local wine is incredibly strong—pure grape juice. I nearly died on the first night of it. No more of that, I tell you. Rumor has it that we may be involved in the initial landings this time.

SEPTEMBER

WEDNESDAY, 1st
Sicily

Left Ionia on the 30th of August and traveled north, coming within 10 miles of Messina. We positioned our guns along a very long beach. We are here to defend the embarkation of invasion troops and motor transport for the invasion of Italy. Italy is just 16 miles away across the water, and we can see roads and habitation quite clearly. We'll be going over with the 51st Division. A reconnaissance is scheduled to assess the positions before we move in, which is set to take place within the next few days.

A squadron of battleships arrived and sent in their broadsides—no opposition at all. Our fighters are up continuously, and Yank bombers are flying over in the hundreds. There doesn't seem to be any life on the other side. Behind us, there's a little village, but it's bloody filthy. The locals come down to the beach to relieve themselves, fully visible to everyone. The streets and houses are in horrible condition; the people are like animals. They have nothing to eat and clamor all day for biscuits. Everyone approaches us for food.

There's a huge concentration of troops around here already, all waiting for the push. I've got about six pays to my credit, but there's nothing to spend it on—nothing in the shops. I managed to get some cosmetics for Joan and sent it off home. I also received some letters from her; it took a month for them to travel back and forth. All is well at home. Harry's in Ireland, and he seems to be doing okay as an L.H.C.

There are plenty of women around here. All the men are either prisoners of war or dead.

After quite an interesting time coming up from Southern Sicily, we paused near Mount Etna whilst battering "Catania". I took this of Etna at sunset, a lovely sight indeed outlined against a lovely sky. With a great plume of white smoke rising from it. At night, the sky was lit by hundreds of our guns in action and by the light of Catania burning.

The campaign in Sicily is over. We are here on a beach defending the organization of invasion craft, just 2 days before our forces set out from this and many like it to Italy, 12 miles away. The coast of Reggio Calabria can be seen here. Whilst here, 1200 guns of every caliber at night laid a barrage across the strait into the defenses of the coast. Craft can be seen here loading up and some going up the strait. 2 monitors of the Navy can be seen firing salvos into the coast near Messina.

Chapter 9:
Italy September 8, 1943 -
May 2, 1945

WEDNESDAY, 8th

Italy

We moved off the beach on the 5th (Sunday) and headed to another site, where, after a wait of 16 hours, we embarked on an ALC. The invasion of Italy had begun the morning before (September 3rd), so we were a day behind. We landed on a beach near Reggio and made our way to a park. This place is completely flattened. The docks and the town are in terrible mess. The people and the Gerrys having pulled out and left everything behind.

We've advanced 45 miles inland, capturing several ports and cities. Mass bombings are ongoing. We went through some of the houses and found some bloody fine furniture, bedding, clothing, and other costly items. One place we entered had nearly everything stamped with a crown. I picked up a gold watch with a fluid movement, worth at least 10 quid. There was some marvelous ladies' wear, and I also snagged some gloves.

A lot of the local population is up in the hills. They seem somewhat different from the Sicilians—much cleaner and more modern. We took over a position on a bridge overlooking the docks. The town is just behind us, not a bad place at all. We've picked up lots of supplies, including a guitar, a ukulele, an accordion, beds, sheets, and quilts.

This is of POW's who have just surrendered to our troops a few miles away. I took this from our gun position (the first in Italy) at Reggio opposite Messina across the straits. This town is in terrible condition, blasted to ruins, looted, and burned. These POW's are mostly Italian. It was while we were here that Italy threw it in. Alas, something else I shan't forget.

THURSDAY, 9th
Reggio Italy

What a great day this is! Italy has asked for an unconditional surrender. General Badoglio and Eisenhower have signed the terms. We are now moving passengers through Italy, and the Italian Army will cooperate with us against Germany.

FRIDAY, 10th
The Allied landing at Naples involved British and Canadian forces. Fighting between the Allies and the Gerrys is ongoing north of Naples, with airborne troops landing at Taranto and securing it. The Italian fleet escaped to the Mediterranean, though some vessels were scuttled. Things are going well; we are advancing rapidly. Italian prisoners pass by here all day, marching miles in this heat, suffering from bad feet, poor clothing, and inadequate equipment. However, they seem pretty happy about returning home. They went wild over the armistice, singing, laughing, and dancing—not just the soldiers but the civilians as well. We managed to score a couple of bottles of rum and marsala wine, and I got somewhat oiled on the rum. This is the norm for the Brits and Canadians; the Yanks have not landed yet. No mail has come in so far, and it looks like we're due for a move shortly.

WEDNESDAY, 15th
Just as I feared, I was evacuated on the 12th of September to the 15th GCS. I received the needles on the 14th and am now on a course for the next nine months. Holy smoke, I'm appalled at the thought! The needles are enormous (three inches). Well, I've resigned myself to it; it's a tough pill to swallow, but I've got to do it, and by hell, I will. There are about 40 of us—Yanks, Canadians, and British.

There is stiff resistance from the Gerrys at Naples, as they occupy the entire north with about 16 divisions there. The 8th Army is advancing from Taranto, while the Yanks were pushed back at Naples. The Italian fleet has escaped to British ports, including six battleships, seven cruisers, and several destroyers. Unfortunately, the Gerrys managed to sink one battleship. I haven't heard from Joan for some time.

SUNDAY, 26th

I've been transferred to 4 CSS, and it's still pretty bad. We've been here for about two weeks now, and it's bloody monotonous. The regiment at Contorni has to make their way up there somehow. The battle is progressing well in Italy, but Naples is still in German hands. I haven't received any mail; I guess it's stuck at Regiment 83.

The men have moved in, fixed up, and discharged. I made my way to Contorni, only to find that the regiment had moved to Taranto" so Iwent up there to find they had moved to "Bari". Had a few days at Taranto, via town and port, I learned that the Italian fleet, sunk by the R.F two years ago, can still be seen sticking out of the water. The shops are open and selling goods, with big, wide main streets and parks. The town stinks, though, like all Italian towns.

I finally made it to Bari, which is a very nice city—big and clean, hardly touched by bombing. After that, I moved on to Foggia and caught up with the regiment. I got to RHQ, then to THP. Everyone is cold, but I plan to be back in my bed soon, God willing.

I returned to the site and the team again, but everything feels strange now; it's not the same. I'm not the man I was—I feel finished and done in. I know I'll get over it, but it will take some time. Honestly, I feel like I'm finished with soldiering; I've been at it too long. I can and will see this through, even though I don't want to. Why should we endure this after three years of suffering—heat, rain, flies, mosquitoes, mud, dirt, bad living conditions, and poor food? There's no rest, no leave, no fags, soap, or razor blades. My clothes are dirty, the guards at night are cold, and I barely sleep. Most of the time, there's nothing to read on the road.

We're moving in the rain and mud, struggling with bad roads and vehicles getting stuck, floundering about getting one out. Getting wet, wet blankets and kits. We drivewith no cover, no water, trees, bugger all. Sticking a Bivvy (tent) on sodden ground, sleeping with only two blankets and a ground sheet. Tons of fleas and mosquitoes keep me awake. Sharing and washing in a pint of water is the norm. The rain has been relentless for two weeks since I joined the crew. No signs of improvement and I feel rough with it. God help me to keep going.

The armies are progressing slowly. Meanwhile, the Russians are invading Poland in the north, and so it goes on. Those at home don't know the half of it—thank God she won't. God, can I endure another eight months of this? Yesterday, I received about ten letters from Vi, Joan, Harry, and Pop. All are well. Joan is under the doctor's care; I think long hours are the cause of her troubles. God grant that she pulls through okay. If I don't get back soon, I fear I might go nuts.

Took this on the plane while flying to "Foggia". Boy! was she shoving the stuff out. The fumes were terrific and the heat!

Drone at "Foggia". This is of Nobbies Café, cookhouse, dining room, sleeping quarters and what have you. The lads are the gun crew. A turkey has just been killed, and Nobby is about to operate on it. The design of the tent is my own. with the gun is in the background. It was very hot then and at night droves of mosquitoes came out and made life miserable for us.

This Heinkel got very brave and came down for a strafe. He missed us but we didn't miss him. We got him with our fourth shot.

343

OCTOBER

FRIDAY, 15th

Foggia

I've been at this position for a week now. It's quite a large field here, with about 50 German planes wrecked—demolition by the looks of them. There are Ju 88s, Dorniers, and some Messerschmitts scattered about. Three squads are here: the Yanks, the Boneheads, and the Comanches and Eagles, all flying Kittyhawks—fighter-bombers that can strike 35 miles from here.

Even as I write, our field guns are battering away at the German positions. We're facing strong opposition, compounded by bad weather and conditions. The ground is muddy, and the rivers are swollen. It looks like this campaign will drag on for months. The Russians are doing well, with the Gerrys in retreat there. The R.A.F. has wiped out Düsseldorf and other cities in a systematic campaign, which is starting to affect German production.

I'm receiving mail okay. Joan has been ill due to night work, but she has a better job now, thank God. I still have an open wound and a lump, and I've been in great pain for the past week. Laying down is excruciating. Every day has been damp, and the bivvy is constantly wet. I don't know if I should report it; I hope it will heal, but it may get worse.

Well, we'll see. I'll survive it, but I worry about how I'll come out on the other side. God help me. It's my own fault; I asked for it, and I'll see it through. But hell, what bad luck!

Whilst flying over "Naples" prior to landing. On my way to the hospital

Taken from the hospital ship that brought us to Leghorn. It's another view of Vesuvius in eruption. I took this from the hospital boat in the Bay of Naples as I was leaving for Leghorn.

MONDAY, 25th
Foggia

We went into dock on the 17th of October, about 150 of us—Canadians, Yanks, and others. All pretty cheerful. The grub is good, and the billets are decent. It's a big hospital here, dealing with TB, maternity, and other peacetime matters. Valuable apparatus is available, like X-ray machines. I'm fine now; the soreness and lump are gone. I'm ready to be turned loose. The unit is still here, and the weather is good.

Some horrible sights in the town—sickening, too. The Brits and Yanks have smashed it flat. They're digging out bodies everywhere, and there are some horrific scenes. There's nothing in the town, no shops, etc. The 8th Army has taken Campobasso and crossed the Volturno. Good progress is being made.

Every day, 250 Fortresses and Liberators go out, along with innumerable fighter-bombers, both long and short range. Medium, heavy, and light bombers are going out continuously from the Dromes around here. We're meeting stiff opposition up there. He's supposed to have 18 divisions. There are perpetual rumors of going home. A lot have already left: the 50th, 51st, armored units, and so on. Some units are sending men who have served three years home. I wonder? The Russians are doing well indeed, advancing everywhere.

NOVEMBER

THURSDAY, 11th

Foggia

I managed to get out okay. The weather is clear now, but I'm still on the medication. Nothing unusual happening—it's bloody cold and wet, and miserable. The grub isn't great; we're still stuck with the eternal bully beef. We're in bivvies, and they are damp and cold. Even with three blankets, it's freezing at night.

We managed to buy turkeys, geese, chicken, and a small pig, so the food situation is a bit better now. The Yanks are okay; they get lots of cigarettes and have everything—a fine kit, good equipment, and plenty of pay. What a contrast to us, who haven't even got a decent bloody tent to sleep in. I managed to knock one off yesterday, fixed it up, and I'm now in it. I also found a bed and have six blankets so ok now. Get my medicine each week, ok now. Big raids are happening from here, targeting Germany and Italy. We're advancing slowly, but it's tough going; everything is so bloody sticky with mud. The Russians are driving forward like hell. They've taken "Kiev" and Crimea and crossed the Dnieper River. The Gerrys can't stop them. The Yanks and Aussies are causing havoc in the East.

I'm hearing from home okay, but Joan may need an operation that could prevent her from having children. God, what a sacrifice! After three years of this, she may suffer the consequences. I sometimes feel a sense of madness—fury at times, unreasoning and blind. To think that I'm enduring this, the fool that I am. Everyone is well at home, but there are no signs of leave. I guess we'll go the whole distance, alright.

A view of Naples, the fort, and the bay, including the esplanade and coast road around the bay.

A view of the Bay & Vesuvius, also the coast road leading to Sorrento. Vesuvius is still in eruption here.

Another view of Vesuvius in eruption. Clouds of smoke and flame. One could see the lava flowing away from the crater. There was ash & soot rolling around me as I took this snap.

A view of Naples.

A street view of Naples. It's quite decent here. While this is the main thoroughfare, the back streets are narrow, dirty, and poorly constructed. The trains are likewise and offer no comfort at all.

Lovely gardens these & a view of the outskirts of Naples.

DECEMBER

SATURDAY, 18th

Termoli Italy

Termoli is 60 miles north of Foggia on the Adriatic. I left Number 3 after a week out of dock and managed to knock together another tent. We arrived in Termoli, a small port on the Adriatic coast, about 100 miles from Yugoslavia. The trip up was uneventful. We were at the Yanks' airbase for three days before heading to Termoli.

We all got camp beds at the airbase, and now I'm on rest for four weeks. The position in Termoli is decent, located on the outskirts of town. However, the town itself is in bad shape. Both German and our own troops have passed through, leaving devastation in their wake. Everything has been looted; the girls have been raped, and there is death everywhere. German and British graves are scattered throughout the area.

1944

The mighty "Sangro" and the longest and biggest Bailey Bridge yet constructed. It took some crossing the river. Weeks of terrible fighting in mud and continuous rain. We had to swim across at first. After we had passed, the bridge was put under continuous Gerry gunfire.

Erecting the Bailey Bridge. Arno Italy

Crossing the Sangro

Bridging and crossing the Sangro River– 8th Army May 1944

The hero shown here is holding "The Crow" and "Pup Betty, " along with S.B. and "The Crow." This was taken while the crew was enjoying a fag in San Vito, May 1944.

Newspaper article cut out by Joan. Me seated in front

Doss house complete with highbrow name.

The method by which the Italian peasants work their fields. Here, they are sowing with oxen. The gun position is high, overlooking the Adriatic. We engaged a U-boat here and succeeded in scaring it away. Ortond, June 1944.

Liberators at the Drome. They had just returned from a bombing mission over Vienna. Highly successful, too. These Libs had been damaged and had casualties aboard, so they came down here. May 1944.

A Ju 52 taking off at Pescara Drome. Taken from the gun position.

Forts, Libs, and rocket-firing Hurricanes on the drome at Pescara. Actually, this drome is a Boston drome; the forts and libs came down in an emergency after being damaged by flak on their bombing trip. The rocket firing Hurry's were helping Tito in Yugoslavia. May 44.

Our gun position was located in the middle of one of the most famous beaches in Italy—San Giorgio. People came from Rome, Naples, and all over Italy for the lovely beach and bathing facilities. The town front, boulevards, and surrounding areas are marvelous, with lovely hotels as well. Here is an example of the bathing beauties who gathered around all day, curious about the gun. The sea was about 15 yards away. Oh boy, what swimming! July 1944.

A crew and 25 pounders in action in "Montelupo" our 1st place as Infantry. We were waiting to go in that night under cover of darkness. There were 25 guns all barking at once. They were very accurate too. 2-3 shots were sufficient to knock out their target. The crew as I took this were realigning a new range and bearing.

Cleaning up just before leaving "Anzio," we left our gun and moved on to "Florence." What a mess! We slept on the ground, up at 4:00, had grub, and away

Wreckage of 80mm dual guns, Italy.

1944
AUGUST

The Colosseum, where Christians were tortured to death and great sports events were held for citizens. The interior is amazing, featuring a maze of underground tunnels, rooms, and cells where animals were kept. This was taken at night.

A monument dedicated to King Victor Emmanuel. It is a palatial structure, incredibly beautiful. The stonework and sculptures are remarkable, with all statues life-size, while the horses at the top are five times their size.

*The Forum: Meeting place of the Romans in ancient times.
Marvelous sculptures here. A huge place as well. The Church in
the background dates back to BC. Taken in the moonlight.*

*St. Peters, the largest church in the world. Its colossal size and
interior beauty are spellbinding. It is lit up here as part of the
Birthday celebrations of the Pope. Note the hundreds of statues
on the building. Taken at night while on 7 days leave.*

Enemy transport caught on the road north of Rome. Hundreds of vehicles, carriers, tanks etc. were bombed and shot to pieces along this line of retreat for Gerry.

This was taken while I was walking down one of the streets of Rome during my leave there. I've managed a smile here. You can just see the strap attached to my camera hanging from my shoulder.

Men of "C Troop" taken at Castel Nuovo (near Siena) while waiting for the disbandment of the regiment. This marks the end of friendships that lasted nearly 4½ years. I was in the hospital in Siena at the time, so I am not in this photo. November 17th, 1944.

January 4th, 1945. 8th Army, Italy. The badges are as follows: 1st— the 8th Army shield; 2nd—regimental colors; 3rd— the Maltese Cross for our good work in Malta.

EPILOGUE

TUESDAY, 8th

The end at last. I was unable to finish this diary due to a lack of paper and a lack of desire. Poor old Batch was killed in the last few days, my old buddy throughout the war. The troop ship Britannia docked in Naples. Not many are left from the old squad. I crossed paths with a B.S.M. now—a nice guy. I feel sick, old, and tired. Can I ever be the same? I've been through so much, seen so much, and lost my buddies.

Anyway, it's back to my wife and civilian life in Southall. I'll make an effort to get back to Canada. Ah yes, I will concentrate on that—my homeland. What's ahead, I wonder? This war has changed so much. I lost most of my snaps in Malta. So ends this diary.

GLOSSARY

A

A.A - Anti Aircraft

Ackers - British Money (slang)

Airdrome - Airstrip

Ambique - Whiskey

B

BBD - Bombardier

B.F. - British Forces

B.H.Q. - Battery Headquarters

Billets - Room/Lodgings (for Sleep)

Billy can - For food (2 parts, top & bottom)

Blanco - Boot Polish

Blighty - Britain

Bomb Stick - Bombs tied together

B.Q.M.S. - Battery Quartermaster Sergeant

Brag - Card Game

Bren - Machine Gun

Broadsiders - Naval Cannon

B.S.M. - Battery Sergeant Major

Buckshee - Free, no cost

Buffs - East Kent Regiment

Bumboys - Beggars

Bunfight - Tea Party or function

C

Castle Boats - Name of Ship Line

Civies - Civilian Clothes

Columnists - Spies

Companionway - Staircase

C3 - Company 3

D

D.A. - Delayed Action Bomb

Dear - Expensive

Deepcut - Ammo Depot

Dixie - Pot, Bucket

Dhobeying - Washing Clothes (slang)

Dog Ends - Cigarette Butts

Dopes - Idiots

Double - Trotting

Dumdums - Bullets

E

Express Dairy   -   Store

F

F.A.B.   -   Field Artillery Bridge

Fags   -   Cigarettes (slang)

Fatigues   -   Chores, Work

Flogs   -   Sells (slang)

French Letters   -   Condoms

G

Gerry   -   Germans

Gharries   -   Small horse drawn cart/buggy

Glass House   -   Prison

H

H   -   Hitler

H.E. Bombs   -   High Explosives

Hurry Bird   -

Hurricane –   British Fighter Plane

Housey Housey   -   Bingo Game

I

Imperial Troops   -   Host Countries Troops

J

J   -   Joan

Ju   -   Junker - German Bomber Plane

K

K.D.   -   Khaki Drill

Kipped   -   Slept

Kites   -   Planes (slang)

Knicked/Knocked off   -   Stole, Robbed, Lifted

L

L.A.Sergeant   -   Lance

Lance Jack   -   Corporal

Laying   -   Gun on target

Layer Gunner   -   Sits on gun, sights with handle

Lewis Gun   -   Machine Gun

Lime Juice   -   For Sea Sickness

Line   -   The Equator

M

Maconochis   -   Stew

M.B.   -   Mine Bomb

M.E.   -

Messerschmitt - German
Fighter Plane
Med. -
Mediterranean
M.O. - Medical
Officer
M.T. -
Mosquito – British
Fighter Plane
M.T.B. - Motor
Torpedo Boat
Mungy -
Food
Musso -
Mussolini - Italian
Dictator
M.V. - Motor
Vehicle

N

NAAFI - Canteen/Cafeteria
Night Fighters - Spitfire
British Fighter Planes
Nowt - Nothing

O

O.C. - Officer
in Command
O.O. - Orderly
Office
Oiled - Drunk

P

Palliasse - Mattress
made of straw
Passout - Inspection

Pence/D - British
money (penny)
Pills - Bombs
Pom Poms - Guns-
British 37 mm auto cannon
Pox - Syphilis
P.T. - Physical
Training
Piastere/Pt - Money
(middle east)
Predictor/Pred. - Machine
for spotting Planes
Primus - Stove
Puttee - Cloth
wrapped around ankle up to
knee (for support)

Q

Q.M.S. - Quartermaster
Sergeant
Queer - Strange,
Odd

R

Raider - Enemy
Ship
R.A.S.C. - Royal
Artillery Service Corps
R.C.S. - Royal
Canadian Service
R.C. - Roman
Catholic
R.E - Royal
Engineers
Recco - Reconnaissance

Reels - Dance type

Rounds - Shells

R.S.M. - Regimental Sergeant Major

S

Screws - Propellers (slang)

Short Arm - Penis

Singlet - Vest

S.M. - Sergeant Major

Snap - Photograph

S.S. - Screaming Shits (diarrhea)

Staff - Staff Sergeant

Stag - On Duty

Stand To - All ready for duty

Strafing - Machine gunning

T

Tender - Boat

Toch H - Organization (like WMCA)

T.H.Q. - Troop Headquarters

Tombola - Card Game

T Gun - Tommy Gun

Toppee - Hat

Torpor - Semi conscious

Tub - Ship

Tube - Underground Train

V

V.P. - Vantage Point

W

Wallahs - Men (African)

Wimpys - Wellingtons British Bombers

ABOUT THE AUTHOR

Sydney Lewis Palmer was born on April 10, 1918, in **Pennygraig**, Wales, to a coal miner father, a mother, and six siblings. In 1927, the family emigrated to Canada and homesteaded in **Naicom**, Saskatchewan. Sydney lost his mother to peritonitis when he was 14. Life was very hard on the Prairies, and with the Depression, he was forced to leave home, his father, and younger twin siblings. He found himself riding the train tops to **Vancouver**, British Columbia, where he eventually got a job building the Trans Canada Highway for room and board. From there, he went on to work as a lumberjack, then as a stoker on ships, and later as a Merchant Seaman, traveling to many foreign ports.

Eventually, he returned to **London**, England, where his family had resettled. Through a favorite sister, he met and married Joan Puddy just a few months before he was conscripted into the war. After the war, Sydney returned to England and had two daughters, Cheryle in 1946 and myself, Jacqueline, in 1952, with Joan. He moved his family to his beloved Canada (Vancouver) in 1956, where he had another daughter, Michelle, in 1960. Joan died in 1992, and Sydney died in 2013 at the age of 94, leaving behind his three daughters, seven grandchildren, and ten great-grandchildren.

Sydney was a wonderful son, brother, husband, father, grandfather, and friend. I was aware of his diary, but he always told me I was too young to read it. I came across the diary when I was moving him to a care home in 2011. I attempted to read it, but due to the diary's age, the small writing in pencil, and British slang and abbreviations, I found it impossible. With Dad's help and a large magnifying glass, he read it to me, and I transcribed it. Dad died two years later when the diary was three-quarters finished. I was able to finish it off, fortunately, so that others can now enjoy it.